William Shakespeare

THE TRAGEDY OF

HAMLET

PRINCE OF DENMARK

William Shakespeare

THE TRAGEDY OF

HAMLET

PRINCE OF DENMARK

Editors
Bernice W. Kliman
Nassau Community College,
State University of New York

James H. Lake
Louisiana State University,
Shreveport

ISBN: 978-1-58510-140-5
ISBN 10: 1-58510-140-0

TABLE OF CONTENTS

Publisher's Note

George Lyman Kittredge's insightful editions of Shakespeare have endured in part because of his eclecticism, his diversity of interests, and his wide-ranging accomplishments — all of which are reflected in the valuable notes in each volume. The plays in the *New Kittredge Shakespeare* series retain the original Kittredge notes and introductions, changed or augmented only when some modernization seems necessary. These new editions also include introductory essays by contemporary editors, notes on the plays as they have been performed on stage and film, and additional student materials.

These plays are being made available by Focus Publishing with the permission of the Kittredge heirs.

Ron Pullins, Publisher
Newburyport, 2007

Acknowledgments

The editors wish to thank their publisher Ron Pullins and his excellent staff at Focus Publishing, especially Cynthia Zawalich and Linda Diering, for their patience and continuous support throughout the project.

Bernice W. Kliman would like to thank Merwin Kliman for constant encouragement; Eric Rasmussen for his insightful comments about textual matters; David A. Smith, "librarian to scholars" at the New York Public Library, for his helpful aid at every turn; and last but certainly not least the Humanities and Social Sciences Library at the New York Public Library for providing a carrel and a shelf in the Allen Room for her research on *Hamlet*.

James H. Lake would like to thank his family for endurance and encouragement; Herbert R. Coursen, Samuel Crowl, and Kenneth S. Rothwell for friendship and inspiration over many years; LSUS Chancellor Vincent J. Marsela, Liberal Arts Dean Larry Anderson, and English Department Chair Terry Harris for generous support; English Department secretary Deloris Wright for frequent assistance; and Noel Memorial Library staff, especially Carla Clark and Susie Davis, for expert and invaluable service.

INTRODUCTION TO THE
FIRST KITTREDGE EDITION[1]

Dating the play

On July 26, 1602, "The Revenge of Hamlet Prince Denmarke as yt was latelie Acted by the Lord Chamberlyne his servants" (Shakespeare's company) was entered into the Stationers' Register, indicating an intention to publish, by James Roberts; but Roberts did not bring the book out until 1604. Shakespeare's play, then, must have been in existence by 1602. Meantime, in 1603, a much shorter version appeared: "The Tragicall Historie of Hamlet Prince of Denmarke. By William Shake-speare. As it hath beene diuerse times acted by his Highnesse seruants in the Cittie of London: as also in the two Vniuersities of Cambridge and Oxford, and else-where. At London printed for N[icholas]. L[ing]. And Iohn Trundell. 1603." This is the First Quarto (Q1). The play was not, it seems, known in 1598, for Francis Meres, in *Palladis Tamia, Wits Treasury* published that year, does not mention it among notable plays, and it is unlikely that in a list of great plays he would have omitted *Hamlet* if it had been performed by that time. 1600 or 1601 is thus a reasonable date for the play.

Sources

More often than not, Shakespeare derived his plots from known sources; this practice affords readers opportunities to note what he changed and to speculate about his intentions. For *Hamlet*'s plot, Shakespeare went to Belleforest's French *Historie Tragiques* (1576). Belleforest worked up his *histoire* from the Latin *Historia Danica* of Saxo Grammaticus (ca. 1200; first printed in 1514). An English translation of Belleforest's tale was printed in 1608 but may have been circulating in manuscript before that time.[2]

---

1   The present editors have shortened and adapted Kittredge's introduction to make room for discussion of recent developments in scholarship. All the footnotes in this section are those of the Focus editors.

2   See Bullough's discussion of the play's sources, 7: 3-59, and translations of the sources themselves, 60-189.

In Belleforest there is no mystery about the King's death. His brother kills him at a banquet and justifies the act by alleging that it was done to rescue the Queen from a murderous plot by her husband. Hamlet is a mere stripling, absolutely in his uncle's power. He feigns madness to protect himself until there shall come an opportunity for revenge. The ancient idea that madmen are sacred is implied, though not expressed. His uncle is suspicious, and resolves to put him to death at once if he can satisfy himself that the boy is not mad indeed. He attempts to entrap him by means of a young woman (who provided Shakespeare with the idea for the Ophelia character and the nunnery scene of 3.1.89-169), and also by the agency of a spy who hides in the Queen's chamber; but in vain (Belleforest's spy is related to Shakespeare's Polonius, 3.3.27-35; 3.4.1-5). The repentant Queen becomes her son's confidante in his plan of revenge (as in Q1 *Hamlet* but not in Q2). After a riotous feast, Hamlet sets fire to the hall and burns the drunken courtiers to death. His uncle, who has retired to his chamber, he decapitates. Then Hamlet delivers an oration to the people, explaining all the facts, and is crowned as king. His further history does not concern us, but he is finally killed in a battle with another uncle.

Between Belleforest's story and Shakespeare's *Hamlet* an old play on the subject intervenes. A performance took place on June 11, 1594, and writers of the last decade of the sixteenth century allude to its ghost, who cried 'Hamlet, revenge!" Further than this, we have no knowledge of its contents. Thus it appears that the ghost was not Shakespeare's invention. Since the murder of Hamlet's father was not accomplished openly, as in Belleforest, Shakespeare needed a figure like the ghost to reveal how the old king, Hamlet's father, had died, and apparently so too did the older playwright. Both in Shakespeare and in Belleforest we have a story of necessarily deferred revenge, but the situation at the outset is not the same, and the ground of the necessity differs accordingly. In the old tale the murder is no secret; but the avenger is helpless, a mere boy in his uncle's power. In the drama, on the other hand, the murder is suspected by no one until the ghost reveals it.

Kittredge's performance of the mind[3]

At first, Hamlet believes that the apparition is indeed the ghost of his father and that it has told the truth. But later it occurs to him that it may be a demon in his father's shape, tempting him to kill an innocent man. Hamlet is not a procrastinator, a vain dreamer, an impulsive creature of feeble will. Shakespeare has done his best to enforce the imperative scruple as to the apparition's nature. It inspires and dictates Horatio's challenge (1.1.46-9); it is implicit in Bernardo's assent (109); it is manifest in Hamlet's declared resolution (1.2.244–6); and it finds solemn utterance when he

---

3   Kittredge envisions a production that exonerates Hamlet from the frequent criticism that he is not strong enough to accomplish what he should. He puts aside Hamlet's lines that are self-accusatory. Kittredge also interprets the play to make taking revenge a holy duty. Many agree with him. But others, from Shakespeare's time to now, have viewed revenge as an evil and regicide as the most heinous of sins. Kittredge does not consider the roles that other characters play—not the Ghost, nor Gertrude, nor Ophelia; he concentrates attention on his two main characters, Hamlet and the King.

adjures the Ghost to speak (1.4.40-4). Nothing could be clearer, in this regard, than Horatio's warning (1.4.69-74). All this leads up to Hamlet's soliloquy at the end of Act II, where he concedes that the Ghost may be evil and that he needs proof to the contrary (2.2.626-32). And the substance of this soliloquy is repeated and enforced when Hamlet explains to Horatio that the purpose of the play within the play is to confirm the King's guilt (3.2.73–85).

The necessity for some device like the play within the play is due to the failure of Hamlet's assumed madness to achieve its purpose. In Shakespeare's drama Hamlet's motive for acting the madman is obvious. We speak unguardedly in the presence of children and madmen, for we take it for granted that they will not listen or will not understand; and so the King or the Queen (for Hamlet does not know that his mother is ignorant of her new husband's crime[4]) may say something that will afford the evidence needed to confirm the testimony of the Ghost. The device is unsuccessful. The King is always on his guard, and the Queen is not an accomplice.

The earliest moment at which Hamlet is justified in striking the blow does not come until the end of the third scene of the third act, when Hamlet finds his uncle at prayer (3.3.73). Obviously, up to this point, we must acquit Hamlet of procrastination. He had adopted the device of madness on the instant, immediately after the Ghost's revelation; and, when this failed as a detective agency, he had utilized the first opportunity for a further test—the play within the play.[5] Note the promptitude of his action in this regard. No sooner had he heard the players' declamation and observed its emotional effect than his plan was formed. Partly from love of the drama, partly to distract his mind from a hitherto insoluble problem, he calls for a "taste of their quality" (2.2.451). The emotional effect of the Pyrrhus declamation suggests a device which he instantly puts into action.

The sight of the King on his knees gives the finishing touch to the testimony of "The Mousetrap." Now at this the first opportunity is Hamlet, if ever, in the mood to kill the King. Yet it is impossible for anyone but an assassin to strike. The avenger Laertes would not have hesitated. But such an act is not in Hamlet's nature and education. This does not mean that he is a weakling. For we must accept the tribute of young Fortinbras, when he declares that Hamlet "was likely. . .to have proved most royal" (5.2.384-5).[6] Hamlet cannot butcher a defenseless man. Nor would

---

4   The queen's innocence is based on one line, her response to Hamlet's accusation "As kill a King, and marry with his brother." She responds, "As kill a King" (3.4.30, ending with a period in Q2, with a question mark in F1, and an exclamation mark in Q1). Her innocence depends on her intonation and perhaps can be inferred from the fact that Hamlet does not accuse her again of murder but speaks in the rest of the scene only of her sexual relationship with her new husband.

5   But having failed with the madness scheme, Hamlet has not made further plans to discover the truth. The players' arrival is accidental and fortuitous.

6   There is no evidence that Fortinbras is in any position to judge Hamlet's valor, but Shakespeare uses Fortinbras to create a stirring valedictory for Hamlet.

such an act accord with the emotional mood of the audience at this juncture. It is a dramatic, a moral, almost a physical impossibility.

Shakespeare is face to face with an exacting problem. He has brought his two main personages together in such a way that it is impossible for Hamlet to strike, though the opportunity is ideal, and though it is, in theory, his sacred duty to kill his uncle as soon as he can. How is he to extricate his characters from the situation in which he has deliberately involved them?

Manifestly, it is out of the question for Hamlet to give the real reason for sheathing his sword; for that would be to make him repudiate the traditional code to which he subscribes, though he has outgrown its literal savagery.[7] The only excuse for inaction now must consist in his persuading himself that the moment is *not* favorable; and he can so persuade himself by proving that, if he strikes now, his vengeance will be ineffectual. He does not really postpone his uncle's death in order that he may consign him to perdition. The problem is not, "Why does Hamlet entertain such infernal sentiments?" but rather, "How happens it that such a pretext occurs to him?" And the answer is obvious: Because the views in question accord with an old-established convention with regard to adequate revenge. With this convention the Elizabethan audience was familiar, and it made allowance accordingly; for language means only what it is meant to mean by the speaker and what it is understood to mean by the hearer.

The delay is not for long. The moment comes in the very next scene, when Hamlet is nerved to strike, in his mother's chamber, when he thrusts his sword through the arras and kills Polonius, mistaking him for the King. This is the turning point of the tragedy. The King, who knows now that Hamlet means to kill him, lays his plans accordingly. There is no moment until the very end of the play when Hamlet has Claudius at his mercy. Both before Hamlet's embarkation for England, and after his return, Claudius is well guarded and Hamlet is under surveillance. And finally, when vengeance comes, it involves the avenger as well as the criminal. He kills the King in hot blood—as it were in a hand-to-hand struggle—and he acts, to all intents and purposes, in self-defense, for Claudius (by the trick of the poisoned rapier and the poisoned drink) has struck the first blow.

King Claudius repays careful study.[8] It is a mistake to regard him as a usurper. In Hamlet's Denmark, as in Macbeth's Scotland, the crown was elective within the limits of the royal family. Nowhere in the play is the question of usurpation raised. The nearest approach to such an idea comes in Hamlet's passionate outburst to his mother (3.4.98–101). And this ambiguous evidence is vacated by his words to Horatio when he is setting forth, with relentless logic, the "perfect conscience" of his vengeful plan (5.2.64-7):

---

7   Here is an instance where Kittredge and those who agree with him must lean on unscripted ideas that might be difficult to convey in performance.

8   Kittredge depicts the king as a "mighty opposite" as Hamlet calls him very near the end (5.2.60-1) and not the "king of shreds and patches" that Hamlet also labels him (3.4.102), and as many productions shape him.

> He that hath killed my king, and whored my mother;
> Popped in between th' election and my hopes . . .

Hamlet's deliberate use of the term election, and of "my hopes" instead of "my rights" is decisive. The council of nobles has elected Claudius. This fact, indeed, is implied when, in his first speech from the throne. Claudius has wronged his nephew by excluding him from the succession, but the wrong—if it was a wrong—was effected in strict accordance with legal procedure.

King Claudius is a superb figure—almost as great a dramatic creation as Hamlet himself. His intellectual powers are of the highest order. He is eloquent—formal when formality is appropriate, graciously familiar when familiarity is in place, persuasive to an almost superhuman degree (as in his manipulation of the insurgent Laertes)—always a model of royal dignity. His courage is manifested, under terrifying circumstances, when the mob breaks into the palace. His self-control when the dumb show enacts his secret crime is nothing less than marvelous. It was no accident that Shakespeare gave him that phrase which has become the ultimate pronouncement of the divine right of monarchy: "such divinity doth hedge a king" (4.5.123).[9]

Intellectually, then, we must admit Claudius to as high a rank as Hamlet himself. What are we to say of him morally? On this point there is danger of misinterpretation. Claudius is often regarded as a moral monster—subtle and cold as a serpent. From such an error we are rescued by the King's soliloquy after "The Mousetrap" has caught his conscience (3.3.36-8):

> O, my offence is rank, it smells to heaven;
> It hath the primal eldest curse upon't,
> A brother's murder!

In this soliloquy Claudius reveals himself not only as passionately remorseful but as so clear-sighted, so pitiless in the analysis of his own offences and motives that he cannot juggle with his conscience. To neglect or undervalue Claudius destroys the balance of the tragedy. The play is a contest between two great opponents. This Hamlet understands; and he expresses the truth in his words to Horatio (5.2.61–2), which might be a summarizing motto for the play: "the pass and fell incensed points / Of mighty opposites." (5.2.61-2)

GEORGE LYMAN KITTREDGE

---

9   The King's hypocrisy is marked. No divinity protected his brother from murder. But Kittredge is referring mainly to his bravery.

INTRODUCTION TO THE FOCUS EDITION

Context

In the last twenty years, interpreters have considered it vital to take into account the social fabric of English society—aspects of religion and politics that could affect both the production of and the response to Shakespeare's plays. Religion was complicated for Elizabethans. A nation long Catholic had been compelled, in 1534, to acknowledge that Henry VIII was not only King of England but also Supreme Head of his new Protestant church. In just over a decade, between King Henry's death, in 1547, and the coronation of his daughter Elizabeth, 12 January 1559, the Tudor government had changed the national religion four times: from King Henry's Protestant version of Catholicism to King Edward VI's more stringent brand of Protestantism to Queen Mary's brief return to the Old Faith, and then lastly to Queen Elizabeth's religious "compromise," which riled Catholics and Protestants alike.

By the time of Shakespeare's adulthood, the Church of England had survived a quarter of the century, despite continuing religious unrest. The Church retained much of the Catholic liturgy, now spoken in English, but discarded such "Popish" accretions as transubstantiation (the belief that the sacramental bread and wine are transformed, during the consecration, into the actual body and blood of Christ), the commemoration of saints' days, and prayers for the dead in purgatory (since their fates were supposed to have been sealed upon their deaths or, in some Protestant views, even before). These doctrinal changes displeased Catholics, and some were martyred for professing their faith; but just as other peoples in history have hidden their true religious beliefs for hundreds of years, so did many Catholics await the full restoration of their church. Nor did the compromise please those more conservatively Protestant than their Queen, and some factions worked assiduously toward the church's further "purification."[1] And while Elizabeth proclaimed that

---

1 None of these religious-political issues should be strange to us, since we too are living at a time when passions run high about the "true" religious-political path. Some people then as now were willing to kill and die to advance their cause, and others stood by ready to join a movement that might further their cause. For a review of early modern beliefs about purgatory and other topical matters, see Greenblatt.

she had no wish to look into anyone's soul and so was relatively tolerant to those who swore their allegiance to her and attended her church, even though they might secretly practice their old faith at home, authorities imposed harsh fines on those who refused public Protestant worship.

Religion could be a reason for regicide, and often was—as in the case of the political execution of Mary Queen of Scots, who, as a staunch Catholic and a valid heir to the Tudor throne of England, was a threat to the continuation of Elizabeth's reign. Simply put, Mary was too dangerous to Elizabeth to be allowed to live. In these few pages, it is impossible to develop fully the religious and political turmoil churning in England, at the turn of the seventeenth century, and show its connection to *Hamlet*. Suffice it to say that Shakespeare when locating a play in a Catholic country had no difficulty presenting at least a superficially Catholic milieu, as in *Romeo and Juliet*, and a play set at a time long before the Protestant Reformation could also include Catholic rites. Thus, Shakespeare could allude to purgatory in *Hamlet*, but he also managed, anachronistically, to mention Hamlet's school in Wittenberg, which his audience would have recognized as a primary site of Protestantism.

By 1600, when *Hamlet* was first performed, James VI of Scotland, Mary Stewart's Protestant son (separated from her virtually from birth), was the unannounced yet expected heir to Elizabeth's throne. James had written, in some of his theories of kingship, that no king could be removed from his holy office no matter how he had come to the throne. In general, strongly held beliefs, promulgated through the pulpit, condemned any kind of regicide, even regicide that was a punishment for crimes against the state. Thus, the killing of a monarch on stage, no matter how he had attained his kingly position, was a daring act by Shakespeare. Shakespeare had polished off kings long before *Hamlet*—in *Richard the Third,* for example. In that play, however, the events of English history could excuse the depiction of regicide; moreover in that play Shakespeare was honoring the Tudor (and thus the Elizabethan) succession. Perhaps one of the reasons Shakespeare had Hamlet delay the killing of the king until the last possible moment is that he had to make the motive not only revenge but also self-defense, thereby lessening offence to official censors, who had to approve every play before it could be performed.

The manner of the killing also could protect Shakespeare from accusations of promulgating regicide. If Hamlet merely scratches the King with the weapon Laertes has anointed (4.7.148-9), it will kill the King only if he and Laertes are guilty of attempted murder. Similarly, the drink that Hamlet forces on the King will kill him only if he has poisoned it to murder Hamlet. But this is only one way that the final scene has been performed over many years.

Hamlet 1603-1623

Given the seventeenth-century *Hamlet* editions available to us and given what we know about seventeenth-century publishing and staging, the openness we discern today in characterizations of Hamlets on stage and film may be a lucky illusion. That is, since Shakespeare was a member of his troupe of players, as well as shareholder and part-owner of the Globe Theater at that time, it is likely that in some sense he played the role of director—as well as performing, as some think, the role of the Ghost. He would have been able to fill in details of missing stage business and characterization. On the other hand, the fact remains that while the nature of persons in the play other than Hamlet is clarified through their speech and through the responses of other characters, Hamlet's personality remains today much more open to interpretation than that of any other character in this or perhaps any Shakespearean play.

The three original editions of *Hamlet* are distinct entities with, however, substantial similarities.[2] Like most editors, Kittredge combined features of all three editions, with, of course, modernized spelling and punctuation. He incorporated additional stage directions that other editors have included over the years and added new ones to help readers interpret the play in performance. Stage directions added to the original texts are in brackets; most of these additions are by Kittredge and his predecessors.

Looking at all three early editions at once, we see their strong similarities and differences. In brief, the First Quarto (Q1, 1603) is about half the length of the other two. Since it is an ideal length for performing and its title page states that it has been performed "diverse times" in London and at the Universities of Cambridge and Oxford, scholars sometimes consider it a text prepared for a road tour. With 2,221[3] lines, it would take about two hours to perform. The Second Quarto (Q2, 1604/5) is about twice as long. The First Folio (F1, 1623), which contains almost all the plays currently considered to be by Shakespeare, has a version of *Hamlet* somewhat shorter than Q2 (about 15 minutes), but not sufficiently so to make it a better choice for a performance. Revision by Shakespeare himself or in conjunction with his fellow actors is sometimes deemed the cause of the variations among the three texts. Many of the changes in the folio, however, are modernizations: it was published under the direction of Shakespeare's fellow actors about seven years after Shakespeare's death, ostensibly from manuscripts by Shakespeare held at the Globe but sometimes from published quartos. At a time when language and grammar were changing rapidly, editors and publishers in 1623 felt, evidently, no obligation to retain earlier forms that had been superseded. Republished three times in the seventeenth century, the later folios continued the process of modernization in some degree: each is thus further removed from Shakespeare's originals.

---

2   They can be conveniently surveyed in *The Three-Text* Hamlet: *Parallel Texts of the First and Second Quartos and First Folio.*

3   The number of lines in editions varies depending on whether editors count a set of partial lines as one complete iambic pentameter line (as Kittredge does), or whether they count each part line as a separate line. Lining of prose lines varies considerably from edition to edition. Early texts had no line numbers, which were finally introduced in the 1860s in the form we recognize now.

Hamlet 1676-1703, Players Quartos

In the latter half of the seventeenth century, players texts began to emerge in quarto format (the first five referred to as Q6-Q10). The title pages of these five editions, which are on the whole very similar to each other, claim to be *Hamlet* as "now Acted at his Highness the Duke of York's Theatre." The text provides a list of characters, a helpful aid not found in the earlier editions, with the names of the actors playing each role. A note "To the Reader" declares that since the play is too long to be "conveniently acted," it is much cut. But so as not to "wrong the incomparable Author," the cut lines are printed but distinguished from the playing text with quotation marks. These editions were meant for play-goers to carry into the theater to facilitate their experience of the play (as some today will read a libretto while attending an opera) or for groups to read aloud as a pastime or for individual perusal. These editions are worth looking at, if only to see what their editors considered to be to be extraneous to the plot and to weigh what these seventeenth-century versions lose in meaning, characterization, and intensity. They are modernized; sometimes they update puzzling words (dictionaries then were not what they are now) and sometimes they misunderstand an older form or a Shakespearean neologism. For example, instead of Hamlet describing his dead father's love for his mother thus:

> so loving to my mother
> That he might not beteem the winds of heaven
> Visit her face too roughly. (1.2.140-2)

the 1676 quarto translates the difficult "beteem," losing the original's smooth rhythm:

> So loving to my mother,
> That he permitted not the winds of heaven
> Visit her face too roughly:

These editions have no explanatory notes.

Editors today generally return to the words recorded in Q2 and F1, basing any emendations of the text on what scholars have deduced about printing-house practices (including typical errors) and likely misreadings by the printers of Shakespeare's apparently difficult handwriting.

One of the reasons for the many textual cuts in the latter part of the seventeenth century was the revolution that had taken place in stagecraft with the Restoration of the monarchy and the defeat of the Puritan government, which had closed the public theaters from 1642 to 1660. Puritans disapproved of, among other issues, the mixing of classes and sexes in the theaters and the subsequent opportunities, they thought, for sinful behavior and Godlessness. Shakespeare plays before the closings had for the most part been performed in court and in public theaters, with platform stages about four feet high, no curtain, no scenery, with two entrance doors from the dressing rooms behind the back wall and only costumes, props, and, above all, words to project the idea of time and place. With the advantage, upon the reopening of the theaters, of stages separated from the audience within a picture-frame-like structure (the proscenium arch as it is called) and with a curtain behind which scenery could be changed, many of the lines that described the setting could be dispensed with. For over 250 years, architectural scenery held sway, but in the last hundred years or so directors of Shakespeare and other early modern English dramatists have made a notable return to the minimalism of early staging. But regardless of the presence or absence of scenery, practitioners thought *Hamlet* too long to please many audiences. The few instances of full-length productions have, however, generally proved this criticism wrong.

Hamlet in performance

Cuts—and modernizations—in acting texts, sometimes called promptbooks, continue today. The difference is that now each production is apt to create an individualized promptbook with cuts or substitutions different from those of other productions, and many theater companies publish these promptbooks with directors' notes. (We list several in Works Cited and quote some below.) The difference in seventeenth- and eighteenth-century promptbooks from those published today suggests a change in attitude toward the play. Professionals now seem to go out of their way to create something new and different rather than rely on tradition, as did earlier theater practitioners through at least the mid-nineteenth century.

Each actor, particularly in the main role, strives to put his/her own stamp on the role (*her* stamp, because Hamlet is one of the few male Shakespearean roles sometimes played by a woman). In fact, the first Hamlet performed on film (1900) was played by Sarah Bernhardt, a French actress.

One production that relies on a fairly full, conflated text (using Q2 and additions from F1) is the BBC version, part of the series *The Shakespeare Plays,* broadcast on television in Britain and the United States, from 1978-1985. The BBC playtext that accompanied the release of the TV program indicates, like the late seventeenth-century texts, which lines were cut in production. It also has helpful notes about performance decisions by the series' literary advisor John Wilders and by people on the production team. Another that uses a full, conflated text is Kenneth Branagh's 1996 film, discussed below.

The development of performance possibilities

In the first quarter of the twentieth-century, the Freudian theory espoused by Ernest Jones and others led directly to several notable Hamlets, whose Oedipal fixations prevented them from doing what they "should" have done: the father is still "he who must be obeyed." Laurence Olivier's stage (1937) and screen performance (1948) can stand for many in the psychological mold (see Kliman, 1988, 23-36; Dawson 110-13). While Freudian scholars sometimes sketch a pathetically neurotic Hamlet, in Olivier's materialization Hamlet was attractive enough to influence followers for half a century. His is, one can imagine, an enactment of which Kittredge would approve.

Olivier, though melancholy, was vigorous and excitable when he felt himself called upon to act suddenly; handsome and muscular, this prince could only have been kept from fulfilling the ghost's command by inner demons. Goethe had called attention to the external, political frame (the pending war at the play's opening, for example), but many Freudian productions found the Fortinbras elements distracting. The Freudian family drama does not require external forces.

A shift in opinion about Hamlet comes from two directions, one emanating from the text and the other from social and political consciousness. From the beginning of commentary on the play, there were always some who doubted that fulfilling the ghost's behest would have been the noblest achievement of Hamlet's life. As Kittredge had pointed out, textual evidence abounds about the ghost's ambiguous nature. Stephen Greenblatt underscores, in *Hamlet in Purgatory*, the difficulty Shakespeare's audience might have had in taking the ghost's "word for a thousand pound" (3.2.297-8).

It is important to emphasize that the ghost's unreliability as a guide to moral behavior does not explain Hamlet's inaction; he never says that he cannot fulfill the ghost's behest because he does not believe revenge is justifiable. He fails (textually) to give voice to the ghost's ethical or moral limitations. With his "Mousetrap," for example, he proves to his own satisfaction the truth of the ghost's story; but according to what he says, he is unaware that an accurate ghost may yet be a demonic ghost, unfit to follow; that is, he seems to think that once he has proven the accuracy of the ghost's story he no longer has to worry about the ghost's evil nature, as he did earlier, in act two (2.2.627-32), and he never weighs the evil of the revenge the ghost has requested.[4] Some, like Eleanor Prosser, who believe that Shakespeare intended a malign ghost, assert that Shakespeare meant audiences to condemn Hamlet for *wanting* to wreak vengeance (even the impotent wish is culpable in her view), just as we censure virtually every other tragic Shakespearean protagonist for corrupt, immoral or ineffectual motives and actions—regardless of their grandeur. Prosser asserts that to achieve the Post-Reformation dignified ghost and blemish-free protagonist the text had to be thoroughly expurgated (244). But she cannot point to a textual condemnation of revenge. With or without cuts, productions can manipulate audience response to Hamlet's action and inaction, and the effect that the ghost makes must have a strong impact on that response. Productions that introduce ambiguous ghosts can mix Hamlet's despicable and honorable attributes (as does Branagh's 1996 film); or they can complicate the mix, if Hamlet knows that

---

4   Banquo, for example, warns Macbeth about listening to supernatural agents:

>   oftentimes, to win us to our harm,
>   The instruments of darkness tell us truths,
>   Win us with honest trifles, to betray's
>   In deepest consequence.—

>   (*Macbeth*, ed. Castaldo, 1.3.123-6)

he must cleanse the state, whatever the nature of the ghost (Kozinstev's 1964 film). These productions like all others work both with and between the lines of the text.

The impetus of the anti-Vietnam-War movement in the 1960s helped to bring political *Hamlet*s, temporarily, to the fore. The idea that the ghost is unreliable made possible Hamlets in revolt against society. Such productions have been more trenchant outside the West, perhaps, where Aesopian interpretations[5] can move audiences stifled by politically repressive states. In addition to the Kozintsev version, Akira Kurosawa's *The Bad Sleep Well* is a flawed but fascinating early film (1960) of a *Hamlet* used·for social commentary.

One of the important twentieth-century stage productions that views Hamlet in a political light is Peter Hall's 1965 Royal Shakespeare Company production with David Warner. Influenced, as Anthony Dawson points out, by the Angry Young Men movement of the 1950s, Hall and Warner created a corrupt world, stuffed with sycophants, and a Hamlet more moved by disgust at political corruption than by love for his father or horror at a single murder (Dawson 132-46). Hamlet's lassitude is engendered by the hopelessness of stopping the smooth bureaucratic machinery of government.

Four Notable Productions

Franco Zeffirelli (1990)

Franco Zeffirelli declares that his 1990 film is an adaptation rather than a faithful production of the play. Famously, it stars a seemingly miscast Mel Gibson, who had played, among other action roles, the murderous cop of *Lethal Weapon* (1987). Gibson, however, doesn't mistake Hamlet for Superman-surrogate Clark Kent, but extracts from Shakespeare's play the hero's capacity for introspection as much as for action. John Nettles has argued that Hamlet's story is the prototype for those action heroes today who find themselves driven to avenge parental deaths and expiate social corruption (44-7). Mel Gibson's portrayal of an energetic, multi-faceted Hamlet supports this premise. While many Hamlets in performance overshadow all other characters in the play, Gibson does not carry the movie alone but shares the honors with Glenn Close, whose magnetic Gertrude has drawn critical acclaim.

The setting seems unlikely at first. There are the battlements, small spaces, and corridors naturally associated with *Hamlet*, but there is also a plethora of sunshine and sky, with windows opening to illuminate everything, and any suggestion of the claustrophobic darkness implied in the play and captured so well in Olivier's *film noir* production becomes mostly metaphoric; there's lots of spying, as critics frequently note, but there are few dark corners for spies to hide in and lots of bright lights. And

---

5   As in Aesop's fables, Aesopian productions have a hidden, usually a political, moral.

of course, Zeffirelli's trademark: operatic spectacle.[6] The bright lights and spectacle do not mask the corruption ingrained in this Elsinore. Zeffirelli gives viewers their first indication of all the secrets and spying in the extra-textual opening sequence set in the royal crypt. Ubiquitous uneasiness settles in among the mourners, which is sustained or but slightly masked throughout the film. Spying and watching commence at once: a steely-eyed Claudius gazes sternly upon his nephew, shrouded in a heavy cowl, pouring earth from his hand over his father's armor-clad body, while watching his mother weep uncontrollably at the coffin; everyone exchanges furtive and telling glances. It is clear, right from this opening scene, that the film's most important visual figure is Glenn Close's Gertrude. Surrounded in the family crypt by those who so obviously feel her influence and in whose deaths she will unwittingly participate, she makes an indelible impression.

Three men—two husbands and a son—will have loved her, in their time. And though the Oedipal theme found by Freud and his disciples may not be as clearly featured in Shakespeare's play as some have thought, it most certainly is in Zeffirelli's film and others, with the obvious difference that Close's Queen spreads her charm and affection more broadly and generously than is customary. She is an unabashed extrovert, who loves to laugh, finds delight in both hunting and dinner parties, and thoroughly savors male company, both Claudius's and her son's. Gibson's Hamlet, however, is repelled by his mother's lack of restraint and public display of affection for his uncle, portrayed by Bates as very much "the bloat king" (3.3.182). Hamlet's repressed rage finally explodes in a violent and incestuous encounter with his mother (3.4), interrupted only by the final appearance of his father's Ghost. However violent, the scene ultimately restores amity between Hamlet and his mother.

Though certainly not the first Gertrude to capitalize upon the role's potential, Close's performance is remarkable for its exuberance, sheer range of emotion, and the high degree of power and strength invested in the part, despite its few lines. Critics repeatedly comment upon the sexuality she brings to the role and have noted that she appears nearer in age to her son than to her new husband. Certainly, it is possible that she could be a young forty to Hamlet's twenty. Zeffirelli intends the Oedipal motif and, because of Gertrude's beauty and apparent youth, he makes it believable. Hamlet's attachment to his mother does not preclude a strong relationship with Ophelia, who in this film is his "intellectual soul-mate," as H. R. Coursen rightly says (58). Not surprisingly then, Hamlet transfers to Ophelia much of his ambivalent feeling for his mother, especially in his harshness to Ophelia in the nunnery scene (3.1).

With his woman-centered focus, Zeffirelli did not need certain aspects of the play and thus omits Fortinbras, with the political ramifications of that role.

---

6   Critics have long noted that Zeffirelli's experience in opera has influenced his films. In the opening remarks to his December 1991 interview with Zeffirelli, John Tibbetts writes that "Zeffirelli has been frequently criticized for a style he describes as 'lavish in scale and unashamedly theatrical.' Yet, undeniably his pictures…have appealed to a mass audience with their blend of flamboyant imagery and spectacle with scrupulous care and craftsmanship" (136-7).

Directors over the years have considered Fortinbras dispensable. If he remains in a production, he can be a type of savior as in Kline's film or a conquering tyrant, as in Branagh's. Much more often, however, he appears as a rather shadowy, undefined figure, as in Kozintsev's film. By omitting him, Zeffirelli evades the challenge of making something important of him and, more usefully for his purpose, avoids distracting his audience from the focus he has chosen.

Zeffirelli uses the time that a Fortinbras entrance would require for a loving interlude between Hamlet and his now-dead mother, whose hands he kisses in a sorrowful farewell, reminiscent of Juliet's kiss of dead Romeo that Zeffirelli filmed some twenty years earlier. The often noted incest trope imaged elsewhere in this film and others gives way in the final moments of Zeffirelli's *Hamlet* to the domesticity of the tragedy and so narrowly focuses that image that other memories of the film are inevitably overridden and must be intentionally recalled to mind. By omitting what he did not want and shaping what he kept, Zeffirelli imposes his interpretation.

Kenneth Branagh (1996)

Like Zeffirelli, Kenneth Branagh frames his film with memorable visual images, but Branagh also interprets the play throughout with added visuals of unscripted actions and with characters' mental images. Branagh's *Hamlet* exemplifies how a director, while retaining the full text of the play, can manipulate audience response by the addition of extra-textual shots and sequences.

Branagh's movie opens and closes with his camera slowly tracking to reveal an enormous statue of the dead king of Denmark, a warrior king all in black, a fearsome presence looming over the men beneath it. The film's ending is a reprise of this opening scene, as Branagh's camera reveals, in slow motion, the methodical demolition of the great statue, which has been encoded in one's memory from the opening sequence. The Ghost, an animated version of the statue, is more terrifying than any child might attach to the memory of even the most frightening of fathers.

Through his imagery, Branagh connects Old King Hamlet and warrior Fortinbras. Branagh interpolates visual images of a tyrannical if not crazed Fortinbras, ending with his brutal attack on Denmark. It's at his command, clearly, that the statue of Old King Hamlet is destroyed. The audience can be fairly certain that the new regime will carry on business just as it had been done in the days of the Old King, so that Claudius' reign may be remembered, by those who love peace, as a pleasant hiatus sandwiched between that of two warmongers.

A tyrannical Fortinbras, as in Branagh's film, is not unique. What is important is that such a negative interpretation must be based on something other than the text of the play. Without changing a word, Branagh shaped Fortinbras to serve his purposes.

If old King Hamlet and Fortinbras are darkened, so too are Polonius and Hamlet. Two related examples of Branagh's extra-textual manipulation of audience response demonstrate his method. The first involves the ironic visual interpolation of a prostitute silently vacating Polonius' bed during his discussion with a sly Reynaldo

(2.1), evidently the pimp who had brought the girl, who is perhaps Ophelia's age. Moments after the Reynaldo scene, Ophelia climbs into that bed just after Polonius overtly expresses his affection for her. The subliminal father-daughter incest visually implied here deflects from and replaces the mother-son incest sometimes associated with Gertrude and Hamlet, as it is in the Olivier and Zeffirelli *Hamlet*s.

An earlier extra-textual interpolation shows shots of Hamlet and Ophelia making love; her mental image of their past love-making punctuates Polonius's fierce, angry demand that she refuse to see Hamlet (1.3). His concern for her virginity has obviously come too late. Though the love-making is sweet and gentle (and images of it occur twice more), it casts a negative light on Hamlet: what Laertes and Polonius thought about him is true, not, as in the text, a reflection of their own natures. Later, when Ophelia cries out to Hamlet for support after soldiers search her bed for him (added to 4.2), he rejects her completely—a negative shaping of Hamlet's nature, again accomplished by interpolated images not derived from the text.

With negativity tainting the Ghost and therefore the old King, Fortinbras, Polonius and Hamlet (as well as other characters we do not discuss), a viewer scarcely knows where to turn to find someone to admire, but perhaps that's Branagh's point. All the men are flawed, all caught up in the blindness of their own personalities.

Michael Almereyda (2000)

In some ways the film by Michael Almereyda, with Ethan Hawke (2000), springs from the same aims that drove Hall's version (see above)—release from the gentlemanly Hamlet and an opportunity to comment on society. In its low-budget modesty (shot in super 16mm for under two million dollars, about one-tenth of the budget for Baz Luhrmann's *Romeo + Juliet*), the adaptation, as Almereyda calls it, is a refreshing relief from the glossy pretentiousness of some Shakespeare films. The film is reminiscent of Ragnar Lyth's 1984 television film, which did much with found locations, such as the derelict Nobel dynamite factory. Each filmmaker makes do with what is available and allows the spectator to fill in the details. But adversity led Almereyda to daring experimentation and gives the film its real-life, impromptu, improvised luster. Never meant to be a definitive *Hamlet,* it is an essay on the play, influenced by Almereyda's considerable knowledge of literature, philosophy, theater and film. As released, the film excised much of the text, one-third or more (no more than Booth's and other famous stage versions), and transposed many scene segments.

This *Hamlet* is about corporate America, about medium tech and high tech saturation. Almereyda integrates closed-circuit monitors, faxes, home video equipment, voice mail, Hamlet's raw video scenes in grainy black and white, Ophelia's photography, omnipresent computers, and allusions to major and minor brands, magazines and stores. The film is about consumerism, from which none of the characters is free. Almereyda engages in aggressive product display, making his film fully complicit in corporate society. This product placement is not an extraneous gesture to glean some extra funding, as some reviewers claimed, but integral to the film. The Ghost fades into a Pepsi dispenser; Hamlet ponders "To be or not to be" (3.1.56-88) along the empty aisles of a Blockbuster Video Store, with every rack blaring "Action" and with bombs blazing on TV monitors; Fortinbras's photo is on the front page of *USA Today* and on the screen of television sets.

An early Almereyda script calls for the Ghost (Sam Shepherd), who appears on the balcony of Hamlet's apartment, to walk through the glass; instead of this special effect, Shepherd opens the door and walks in. The low-tech solution may have been an accident of the budget, but the effect is to humanize the Ghost: though Shepherd has charisma and presence, his Ghost is not a metaphysical entity; he is dead, but with humanity intact, including a smoking habit. Almereyda states (133) that his *Hamlet* was influenced by the conception of filmmaker Andrei Tarkovsky, who had expected to stage *Hamlet*. In his diary, Tarkovsky had outlined his plan to humanize the Ghost, who, he says,

> walks out perfectly normally, factually, he doesn't vanish in a theatrical way. Altogether the Ghost ought to be the most real, concrete character in the play . . . . All the pain is now concentrated in him, all the suffering of the world. He could even have a handkerchief in his hand, and put it to his ear, as if he could still feel the poison there, as if it were still seeping (Tarkovsky 381).

Interestingly, the Russian filmmaker thought he could better fulfill his aim with a staged production. Almereyda shows that the aim could also be realized on film. Like Tarkovsky's Ghost, Almereyda's, recounting his grievances to Hamlet, holds a handkerchief to his ear, mopping up the oozing poison. Once he has delivered his message to Hamlet, he hangs around looking as if he were pained by the world's ills.

Humanizing the Ghost, which can also be effected in more traditional productions, is one way to explain the play. As a revenant, who carries with him the baggage of his humanity, he is not the grand presence whom Hamlet must obey unquestioningly. In Almereyda's version, Hamlet has to make the moral choices without supernatural solicitings. Shepherd's compassionate Ghost, with deeply pitying eyes, is only a model and as limited as any human mentor might be.

Of course Almereyda's updating of the film clashes with the Shakespearean language: Why would a king lead the Denmark Corporation in New York City? However, given the more experienced Shakespeareans in the cast, like Liev Schreiber (Laertes) and Diane Venora (Gertrude), we cannot regret the disjunction between image and language in Almereyda's film.[7] The rest of the cast—stellar actors all— are sometimes merely adequate verse speakers, but their awkwardness with the language throws them back into what film does best—that is, revealing, through closeups of faces, characters' inner thoughts and feelings. In Shakespeare, reaction

---

7   Venora and Schreiber played Hamlet at the Public Theater in New York City, she in 1982, directed by Joseph Papp, and he in 1999, directed by André Serban. Schreiber deserved a chance to play Hamlet in a better production.

is as important as speech; not all of *Hamlet* is in the lines. It is no accident that some of the most highly prized Shakespeare films are, at most, subtitled in rags of Shakespearean verse, or they are altogether without Shakespeare's language. That such a fine *film* set in contemporary New York City could be made with Shakespeare's language is a small miracle.

The mise en scène and the film personalities do much of the work, but the protagonist's age also contributes mightily to the film's emotional effect. Many have written and speculated about Shakespeare's intentions for Hamlet's age, but the best guess is that he is a youth at the beginning (young enough for the King to lecture him) and a young man of thirty at the end (though only about two months separate beginning from end). Almereyda's Hamlet is as immature as his poem to Ophelia suggests he is. Along with the Ghost's humanity, Hamlet's callow youthfulness, his adolescent bewilderment, does much to explain his disgust with his beautiful mother's sexuality (Diana Venora is a stunning Gertrude), and his difficulty stomaching the corporate world of Claudius and Polonius. He would have had similar difficulty while his father was in charge; the life of a CEO is not for him. A note in the published screenplay implies that Hamlet's conversation with his father is probably the most intimate they have ever shared: "His father, we might sense, never spoke to him so directly while alive" (31).

Infantilized by her loving but controlling father, Ophelia is a few years younger than Hamlet (Julia Stiles was seventeen in 1998 and had made a career up to then of playing teenagers). Wounded by her father's betrayal of her, Ophelia's first thoughts of suicide come when Polonius reads Hamlet's poem to Claudius and Gertrude (2.2): standing at the edge of the executive pool, where the scene takes place, she imagines drowning herself in the water. For the nunnery scene, Polonius outfits her with a recording device, which Hamlet discovers when he reaches under her shirt while kissing her. She fails him miserably, but Hamlet's video shots of her in quiet poses, reading in some and joyously skating in others, sweeten and expand their relationship. Almereyda has metafilmic impulses; his Hamlet frequently works with his video camera and video images; Hamlet's video-within-the-film takes the place of the play-within-the-play; Hamlet's last images are of his father and Ophelia as he had captured them on video. Images over and between the words, and images within images, forge Almereyda's interpretation—augmented of course by the nonverbal elements always added to the text—design, sound effects, nonverbal actions and reactions. Through his images within the text's interstices, Almereyda offers yet another possible version of the play's meaning. Hawke's Hamlet is not heroic; there is no room for heroism in this New York City world. But neither is he ineffectual. He is confused, sad, and sympathetic.

The conclusion of *Hamlet* has real-life journalist Robert MacNeil, on television, seated beside an on-screen photo captioned "Fortinbras, Denmark's New King." [8]

---

8   Almereyda perhaps had his inspiration from Baz Luhrmann's 1994 film *Romeo + Juliet*, which featured a television announcer.

MacNeil intones a few lines from the end of the play, including "This quarry cries on havock" (5.2.375) and "The sight is dismal" (5.2.378), ending with two lines, creating a couplet, from the play-within-the-play: "Our wills and fates do so contrary run" (3.2.221) and "Our thoughts are ours, their ends none of our own" (3.2.223). The couplet exonerates Hamlet—and the Ghost—by suggesting that intentions and results do not often match. The couplet might be an epigraph for the production itself, which had to compromise so often and yet achieved so much.

John Caird (2000-1)

In contrast to Almereyda's shaping of a clueless Hamlet, a modern production that comes close to Kittredge's ideal (see above) is the stage version acted by Simon Russell Beale (directed by John Caird, 2000-1)—but without Kittredge's theory of the King and Hamlet as "mighty opposites."[9] A theatrical production—unlike an essay like Kittredge's analysis—has to take into consideration all the characters that will appear on stage, not merely Hamlet and the King. Mature and lovable, Beale is the most believable in a long line of Hamlets played as exemplary human beings: kind, compassionate, and intelligent.

Beale showed brilliantly that a sensitive, gentle, and sweet-tempered Hamlet is a viable possibility that does much to unify and elucidate the play. Beale on the surface is not an heroic figure. Above average in girth and below average in height, he relies on his sensibility and intelligence to create the character. Solid and quiet, Beale moves quickly when occasion demands (getting out of the way of the funeral procession in act five, scene one; fencing adroitly in act five, scene two), but he is also capable of a focused and generative stillness. One of the finest actors currently on stage, he has range and depth sufficient for the text. He is an actor who can let audiences know what he is thinking, and his thoughts are worth attending to. Through him, the National Theatre production yields perfect clarity about the character (not necessarily every director's goal for the play): this Hamlet has no desire to be a king, no urge to be a hero. He wants to do the right thing. He is deeply grieved by his father's death and mother's swift remarriage but incapable of hatred. One admires him because he has a pleasing wit and a serious intellect. One likes him because he is warm-hearted, lovable and sensitive; he is a better person than most people we know. This is not a popular take on Hamlet these days. What many critics seem to want is a nasty Hamlet, closer to Iago than to the eighteenth- and nineteenth-century Romantic Hamlet. Beale knows how to do Iago, having played a definitive one a few years before, but his Hamlet is sweet and humane, without being a prig. He can become irritated, as he does with Laertes at Ophelia's grave, but he quickly recollects himself. One might multiply adjectives to describe Beale; he is multifaceted and every facet gleams. Many of us have wondered how stocky,

---

9   The comments on Beale are adapted from Bernice W. Kliman's review in *Shakespeare Newsletter* 51 (Spring/Summer 2001): 39, 42, 44, and from her Blackwell essay. In a recent on-line article in the (London) *Times,* critic Benedict Nightingale, after some forty years of reviewing *Hamlet*s, chose Beale as the best of the lot.

fortyish Richard Burbage, Shakespeare's Hamlet, could have played the Dane. Very well, it seems, if he were as superb as stocky, fortyish Beale.

That the production makes more of Ophelia than most do enhances our perception of Hamlet. In the first court scene, her connectedness to him is lovely as she mourns with him, standing comfortingly behind him. Editors, even those whose copytext is the Folio (1623), persist in following the Second Quarto (1604) in omitting Ophelia from the scene. Productions seldom emulate the editions in this respect. With few opportunities for Hamlet and Ophelia to be together, productions take advantage of the opportunity in this scene to show the attachment or lack of it between them—to clarify another ambiguous aspect of the text. After the first court scene, Caird provides further opportunities to enhance Ophelia's status. In act two, scene two, when told by Polonius about Hamlet's love, the king turns to Ophelia (rather than to Gertrude) to ask "Do you think 'tis this?" (2.2.151), furthering Ophelia's presence and dignity. In the nunnery scene, she signals with a gesture that her father, whom she says is at home (3.1.134), is actually present unseen. Hamlet's anger is directed at her father more than at her though he faults her also for playing a part in this entrapment. After the nunnery scene, realizing that their relationship is over, she reads, then tears the letters she had tried to return to him, then tenderly places them in her reticule; she will later withdraw these fragments and hand them out as flowers (4.5.175-85). The relationship between Hamlet and Ophelia is deep and poignant, much of it depending on gestures and blocking rather than on text.

Stage performances are ephemeral, disappearing after a short run, seen by few. But those who missed his stage Hamlet can listen to Beale's excellent verse speaking on a full-cast Arkangel recording (Penguin 1999). For students of the play, reading the text while listening to the performance can focus their attention on the language and intonation and can clarify meaning. Like any production of the play, the director and actors of sound recordings achieve their purposes with pacing, pauses, tones of voice, and all the other unscripted nuances available to the medium. The benefit for listeners is that they can put aside for the time the distracting multiplicity of stage and screen performances to concentrate on verbal effects and then return to page and screen with increased understanding and appreciation for what happens beyond language.

Opportunities to create *Hamlet*

Directors are in a good position to shape the *Hamlet* of their choice—by casting, cutting, creating dynamic, non-verbal interactions among characters and choosing among all the other resources of stage and screen. *Hamlet* is the most refreshing of plays because it is so very open to possibility. A director who comes upon the play without knowing much about Shakespeare or even about the play itself can nevertheless succeed in mounting a version that can move and enlighten audiences. No one version anyone creates will encompass all of the play's potentialities. That's why many people go to see it over and over—and why some directors and actors want to try it repeatedly. Its elusiveness is freeing because it means that no one needs to suffer the burden of total perfection in creating his or her vision of the play.

Thus, we want to encourage students to welcome the contrary opinions that have been held about Hamlet and *Hamlet* and that directors have expressed in widely varying productions. Contraries can serve as an invitation to open your mind, soul, and heart to the words of the play, to tease out possibilities in performance, whether it is a performance imagined in your mind or developed with classmates, or sketched out on paper. Though one might think that after 400 years of existence, the play must be a completely known entity, the fact that hundreds of new essays, books, and performances in all media appear each and every year demonstrates that one need only dip into the play energetically and honestly to reach something powerful that can please you and others.

THE EDITORS

- quartos didn't come out together (1603, 1604, 1623) Q1 (short), Q2, Folio
  ↳ Q1 w/o self questioning - revenge w/o mental
- 1604 new king - second quarto - twice the length
  ↳ James I father was murdered + mother marries lover
  ↳ problematizes the revenge to make it more comfortable for James
- religious + existential questions about revenge - refuses the dramatic function
  ↳ revenge is of the lord → christian world the revenge is violent + problematic
  ↳ Hamlet is the problem within this situation
- Hamlet is cain, old hamlet abel
- protestants would have thought about the ghost as a tempter (form of the devil)

major themes
- action + inaction
- legitimacy - switch of succession   - proving himself to his father (Hal)
- amleth - plays mad

THE TRAGEDY OF
HAMLET
PRINCE OF DENMARK

Dramatis Personae[†]

Hamlet, Prince of Denmark	*Fortinbras,* Prince of Norway
Claudius, King of Denmark	*Norwegian Captain*
Gertrude, Queen, Hamlet's mother	*Clown,* gravedigger
Ghost	*2nd Clown,* gravedigger
Horatio, Hamlet's friend	*Player King*
Polonius, Counselor to the king	*Player Queen*
Laertes, Polonius's son	*Lucianus,* player murderer
Ophelia, Polonius's daughter	*Osric,* landed gentleman
Reynaldo, Polonius's servant	*Gentleman* (4.5)
Rosencrantz & *Guildenstern,* Hamlet's childhood friends	*Priest*
	Sailor
Marcellus, sentry	*Voltemand & Cornelius,* Danish ambassadors
Bernardo, sentry	
Francisco, sentry	*Laertes's followers*

also

Messenger (4.5 and 4.7), *Lord* (5.1), *Ambassadors from England* (5.2)

Scene.—*Elsinore.*

---

†   Not found in early editions, the list of characters is here arranged to reflect importance, family and other groupings, and number of scenes in which each character appears.

       Much doubling would ordinarily take place in almost any stage performance of a Shakespeare play, but particularly so in Shakespeare's time when there were approximately fifteen players who had to undertake all the roles. Filmmakers often expand the number of actors greatly, as in Branagh's film.

ACT I

SCENE I. [*Elsinore. A platform before the Castle*].†

Enter two Sentinels, Francisco and Bernardo.

BERNARDO	Who's there?‡	*partially obscured*
FRANCISCO	Nay, answer me. Stand and unfold yourself.*	*cannot see full person*
BERNARDO	Long live the King	*is outside vs inside*
FRANCISCO	Bernardo?	
BERNARDO	He.	5
FRANCISCO	You come most carefully upon your hour.	
BERNARDO	'Tis now struck twelve. Get thee to bed, Francisco.	
FRANCISCO	For this relief much thanks. 'Tis bitter cold, And I am sick at heart.	
BERNARDO	Have you had quiet guard?	
FRANCISCO	Not a mouse stirring.	10
BERNARDO	Well, good night. If you do meet Horatio and Marcellus, The rivals of my watch, bid them make haste.	

NKS *Hamlet* Editors' Note: The editors have in some instances modified Kittredge's explanatory notes to modernize and shorten them. Additional explanatory notes are marked "EDS." Performance notes, found below the explanatory notes, are all by the NKS *Hamlet* editors.

ACT I. SCENE I.
2. **Nay, answer me:** The implied state of confusion anticipates the general sense of dislocation Hamlet feels when he says "the time is out of joint" (1.5.185). [EDS.] —**unfold:** show who you are. 3. **Long live the King:** a customary exclamation [or perhaps a password. EDS.]. 6. **carefully upon your hour:** on time. [EDS.] 9. **sick at heart:** depressed. 13. **rivals:** partners.

---

†   Almereyda and Zeffirelli omit this scene. Almereyda begins with Hamlet, working on a video project while saying "I have of late lost all my mirth...What a piece of work is a man..."(2.2.306-313). Zeffirelli substitutes a scene showing the interment of King Hamlet, introducing the audience to the main characters and their relationships.

     Klein's version, based on his stage production at the Public Theater in New York City and filmed for television, clearly shows its theatrical origin, with bare boards and minimal set enhancements. Klein cut the text briskly, as do many productions whether on stage or film. Branagh's film, on the other hand, relies on real and realistic outdoor and indoor settings, not only using the full text but also inserting many visuals (flashcuts) between the words and adding unscripted scenes. Olivier's film with a significantly cut script makes extensive use of a moody and expressionistic set, neither precisely theatrical nor conventionally filmic.

‡   Branagh's Bernardo tackles Francisco, who lands face-down in snow; he says, "Nay, answer me" ironically.

*   His few lines (2-18), in which he admits he is uneasy (9), help to set the scene's mood of dread and mystery.

Enter Horatio and Marcellus.

FRANCISCO	I think I hear them. Stand, ho. Who is there?	
HORATIO	Friends to this ground.	
MARCELLUS	And liegemen to the Dane.	15
FRANCISCO	Give you good night.	
MARCELLUS	O, farewell, honest soldier. Who hath relieved you?	
FRANCISCO	Bernardo hath my place. Give you good night.	*Exit.*
MARCELLUS	Holla, Bernardo.	
BERNARDO	Say— What, is Horatio there?	
HORATIO	A piece of him.	
BERNARDO	Welcome, Horatio. Welcome, good Marcellus.	20
MARCELLUS	What, has this thing appeared again to-night?	
BERNARDO	I have seen nothing.	
MARCELLUS	Horatio says 'tis but our fantasy, And will not let belief take hold of him Touching this dreaded sight, twice seen of us. Therefore I have entreated him along, With us to watch the minutes of this night, That, if again this apparition come, He may approve our eyes and speak to it.	25
HORATIO	Tush, tush, 'twill not appear.	
BERNARDO	Sit down awhile,** And let us once again assail your ears, That are so fortified against our story, What we two nights have seen.	30

---

15. **liegemen:** subjects. [EDS.] 16. **the Dane:** the Danish king. —**Give:** God give. 19. **A piece of him:** A mildly humorous affirmative. Horatio is prone to such mild jokes. [The line also implies Horatio's skepticism. EDS.] 23-25. **fantasy:** imagination.—**of us:** by us. 26. **entreated:** asked urgently. [EDS.] 29. **approve our eyes:** support our claim. [EDS.]—**speak to it:** They have not ventured to speak to the Ghost, for it was thought dangerous to address an apparition, except in proper form. 33. **What...seen:** "may make one more attempt to get a hearing from you for our account of what we have seen."

**   Unless the line is cut, at least one of the three men will sit here so that he can rise upon the Ghost's sudden appearance (40). One or more sit again (70), so that they can rise again when the Ghost returns (129). Only Horatio sits in Klein's version, which has the Ghost appear only once.

HORATIO	Well, sit we down,
	And let us hear Bernardo speak of this.

BERNARDO	Last night of all,	35
	When yond same star that's westward from the pole	
	Had made his course t' illume that part of heaven	
	Where now it burns, Marcellus and myself,	
	The bell then beating one —	

Enter Ghost.

MARCELLUS	Peace. break thee off. Look where it comes again.†	40
BERNARDO	In the same figure, like the King that's dead.	
MARCELLUS	Thou art a scholar; speak to it, Horatio.	
BERNARDO	Looks it not like the King? Mark it, Horatio.	*cast doubt on*
HORATIO	Most like. It harrows me with fear and wonder.	*the current King*
BERNARDO	It would be spoke to.	
MARCELLUS	Question it, Horatio.	45
HORATIO	What art thou that usurp'st this time of night	
	Together with that fair and warlike form	
	In which the majesty of buried Denmark	
	Did sometimes march? By heaven I charge thee speak.	
MARCELLUS	It is offended.	50
BERNARDO	See, it stalks away.	
HORATIO	Stay. Speak, speak. I charge thee speak.	

Exit Ghost.

MARCELLUS	'Tis gone and will not answer.	
BERNARDO	How now, Horatio? You tremble and look pale.	
	Is not this something more than fantasy?	
	What think you on't?	55

---

37. **his:** its. 42 **Thou art a scholar...Horatio:** As a scholar, Horatio knows how to address the vision in the right way, so as neither to offend it nor to subject himself or them to any evil influence. His language is formal and solemn, but he does not use Latin or utter an exorcism formula. 43. **harrows:** tortures. A harrow is a farming tool used to rip apart and loosen the soil. [EDS.] 48-9. **Denmark:** the King of Denmark. [Kings were customarily called by the name of their countries. EDS.]—**sometimes:** formerly.

---

†   The Ghost varies considerably in performance—but whether it is an unseen presence (a shadow in Gielgud's version with Richard Burton and a light in Richardson's with Nicol Williamson, both stage versions captured on film); a realistic father figure (as in Zeffirelli's and Almereyda's films); or an otherworldly presence (noble in Kozintsev's and demonic in Branagh's film)—its presentation is a key to understanding the command it gives Hamlet.

Kozintsev's Ghost is remote and terrifying as it stalks majestically on the high battlements of Elsinore, appearing larger than life to the film audience as well as to Hamlet and his friends.

HORATIO	Before my God, I might not this believe Without the <u>sensible</u> and true avouch Of mine own eyes. — *so much philosophy/psychology must trust senses*
MARCELLUS	Is it not like the King?
HORATIO	As thou art to thyself. Such was the very armor he had on 60 When he th' ambitious Norway combated. So frowned he once when, in an angry parle, He smote the sledded Polacks on the ice. 'Tis strange.
MARCELLUS	Thus twice before, and jump at this dead hour, 65 With martial stalk hath he gone by our watch.
HORATIO	In what particular thought to work I know not; But, in the gross and scope of my opinion, This <u>bodes some strange eruption to our state</u>. — *turmoil within* — *land — below*
MARCELLUS	Good now, sit down, and tell me he that knows, 70 Why this same strict and most observant watch So nightly toils the subject of the land, And why such daily cast of brazen cannon And foreign mart for implements of war;

56. **might:** could. 57-8 **the...eyes:** the testimony of my own eyes, which is a matter of the senses and must be true. 61. **Norway:** King of Norway. 62. **parle:** parley; conference between hostile leaders. 63. **smote:** The parley broke up in a battle, in which the King smote (routed) the Polanders. —**the sledded Polacks:** the Polanders, who ride in sledges. 65. **jump:** precisely. 68. **in...opinion:** in the general view or range of my opinion (as opposed to any precise thought). 70. **Good:** my good friend. — **tell me... knows:** Let him who knows tell me. 72. **subject:** That is, "subjects." Compare 1.2.33. 74. **foreign mart:** commerce with foreign countries.

Why such impress of shipwrights, whose sore task   75
Does not divide the Sunday from the week.
What might be toward, that this sweaty haste
Doth make the night joint-laborer with the day?
Who is't that can inform me?

HORATIO   That can I.
At least, the whisper goes so. Our last king,   80
Whose image even but now appeared to us,
Was, as you know, by Fortinbras of Norway,
Thereto pricked on by a most emulate pride,† *masculine*
Dared to the combat; in which our valiant Hamlet *enterprise*
(For so this side of our known world esteemed him) *of war* 85
Did slay this Fortinbras; who, by a sealed compact,
Well ratified by law and heraldry,
Did forfeit, with his life, all those his lands
Which he stood seized of, to the conqueror;
Against the which a moiety competent   90
Was gaged by our king; which had return
To the inheritance of Fortinbras,
Had he been vanquisher, as, by the same comart
And carriage of the article designed,   *now fear*
His fell to Hamlet. Now, sir, young Fortinbras,— *young* 95
Of unimproved mettle hot and full,   *fortinbras*
Hath in the skirts of Norway, here and there,   *one of hamlet's foils*
Sharked up a list of lawless resolutes,
For food and diet, to some enterprise
That hath a stomach in't; which is no other,   100
As it doth well appear unto our state,

---

75. **impress:** Ship carpenters could be drafted in time of war. 77. **might be toward:** could be in the offing. 81. **image:** exact likeness. 83. **emulate pride:** arrogant desire to rival him. 86. **compáct:** accented on the second syllable. 87. **law and heraldry:** heraldic law, i.e., a decree made and ratified by the heralds of both countries; equivalent to what we call "international law." 89. **stood seized of:** held in his possession at that time. 90. **a moiety competent:** an adequate portion (of his own lands). 91. **gagéd:** pledged; two syllables.—**had returned:** would have become. 92. **inheritance:** possession. 93. **comart:** mutual bargain. 94. **carriage...designed:** the **sense** of the agreement drawn up. 96. **unimproved:** unused. To *improve* anything often means to "put it to profitable use." —**mettle:** high spirit. 97. **skirts:** outskirts. [EDS.] 98. **Sharked up:** "picked up without distinction, as the shark collects his prey." —**lawless:** *Lawless* may mean "outlawed." —**resolutes:** desperadoes. 99. **some:** This suggests that he enlisted his desperadoes without telling them just what the enterprise was. 100. **stomach:** valor. 101. **our state:** our administration.

---

† Critics often say that if Fortinbras is to come in at the end (5.2.373-414), a director must mention him here, and keep his name in play (as the text does in 1.2.17-30; 2.1.62-79; 4.4.14 and 48; 5.1.157). Klein manages very well, however, without any preliminary mentions before a mild Fortinbras appears in 4.4.1-7 and at the end. Branagh, on the other hand, expands Fortinbras's role considerably with many silent visuals before he enters in 4.4.1 and 5.2. 373, while Olivier and Zeffirelli omit him altogether (as did most stage productions from 1662-1950).

Branagh's flashcut reveals an angry Fortinbras (Rufus Sewall), snarling into the camera, as Horatio (Nicholar Farrell) explains why Denmark is preparing for war with Norway (1.1.79-107).

fighting over land
But to recover of us, by strong hand   *Fortinbras wants land*
And terms compulsatory, those foresaid lands   *identity + power*
So by his father lost; and this, I take it,   *tied to land*
Is the main motive of our preparations,   105
The source of this our watch, and the chief head
Of this post-haste and romage in the land.

BERNARDO   I think it be no other but e'en so.
Well may it sort that this portentous figure
Comes armed through our watch, *so* like the King   110
That was and is the question of these wars.

HORATIO   *A* mote it is to trouble the mind's eye.
In the most high and palmy state of Rome,
A little ere the mightiest Julius fell,
The graves stood tenantless, and the sheeted dead   115
Did squeak and gibber in the Roman streets;
As stars with trains of fire, and dews of blood,
Disasters in the sun; and the moist star

---

103. **terms compulsatory:** synonymous with *strong hand* in previous line. 105. **motive:** moving cause. 106. **head:** means the same as *source* (compare *fountainhead*). 107. **romage:** intense activity. 108–125. In the Quartos but not in the Folios. 108. **be:** The subjunctive in indirect discourse. The *be* does not express any special doubt in the speaker's mind. 109. **Well may it sort:** It may well be in accord with this state of things. 112. **mote:** a speck of dust. 113. **palmy:** flourishing. 116. **squeak:** alluding to the horribly thin and strident voice ascribed to ghosts. 117. **As:** *As* may mean "and so likewise there were."—**trains of fire:** Among the signs that foretold the death of Cæsar, Plutarch mentions fires in the sky and spirits running up and down in the night.—**dews of blood:** An often-reported phenomenon by ancient writers. 118. **Disasters:** threatening signs. *Disasters* in its astrological sense (*asters* are stars) includes any threatening phenomena in the heavenly bodies.—**moist star:** the moon. According to the old science, which divided all things according to the four categories—moist, dry, hot, cold—the moon was moist by nature. Hence it had much to do with dew, mist, and fog.

Upon whose influence Neptune's empire stands
Was sick almost to doomsday with eclipse.   120
And even the like precurse of fierce events,
As harbingers preceding still the fates
And prologue to the omen coming on,
Have heaven and earth together demonstrated
Unto our climature and countrymen.   125

Enter Ghost again.

But soft. behold. Lo, where it comes again.
I'll cross it, though it blast me. — Stay, illusion.

                                                  Spreads his arms.

If thou hast any sound, or use of voice,
Speak to me.
If there be any good thing to be done,   130
That may to thee do ease, and grace to me,
Speak to me.
If thou art privy to thy country's fate,
Which happily foreknowing may avoid,
O, speak.   135
Or if thou hast uphoarded in thy life
Extorted treasure in the womb of earth
(For which, they say, you spirits oft walk in death),

                              The cock crows.

Speak of it. Stay, and speak. — Stop it, Marcellus.

MARCELLUS   Shall I strike at it with my partisan?   140

HORATIO   Do, if it will not stand.

BERNARDO   'Tis here.

HORATIO   'Tis here.

---

119. **Upon...stands:** by whose influence the sea is controlled (in its tides). 120. **doomsday:** Judgment Day. [EDS.] 121. **precurse:** indication in advance.—**fierce:** terrible. 122. **harbingers:** A harbinger was an officer who went ahead to arrange for the lodgings of a king and his suite, [thus, forerunners. EDS.].—**still:** always. The fates, Horatio implies, always come with an announcement. 123. **omen:** a sign of a dire event. 125. **climature:** country. 126. **soft:** interjection asking for silence. 127. **I'll cross it, though it blast me:** Horatio's courage comes out strongly here, for to cross a spirit, or to let it cross you, was even more dangerous than to speak to it. Horatio shows a scholar's knowledge in his enumeration of the causes that send ghosts back to earth. He mentions (1) some good action which remains undone; (2) some disclosure for the benefit or protection of surviving friends; (3) the revelation of buried treasure. Abundant illustration of all three points occurs in European folklore. 131. **do ease:** relieve thy conscience and let thee rest in peace.—**grace to me:** be set to my credit as a virtuous action. Only on this condition does Horatio promise to carry out the apparition's wishes, for he cannot be sure that it is not a malignant ghost or even a demon. 133. **thy country's fate:** as in lines 108-11, 22 Horatio alluded to already. 134. **happily:** perhaps. 139. **Stay:** The Ghost starts to go. Horatio forgets his learning in his excitement and calls upon Marcellus to "stop it," though that is impossible. 140. **partisan:** a long-handled weapon. [EDS.]

MARCELLUS	'Tis gone.

Exit Ghost.

We do it wrong, being so majestical,
To offer it the show of violence;
For it is as the air, invulnerable,   145
And our vain blows malicious mockery.

BERNARDO   It was about to speak, when the cock crew.

HORATIO   And then it started, like a guilty thing
Upon a fearful summons. I have heard
The cock, that is the trumpet to the morn,   150
Doth with his lofty and shrill-sounding throat
Awake the god of day; and at his warning,
Whether in sea or fire, in earth or air,
Th' extravagant and erring spirit hies
To his confine; and of the truth herein   155
This present object made probation.

MARCELLUS   It faded on the crowing of the cock.
Some say that ever, 'gainst that season comes
Wherein our Savior's birth is celebrated,
The bird of dawning singeth all night long;   160
And then, they say, no spirit dare stir abroad,
The nights are wholesome, then no planets strike,
folktales No fairy takes, nor witch hath power to charm,
So hallowed and so gracious is the time.

HORATIO   So have I heard and do in part believe it.   165
But look, the morn, in russet mantle clad,
Walks o'er the dew of yon high eastward hill.
Break we our watch up; and by my advice
Let us impart what we have seen to-night
Unto young Hamlet; for, upon my life,   170
This spirit, dumb to us, will speak to him.
Do you consent we shall acquaint him with it,

---

146. **malicious mockery:** a hollow mockery of doing harm. 151. **lofty:** high-pitched. 152. **at his warning:** when the cock's crow warns them of sunrise: ghosts, trolls, devils, and the like, according to a very old belief, cannot endure the sunlight. 154. **extravagant:** escaped from its *confine* or assigned limits.—**erring:** wandering. 156. **object:** sight. In Elizabethan English all that the eye can take in at one view may be called an *object.*—**probation:** proof. 158. **'gainst:** just before. 162. **wholesome:** free not only from witchcraft and demonic influences, but from **contagious disease**, which was commonly ascribed to the night air. —**strike:** regularly used of the sudden malignant action ascribed to an evil planet. 163. **takes:** bewitches. All kinds of ill effects were ascribed to malicious fairies and elves—from "pinching black and blue" to idiocy, madness, and even death. 164. **gracious:** blessed. 165. **in part:** Horatio speaks with his habitual caution. 166. **in russet mantle clad:** The dawn is cloudy or misty. *Russet* was a kind of coarse homespun, either brown or grey.

As needful in our loves, fitting our duty?

MARCELLUS   Let's do't, I pray; and I this morning know
Where we shall find him most conveniently.   175

Exeunt.

SCENE II. [*Elsinore. A room of state in the Castle.*]

*Flourish. Enter Claudius, King of Denmark, Gertrude the Queen, Hamlet, Polonius,
Laertes and his sister Ophelia†, [Voltemand, Cornelius,] Lords Attendant.*

KING   Though yet of Hamlet our dear brother's death
The memory be green, and that it us befitted
To bear our hearts in grief, and our whole kingdom
To be contracted in one brow of woe,
Yet so far hath discretion fought with nature   5
That we with wisest sorrow think on him
Together with remembrance of ourselves.   *benefitting others*
Therefore our sometime sister, now our queen,   *than just himself*
Th' imperial jointress to this warlike state,
Have we, as 'twere with a defeated joy,   10
With an auspicious, and a dropping eye,
(With mirth in funeral, and with dirge in marriage,)
In equal scale weighing delight and dole,
Taken to wife; nor have we herein barred
Your better wisdoms, which have freely gone   15

no one stopped it

173. **loves:** These gentlemen are Hamlet's personal friends. The plural of abstract nouns is common when two or more persons are mentioned.

SCENE II.

1.2.1-108. The king's speech is in part pompous and rhetorical (1-41), in part ingratiatingly personal (42-66), in part hectoring (87-108). 2. **be:** is.—**that:** though. —**us:** all of us. Not the royal *we* [or he would have said "our heart" EDS.]. —**befitted:** would befit. 4. **contracted...of woe:** mournful. 5. **discretion:** wise moderation (which teaches us to restrain our natural grief). 7. **ourselves:** myself and all of you. A suggestion that the marriage was not merely a personal affair, but an advantage to the whole state. [See also 1.2.14-16. EDS.] 8. **our:** my. This is the royal *we.* —**sometime sister:** The King has the nerve to point to the incestuous nature of the marriage; according to Biblical rules still adhered to in Shakespeare's time, marriage of a brother-in-law to a sister-in-law was forbidden. [EDS.] 9. **jointress:** heiress; a widow who has *jointure,* an estate which she receives on the death of her husband. [The King has the further nerve to mention the fortune his new wife brings to the marriage. EDS.] 10. **defeated:** destroyed. 11. **auspicious:** happy; [promising a good outcome. EDS.]. —**dropping:** sorrowful. [EDS.] 12. **mirth:** cheerfulness. 13. **dole:** grief. 14. **barred:** shut out; left unconsulted. 15. **Your better wisdoms:** "your wise counsel as to what it was better for me to do." 15-16. **freely...along:** heartily agreed with

†   Though only the Folio has Ophelia enter, few productions omit her; it's an opportunity to show something about her relationship with Hamlet before he encounters the Ghost. Branagh has the King and Queen enter as if in a wedding procession, with a setting reminiscent of Richard Chamberlain's for his 1970 film. The decorous BBC-TV production has the King acknowledge and bring the Queen to his side only when he mentions their marriage (8-14).

With this affair along. For all, our thanks.
Now follows, that you know, young Fortinbras,
Holding a weak supposal of our worth,
Or thinking by our late dear brother's death
Our state to be disjoint and out of frame,   20
Colleagued with this dream of his advantage,
He hath not failed to pester us with message
Importing the surrender of those lands
Lost by his father, with all bands of law,
To our most valiant brother. So much for him.‡   25
Now for ourself and for this time of meeting.
Thus much the business is: we have here writ
To Norway, uncle of young Fortinbras,
Who, impotent and bedrid, scarcely hears
Of this his nephew's purpose, to suppress   30
His further gait herein, in that the levies,
The lists, and full proportions are all made
Out of his subject; and we here dispatch
You, good Cornelius, and you, Voltemand,
For bearers of this greeting to old Norway,   35
Giving to you no further personal power
To business with the King, more than the scope
Of these dilated articles allow. [*Gives a paper.*]
Farewell, and let your haste commend your duty.

COR., VOLT.   In that, and all things, will we show our duty.   40

KING   We doubt it nothing. Heartily farewell.
                    Exeunt Voltemand and Cornelius.

---

me throughout this affair. **17. that you know:** what you already know. The Councilors are acquainted with the demand of young Fortinbras, but not with the King's purposed reply (see lines 26-33). **18. our worth:** my ability to govern. **20. Our state:** my royal administration.—**disjoint and out of frame:** Broken in its structure. **Colleagued...advantage:** with no support except his false notion that now is a favorable time. **22. to pester us with message:** to *annoy* me with *frequent* messages. **24. bands:** bonds; binding covenants and decisions. **28. Norway:** the King of Norway. **29. impotent:** feeble.— **bedrid:** confined to his bed; or ridden (i.e. carried) on a bed. **31. gait:** procedure. **31-2. levies, lists, full proportions:** Three synonyms for his followers. **33. subject:** Collective noun meaning "subjects." **37. To business:** to negotiate. **38. dilated:** detailed. **39, 40. duty, duty:** The repetition is intentional and effective: the ambassadors submissively echo the words of the King. **41. nothing:** not at all.

---

‡   The King variously shows his disdain for Fortinbras, by tearing or crumpling the paper representing his demands, usually with jovial reactions from the courtiers. Richardson's are especially high-spirited and lively, filling the frame in tight shots.

And now, Laertes, what's the news with you?[*]
You told us of some suit. What is't, Laertes?
You cannot speak of reason to the Dane
And lose your voice. What wouldst thou beg, Laertes,   45
That shall not be my offer, not thy asking?
The head is not more native to the heart,
The hand more instrumental to the mouth,
Than is the throne of Denmark to thy father.
What wouldst thou have, Laertes?

LAERTES   My dread lord,   50
Your leave and favor to return to France;
From whence though willingly I came to Denmark
To show my duty in your coronation,   *– Q1 says prior King's burial*
Yet now I must confess, that duty done,
My thoughts and wishes bend again toward France   55
And bow them to your gracious leave and pardon.

KING   Have you your father's leave? What says Polonius?

POLONIUS   He hath, my lord, wrung from me my slow leave
By laborsome petition, and at last
Upon his will I sealed my hard consent.   60
I do beseech you give him leave to go.

KING   Take thy fair hour, Laertes. Time be thine,
And thy best graces spend it at thy will.
But now, my cousin Hamlet, and my son —

42-50. **And now, Laertes…Laertes?** Ceremony over, and the state business dispatched, Claudius falls gracefully into a tone of familiarity, which becomes ever more intimate as he proceeds. At line 45 he abandons the royal *we* and the formal *you* for the personal and affectionate *I* (*my*) and *thou*. He is affable as well as kingly [or possibly politically slick; Laertes and his father Polonius are meant to feel flattered by this attention. EDS.]. 44. **the Dane:** the Danish king. 46. **my offer, not thy asking:** something granted before it is asked. 47. **native to:** naturally associated with; bound by ties of nature to. 48. **instrumental:** serviceable. 49. **thy father:** Claudius is obviously indebted to Polonius for assistance in procuring his election as king. 51. **leave and favor:** gracious permission. 56. **pardon:** permission to depart. 58. **wrung…consent:** [begged until I reluctantly gave permission EDS.] 62. **Take thy fair hour:** A graceful adaptation of the familiar *Carpe diem* [seize the day: take advantage of the time. EDS.]. 63. **graces:** good qualities (of every kind). The verses combine permission for Laertes to enjoy his youth while it lasts ("Time be thine") with the wish that such enjoyment may be guided by the best qualities of his nature. 64. **cousin:** kinsman. [EDS.]

---

[*]   The BBC's Laertes is surprised that he is the first to be called upon after the state business. During this interchange, Almereyda's Hamlet and Ophelia manage to communicate in spite of the efforts of her father and brother to separate them.

HAMLET	[*aside*] A little more than kin, and less than kind.** *both son + nephew — + threat to Claudius' reign* 65
KING	How is it that the clouds still hang on you?† *grief*
HAMLET	Not so, my lord. I am too much i' th' sun. *son*
QUEEN	Good Hamlet, cast thy nighted color off,
	And let thine eye look like a friend on Denmark.
	Do not for ever with thy vailed lids 70
	Seek for thy noble father in the dust. *—earth*
	Thou know'st 'tis common. All that lives must die,
	Passing through nature to eternity.
HAMLET	Ay, madam, it is common. *—whore*
QUEEN	If it be,
	Why seems it so particular with thee? 75

Quean: whore

HAMLET	Seems, madam? Nay, it is. I know not "seems."
	'Tis not alone my inky cloak, good mother,
reflexive	Nor customary suits of solemn black,
aware of a role	Nor windy suspiration of forced breath,
he is playing	No, nor the fruitful river in the eye, 80
(on stage)	Nor the dejected havior of the visage, *appearance*
	Together with all forms, moods, shapes of grief,
	That can denote me truly. These indeed seem,
	For they are actions that a man might play;
	But I have that within which passeth show — 85
	These but the trappings and the suits of woe.
KING	'Tis sweet and commendable in your nature, Hamlet,‡
	To give these mourning duties to your father;

Claudio + mother "seem" to be grieving

Claudio telling everyone how to feel

---

65. **more than kin...kind:** Hamlet fastens on the King's words and continues them with bitter irony: "Yes, nephew and son both. . . a little more than normal kin, and yet not quite kindly in my feelings toward you," [nor do I have your *kind* of temperament. EDS.]. 67. **Not...sun:** more in the position of a *son* than I wish I were. Thus Hamlet bitterly refuses the title *son* which the King has emphasized. [The *sun* may also symbolize the King, as in *Richard II* written about 1597. EDS.] 69. **Denmark:** the King of Denmark. 70. **vailed:** downcast. 72. **common:** universal. 73. **nature:** natural life. 75. **particular:** personal, as if it were an individual experience special to you alone. 79. **windy...breath:** A scornfully elaborate phrase for "heavy sighs." 80. **fruitful:** teeming, abundant. 81. **havior:** appearance. 82. **moods:** moody appearances. 85. **passeth show:** surpasses all mere *signs* of grief [perhaps with an echo of Paul to the Philippians 4:6-9, re "the peace that passeth understanding." EDS.].

** Kline does not say this as an aside; he doesn't care if the King hears him; the words throw the King off and make him ask a question he had not intended.

† In Zeffirelli's film, The King's exchange with Hamlet is set in Hamlet's bedroom, furnished as a scholar's study.

‡ A closeup view of Branagh facing Derek Jacobi shows a family resemblance between them; Branagh hints that Hamlet may be the result of his mother's infidelity. Almereyda's King speaks to Hamlet as they walk on a busy New York City street rather than before the whole court.

But you must know, your father lost a father;
That father lost, lost his, and the survivor bound   90
In filial obligation for some term
To do obsequious sorrow. But to persever
In obstinate condolement is a course
Of impious stubbornness. 'tis unmanly grief;
It shows a will most incorrect to heaven,   95
A heart unfortified, a mind impatient,
An understanding simple and unschooled;
For what we know must be, and is as common
As any the most vulgar thing to sense,
Why should we in our peevish opposition   100
Take it to heart? Fie. 'tis a fault to heaven,
A fault against the dead, a fault to nature,
To reason most absurd, whose common theme
Is death of fathers, and who still hath cried,
From the first corse till he that died today,   105
"This must be so." We pray you throw to earth
This unprevailing woe, and think of us
As of a father; for let the world take note
You are the most immediate to our throne,
And with no less nobility of love   110
Than that which dearest father bears his son
Do I impart toward you. For your intent
In going back to school in Wittenberg,
It is most retrograde to our desire;

Strength in state + man = not grieving

---

90. **bound:** The subject of the verb is *that father*; the object is *survivor.* "That father, by dying, laid his surviving son (your father) under an obligation to mourn for him." 92. **obsequious sorrow:** sorrow befitting obsequies (funeral rites).—**persever:** persevere. 93. **obstinate condolement:** mourning that refuses to be comforted. 95. **incorrect to heaven:** Not submissive to God's will. 99. **As any...sense:** as anything that is the commonest object of sight or hearing. 100. **peevish:** childish, foolish. 101-2. **a fault...nature:** a triple fault, involving (1) rebellion against God's will; (2) unfilial feelings (as if one blamed one's father for dying); (3) revolt against the established order of nature (for death is as natural as life). 103. **whose:** The antecedent seems to be *nature* rather than *reason.*—**common theme:** events in nature show that death must be the lot of all mankind. 104. **still:** always.—**he:** grammatically correct. 105. **corse:** corpse. [EDS.] 106. **We:** The royal *we* introduces the sentence relating to succession to the throne. 107. **unprevailing:** useless. [EDS.] 108–117. The King proclaims Hamlet his heir; and, even in this elective monarchy, such an announcement would go far to determine the succession. [Later, Hamlet refers to himself as fed with meaningless promises (3.2.99-100, 354-9. If his mother is young enough to bear the king a child, the promise might be moot. EDS.] 110. **nobility of love:** distinguished affection. 112. **impart:** express myself.—**For:** as for. 113. **school:** your university studies. The University of Wittenberg (founded in 1502) was at the height of its reputation in Shakespeare's day and was esteemed because of its connection with Luther and the Reformation. [The time scheme of the play varies; later it appears the time is that of the Danelaw, when England was under the control of Denmark, historically in the 9th century; see 4.3.60-4. EDS.] 114. **retrograde:** contrary; literally, moving backward. *Retrograde*, as an astronomical term, describes the motion of a planet when it seems to move backward, i.e., in a direction contrary to the order of the signs of the zodiac.

likeness — Oedipus

In Branagh's film, the likeness between Hamlet and the King (Derek Jacobi) is remarkable, suggesting a closer relationship than nephew and uncle.

	And we beseech you, bend you to remain	115
	Here in the cheer and comfort of our eye,	
	Our chiefest courtier, cousin, and our son.	
QUEEN	Let not thy mother lose her prayers, Hamlet.	
	I pray thee stay with us, go not to Wittenberg.	
HAMLET	I shall in all my best obey you, madam.	120
KING	Why, 'tis a loving and a fair reply.	
	Be as ourself in Denmark. Madam, come.	
	This gentle and unforced accord of Hamlet	
	Sits smiling to my heart; in grace whereof,	
	No jocund health that Denmark drinks today	125
	But the great cannon to the clouds shall tell,	
	And the King's rouse the heaven shall bruit	
	again, Respeaking earthly thunder. Come away.†	

---

115. **we beseech you, bend you:** we ask you to submit to our will. 116. **our eye:** my royal presence. 117. **son:** The King emphasizes once more that title (*son*) which has provoked Hamlet's bitter jest (line 65). 118. The Queen interposes again (as in line 68), thus preventing any further taunts and enabling Hamlet to obey *her* rather than his stepfather. 119. **thy...thee:** The familiar and affectionate form of address. The King has used the more formal *you* [a contrast to his *thou*ing of Laertes. EDS.]. 122. **Be as ourself:** Regard yourself as King, to all intents and purposes. 124. **Sits...heart:** gives me heartfelt satisfaction.—**grace:** honor. 127. **rouse:** drink, especially, a deep draught—one that empties the beaker. *Rouse* is a shortened form of *carouse,* noun and verb. —**bruit again:** report again. This drinking bout is particularly repugnant to Hamlet, educated at a foreign university and also constitutionally averse to heavy drinking. Samuel Johnson (1765) was the first to point out that the King rarely misses an opportunity to drink.

---

†   Ophelia (both Diane Venora in Klein's version and Kate Winslet in Branagh's version) tries to approach Hamlet, but Laertes restrains her and draws her away.

too alive for / suicide (handwritten)

Flourish. Exeunt all but Hamlet.

HAMLET O that this too too solid flesh would melt,‡

Thaw, and resolve itself into a dew.   130

Or that the Everlasting had not fixed

His canon 'gainst self-slaughter. O God. God.

How weary, stale, flat, and unprofitable

Seem to me all the uses of this world.

Fie on't. ah, fie. 'Tis an unweeded garden — *eve* (handwritten)   135

That grows to seed; things rank and gross in nature

Possess it merely. That it should come to this.

But two months dead. Nay, not so much, not two.

So excellent a king, that was to this

Hyperion to a satyr; so loving to my mother*   140

(handwritten left margin: gender differences / man: solid flesh / woman: sullied flesh / women: inability to control sexual desire / sin is a product of that)

That he might not beteem the winds of heaven

Visit her face too roughly. Heaven and earth.

Must I remember? Why, she would hang on him

As if increase of appetite had grown

By what it fed on; and yet, within a month — *sullied flesh* (handwritten) 145

Let me not think on't. Frailty, thy name is woman.** —

A little month, or ere those shoes were old

With which she followed my poor father's body

Like Niobe, all tears — why she, even she

(O God. a beast that wants discourse of reason *animal – primal / sexual nature* (handwritten) 150

Would have mourned longer) married with my uncle;

My father's brother, but no more like my father

Than I to Hercules. Within a month,

Ere yet the salt of most unrighteous tears

Had left the flushing in her galled eyes,   155

---

129. **too too:** A very common doubling of *too* for emphasis.—**solid:** Hamlet wishes that he could melt away, with a wish, or that suicide were not forbidden by God's law. [A few editors prefer *sullied* (*soiled*) or *sallied* (assailed by the demands of the flesh). EDS.] 132. **canon:** divine law. 134. **uses:** Either "custom'" or (better) "enjoyments," i.e., "advantages to be derived from life in this world." 137. **merely:** entirely, utterly. 140. **Hyperion:** the sun god, most beautiful of the divinities. [The comparison of the King to the sun is an Elizabethan commonplace, as is the Queen to the moon. So it is natural that Hamlet compare his father to Hyperion, but he also uses the occasion to contrast him to the present King, his uncle, whom he likens to a satyr, a mythical beast, half man, half goat, always symbolic of lechery. EDS.] 141. **might not beteem:** could not allow. 147. **or ere:** Both *or* and *ere* mean "before." 150. **discourse of reason:** the process or faculty of reasoning. 153. **Than I to Hercules:** Hamlet is strong and active—a good fencer— [but not a doer of great deeds, as was Hercules. His father, however, was Hercules-like in his deeds. EDS.]. 154. **unrighteous:** because they were insincere. 155. **left the flushing:** allowed the redness to disappear.—**galled:** irritated, inflamed.

---

‡   Zeffirelli's Hamlet delivers this soliloquy while standing at his study window.

*   Scott's Hamlet tears a snapshot of his parents, keeping the half with his father's image.

**   Zeffirelli's Hamlet says this line while watching his mother and stepfather below, riding to the hunt, one of many instances of spying in the film.

She married. O, most wicked speed, to post
With such dexterity to incestuous sheets.
It is not, nor it cannot come to good.
But break my heart, for I must hold my tongue. ‑ *none of this can be public*

Enter Horatio, Marcellus, and Bernardo.

HORATIO	Hail to your lordship.	
HAMLET	I am glad to see you well.†	160
	Horatio. — or I do forget myself.	
HORATIO	The same, my lord, and your poor servant ever.	
HAMLET	Sir, my good friend — I'll change that name with you.	
	And what make you from Wittenberg, Horatio?	
	Marcellus?	165
MARCELLUS	My good lord.	
HAMLET	I am very glad to see you. — [*To Bernardo*] Good even, sir. —	
	But what, in faith, make you from Wittenberg?	
HORATIO	A truant disposition, good my lord.	
HAMLET	I would not hear your enemy say so,	170
	Nor shall you do my ear that violence	
	To make it truster of your own report	
	Against yourself. I know you are no truant.	
	But what is your affair in Elsinore?	
	We'll teach you to drink deep ere you depart.	175
HORATIO	My lord, I came to see your father's funeral.	
HAMLET	I prithee do not mock me, fellow student.	
	I think it was to see my mother's wedding.	
HORATIO	Indeed, my lord, it followed hard upon.	

157. **dexterity:** speed.—**incestuous sheets:** marriage to a brother's widow is, Biblically, regarded as incest. See line 8 and note. [EDS.] 160. **I am glad...well:** Mechanically uttered, before Hamlet sees who it is. The next line is spoken in enthusiastic recognition of his friend. 163. **change:** exchange: call each other "friend." [treat each other as equals. EDS.] 164. **And what make you?** And what are you doing?—**from:** away from. 165–7. Shakespeare takes pains to show that Hamlet is not a snob; he speaks easily to those of lower birth. Thus his rudeness to those he dislikes when he puts on madness is all the more deceptive. 169. **A truant disposition:** a feeling that I should skip school. *Disposition* often means a "mood." —**my lord:** Practically a single word (compare French *milord*), thus "good my lord" is equivalent to "my good lord." 174. **your affair:** "your actual business." [Hamlet also asks searching questions of Rosencrantz and Guildenstern (2.2.247-9, 278, etc.); Horatio passes and they fail the test. EDS.] 175. **to drink deep:** Usually said sarcastically in performance: in several places, Hamlet exhibits his disapproval of the Danish predilection for drunkenness.

† **I am glad to see thee well**: Tears blot Kline's eyes so that he does not recognize the men who enter and responds mechanically.

HAMLET	Thrift, thrift, Horatio. The funeral baked meats	180
	Did coldly furnish forth the marriage tables.	
	Would I had met my dearest foe in heaven	
	Or ever I had seen that day, Horatio.	
	My father — methinks I see my father.	
HORATIO	O, where, my lord?	
HAMLET	In my mind's eye, Horatio.	185
HORATIO	I saw him once. He was a goodly King	
HAMLET	He was a man, take him for all in all.	
	I shall not look upon his like again.	
HORATIO	My lord, I think I saw him yesternight.	
HAMLET	Saw? who?	190
HORATIO	My lord, the King your father.	
HAMLET	The King my father?	
HORATIO	Season your admiration for a while	
	With an attent ear, till I may deliver,	
	Upon the witness of these gentlemen,	
	This marvel to you.	
HAMLET	For God's love let me hear.	195
HORATIO	Two nights together had these gentlemen	
	(Marcellus and Bernardo) on their watch	
	In the dead vast and middle of the night	
	Been thus encountered. A figure like your father,	
	Armed at point exactly, cap-a-pe,	200
	Appears before them and with solemn march	
	Goes slow and stately by them. Thrice he walked	
	By their oppressed and fear-surprised eyes,	
	Within his truncheon's length; whilst they distilled	
	Almost to jelly with the act of fear,	205

[handwritten margin note: ironic w/ brother acting as King]

---

180. **Thrift:** mere economy. A bitter jest. The only reason for such haste was, he says, to save the remnants of the funeral feast.—**baked meats:** meat pies. Elaborate funeral feasts were an old and universal custom. 181. **coldly:** when cold. 182. **dearest:** *My dearest foe* means "bitterest enemy." 183. **Or ever:** before ever. 186. **once:** Horatio, though a Dane, was not a courtier; but he has visited the Danish court before [or he has seen him during his wars, as he suggests in 1.1.60-3. EDS.].—**goodly:** handsome. 190. Horatio has been startled by Hamlet's "Methinks I see my father." Hamlet is equally surprised by Horatio's words. 192. **Season your admiration:** Control your astonishment. 193. **deliver:** report. 198. **the dead vast:** endless, desolate, [EDS.] 200. **at point:** completely.—**cap-a-pe:** from head to foot. 203. **oppressed:** overwhelmed by the horror of the sight.—**fear-surprised:** seized upon by fear. *Surprise* usually means to "take captive" or "seize," literally or figuratively. 204. **his truncheon's length:** The truncheon was a short staff signifying military command. —**distilled:** dissolved. 205. **with the act of fear:** by the action of fear.

	Stand dumb and speak not to him. This to me	
	In dreadful secrecy impart they did,	
	And I with them the third night kept the watch;	
	Where, as they had delivered, both in time,	
	Form of the thing, each word made true and good,	210
	The apparition comes. I knew your father.	
	These hands are not more like.	
HAMLET	But where was this?	
MARCELLUS	My lord, upon the platform where we watched.	
HAMLET	Did you not speak to it?	
HORATIO	My lord, I did;	
	But answer made it none. Yet once methought	215
	It lifted up it head and did address	
	Itself to motion, like as it would speak;	
	But even then the morning cock crew loud,	
	And at the sound it shrunk in haste away	
	And vanished from our sight.	
HAMLET	'Tis very strange.	220
HORATIO	As I do live, my honored lord, 'tis true;	
	And we did think it writ down in our duty	
	To let you know of it.	
HAMLET	Indeed, indeed, sirs. But this troubles me.	
	Hold you the watch tonight?	
BOTH [*Mar. and Ber.*]	We do, my lord.	225
HAMLET	Armed, say you?	
BOTH	Armed, my lord.	
HAMLET	From top to toe?	
BOTH	My lord, from head to foot.	
HAMLET	Then saw you not his face?	
HORATIO	O, yes, my lord. He wore his beaver up.	230
HAMLET	What, looked he frowningly?	
HORATIO	A countenance more in sorrow than in anger.	
HAMLET	Pale or red?	
HORATIO	Nay, very pale.	

---

207. **In dreadful secrecy:** under pledge of silence. 216. **it head:** its head. 216-17. **did address... speak:** seemed to indicate that it wanted to speak. 230. **beaver:** visor. Helmets varied in style: some had a piece that lifted up; others hinged down. 232. **countenance:** facial expression.

HAMLET	And fixed his eyes upon you?	
HORATIO	Most constantly.	
HAMLET	I would I had been there.	235
HORATIO	It would have much amazed you.	
HAMLET	Very like, very like. Stayed it long?	
HORATIO	While one with moderate haste might tell a hundred.	
BOTH.	Longer, longer.	
HORATIO	Not when I saw't.	
HAMLET	His beard was grizzled — no?	240
HORATIO	It was, as I have seen it in his life, A sable silvered.	

HAMLET   I will watch to-night.
          Perchance 'twill walk again.

HORATIO   I warr'nt it will.

HAMLET   If it assume my noble father's person,
          I'll speak to it, though hell itself should gape   245
          And bid me hold my peace. I pray you all,
          If you have hitherto concealed this sight,
          Let it be tenable in your silence still;
          And whatsoever else shall hap tonight,
          Give it an understanding but no tongue.   250
          I will requite your loves. So, fare you well.
          Upon the platform, 'twixt eleven and twelve,
          I'll visit you.

ALL   Our duty to your honor.

HAMLET   Your loves, as mine to you. Farewell.
                                   Exeunt [all but Hamlet].
          My father's spirit — in arms? All is not well.   255
          I doubt some foul play. Would the night were come.
          Till then sit still, my soul. Foul deeds will rise,
          Though all the earth o'erwhelm them, to men's eyes.   *Exit.*

---

235. **constantly:** unswervingly. 236. **amazed you:** confused your thoughts. 238. **tell:** count. 240. **grizzled:** grey and black mixed. Horatio responds with what is perhaps a softer expression of the same feature: "a sable silvered" (line 241). Similarly, he responds to Hamlet's "The air bites shrewdly" with "It is a nipping and an eager air" (1.4.1-2). Horatio's wit shows he is a good match for Hamlet. 244. **assume:** Hamlet does not know whether the apparition was his father's ghost or a demon in the shape of his father; [his physical likeness to his father is persuasive, but other of his attributes make him ambiguous. EDS.]. 245. **gape:** Hell-mouth was a familiar figure in medieval art; on the Elizabethan stage, it was an enormous wide-open mouth with huge teeth. 246. **hold my peace:** Hamlet is thinking of the danger of speaking to a demon. 248. **Let it be tenable:** Regard it as something that must be held secret. 254. **Your loves, as mine to you:** Hamlet courteously tells Horatio and the others not to consider him to be their superior but to regard him simply as their friend. 256. **I doubt some foul play:** I suspect a crime.

echo-chamber: views of Hamlet that cast a doubtful light on him that would remain in audience's mind & bias

SCENE III. [*Elsinore. A room in the house of Polonius.*]

Enter Laertes and Ophelia.†

LAERTES	My necessaries are embarked. Farewell.
	And, sister, as the winds give benefit
	And convoy is assistant, do not sleep,
	But let me hear from you.
OPHELIA	Do you doubt that?
LAERTES	For Hamlet, and the trifling of his favor,
	Hold it a fashion, and a toy in blood;
	A violet in the youth of primy nature,
	Forward, not permanent — sweet, not lasting;
	The perfume and suppliance of a minute;
	No more.
OPHELIA	No more but so?
LAERTES	Think it no more.
	For nature crescent does not grow alone
	In thews and bulk; but as this temple waxes,
	The inward service of the mind and soul
	Grows wide withal. Perhaps he loves you now,
	And now no soil nor cautel doth besmirch
	The virtue of his will; but you must fear,
	His greatness weighed, his will is not his own;
	For he himself is subject to his birth.
	He may not, as unvalued persons do,
	Carve for himself, for on his choice depends
	The safety and health of this whole state,
	And therefore must his choice be circumscribed
	Unto the voice and yielding of that body

Line numbers: 5 (line 5), 10 (line 10), 15 (line 15), 20 (line 20)

his birth has been put into question

ACT 1. SCENE III

3. **convoy:** means of transportation. 6. **fashion:** typical behavior for young men of Hamlet's class.—**a toy in blood:** a whim of youthful passion. 7. **in...nature:** in the springtime of life. This passage confirms Hamlet's youth. 9. **The perfume...minute:** the pleasant pastime of a minute. 10. **No more but so?** Only that and nothing more? 11. **nature crescent:** one's nature, as it grows. 12. **thews:** sinews.—**this temple:** the body. The metaphor is carried out in the next lines: "As the body (the temple) grows larger, the services conducted therein by the mind and soul (the priests of the temple) grow more extensive and elaborate." See *1 Corinthians* 6:19. 14. **withal:** at the same time. 15. **soil:** foul thought.—**cautel:** deceit.—**besmirch:** tarnish; taint. [EDS.] 16. **will:** willpower. [EDS.] 17. **His greatness weighed:** when his high rank is considered. 20. **Carve for himself:** choose for himself. 21. **safety:** Three syllables to preserve the line's ten-beat meter.—**health:** welfare. 23. **voice and yielding:** authority and assent.

---

† In Kline's production, a smiling Ophelia is reading a letter; Laertes enters, takes the letter and crumples it. She later manages to retrieve it.

supposed to be hamlet but thats not the case

Whereof he is the head. Then if he says he loves you,
It fits your wisdom so far to believe it   25
As he in his particular act and place
May give his saying deed; which is no further
Than the main voice of Denmark goes withal.
Then weigh what loss your honor may sustain
If with too credent ear you list his songs,   30
Or lose your heart, or your chaste treasure open
To his unmastered importunity.
Fear it, Ophelia, fear it, my dear sister,
And keep you in the rear of your affection,
Out of the shot and danger of desire.   35
The chariest maid is prodigal enough
If she unmask her beauty to the moon.
Virtue itself scapes not calumnious strokes.
The canker galls the infants of the spring
Too oft before their buttons be disclosed,   40
And in the morn and liquid dew of youth
Contagious blastments are most imminent.
Be wary then; best safety lies in fear.
Youth to itself rebels, though none else near.

OPHELIA   I shall th' effect of this good lesson keep   45
As watchman to my heart. But, good my brother,
Do not as some ungracious pastors do,
Show me the steep and thorny way to heaven,
Whiles, like a puffed and reckless libertine,
Himself the primrose path of dalliance treads   50
And recks not his own rede.

LAERTES   O, fear me not—

Enter Polonius.

I stay too long. But here my father comes.
A double blessing is a double grace;

---

26. **in...place:** acting under the restrictions of his rank. 28. **main:** powerful.—**goes withal:** agrees
therewith. 30. **credent:** credulous. [EDS.] 34. **affection:** feelings. [Laertes is advising Ophelia to restrain
herself. EDS.] The military metaphor is carried out in the next line. Laertes, like his father, is fond of
elaborate figures of speech. 36. **chariest:** most cautious and circumspect. 39-40. **canker...disclosed:**
the rose caterpillar *galls* (gnaws) the heart of roses "before the buds are unclosed." 42. **blastments:**
blights. [EDS.] 44. **Youth...near:** Youth often acts contrary to its better nature, even without temptation.
45. **th' effect:** the substance.—**lesson:** with a mischievous suggestion that Laertes is "reading a lesson"
like a preacher. 47. **ungracious:** graceless. 49. **Whiles:** while. —**libertine:** one who is sexually loose.
50. **primrose path:** seemingly pleasant but irresponsible life. [EDS.]—**dalliance:** pleasure. 51. **recks
not his own rede:** heeds not his own counsel.—**O, fear me not:** Don't worry about me! 53. **A double
blessing...grace:** To receive two blessings (at parting from one's father) is a double gift from heaven.

Occasion smiles upon a second leave.

POLONIUS   Yet here, Laertes? Aboard, aboard, for shame.   55
The wind sits in the shoulder of your sail,
And you are stayed for. There — my blessing with thee.
And these few precepts in thy memory †
Look thou character. Give thy thoughts no tongue,
Nor any unproportioned thought his act.   60
Be thou familiar, but by no means vulgar:
Those friends thou hast, and their adoption tried,
Grapple them unto thy soul with hoops of steel;
But do not dull thy palm with entertainment
Of each new-hatched, unfledged comrade. Beware   65
Of entrance to a quarrel; but being in,
Bear't that th' opposed may beware of thee.
Give every man thine ear, but few thy voice;
Take each man's censure, but reserve thy judgment.
Costly thy habit as thy purse can buy,   70
But not expressed in fancy; rich, not gaudy;
For the apparel oft proclaims the man,
And they in France of the best rank and station
Are most select and generous, chief in that.
Neither a borrower nor a lender be;   75
For loan oft loses both itself and friend,
And borrowing dulls the edge of husbandry.
This above all — to thine own self be true,
And it must follow, as the night the day,
Thou canst not then be false to any man.   80
Farewell. My blessing season this in thee.

---

54. **Occasion smiles...leave:** Opportunity treats me kindly in granting me this second good-bye. 57. **There:** Polonius lays his hand on his son's head and gives him his blessing. 59. **cháracter:** inscribe, write. 60. **unproportioned:** out of harmony with reason and good conduct.—**his:** its. 61. **vulgar:** indiscriminate in friendship. 64-5. **But do not dull...comrade:** But do not shake hands so readily and often that you can no longer distinguish between a true friend and a chance acquaintance. 64. **entertainment:** reception, welcoming. 67. **Bear't:** Conduct the affair.—**that:** so that.—**opposéd:** opponent. 68. **voice:** recommendation. 69. **censure:** judgment. 71. **expressed in fancy:** showing its costliness. The next phrase repeats the idea. 72. **the apparel...man:** people often judge a man by his clothing. [EDS.] 74. **Are most...in that:** show their fine taste and gentlemanly instincts more in that than in any other point of manners. 77. **borrowing...husbandry:** A habit of borrowing makes one less eager to economize. 78–80. **This above all...any man:** This precept includes and ennobles all others. [However, the worth of being true to oneself depends on the person's moral quality. EDS.] 81. **season this:** follow my advice by good conduct.

---

†   Maintaining the motif of Hamlet-as-spy, Zeffirelli's Hamlet watches from above when Polonius delivers his advice to Laertes and when Polonius chastises Ophelia for her romantic interest in Hamlet (88-134).

LAERTES	Most humbly do I take my leave, my lord.	
POLONIUS	The time invites you. Go, your servants tend.	
LAERTES	Farewell, Ophelia, and remember well What I have said to you.	
OPHELIA	'Tis in my memory locked, And you yourself shall keep the key of it.	85
LAERTES	Farewell.	*Exit.*
POLONIUS	What is't, Ophelia, he hath said to you?	
OPHELIA	So please you, something touching the Lord Hamlet.	
POLONIUS	Marry, well bethought. 'Tis told me he hath very oft of late Given private time to you, and you yourself Have of your audience been most free and bounteous. If it be so — as so 'tis put on me, And that in way of caution — I must tell you‡ You do not understand yourself so clearly As it behooves my daughter and your honor. What is between you? Give me up the truth.	90 95
OPHELIA	He hath, my lord, of late made many tenders Of his affection to me.	100
POLONIUS	Affection? Pooh. You speak like a green girl, Unsifted in such perilous circumstance. Do you believe his tenders, as you call them?	
OPHELIA	I do not know, my lord, what I should think.	
POLONIUS	Marry, I will teach you. Think yourself a baby That you have ta'en these tenders for true pay, Which are not sterling. Tender yourself more dearly, Or (not to crack the wind of the poor phrase, Running it thus) you'll tender me a fool.	105

---

83. **tend:** are waiting. 94. **put on me:** brought to my notice. 98. **Give me up the truth:** Tell me the truth. 99. **tenders:** offers. 101. **green girl:** immature, naive; also lovesick: green was the color of lovers and of jealousy. [EDS.] 102. **Unsifted:** inexperienced. 106–9. Polonius puns on *tender* in the sense of "an offer" (line 106), of "hold" or "regard" (line 107), and finally of "furnish" or "afford" (line 109): "Hold yourself at a higher rate,—don't make yourself so cheap,—or you'll furnish me with a fool for a daughter (by making a fool of yourself)." 108. **crack the wind...phrase:** make the poor word pant like an over-ridden horse.

---

‡   95-134. Polonius may be dismissive (Kline's and Kozintsev's), confusing her with his calm certainty, or, at another extreme, fiercely domineering (Branagh's).

"He hath, my lord, made many tenders Of his affection to me" (1.3.99-100). Kozintsev's Polonius (Yuri Tolubeyev) scans a book, while Ophelia (Anastasia Vertinskaya) sits humbly at his feet, her hands folded as if in meditation. Polonius' elevation and apparent preoccupation underscore his conviction that he controls the situation and forces her acquiescence.

OPHELIA	My lord, he hath importuned me with love	110
	In honorable fashion.	
POLONIUS	Ay, fashion you may call it. Go to, go to.	
OPHELIA	And hath given countenance to his speech, my lord,	
	With almost all the holy vows of heaven.	
POLONIUS	Ay, springes to catch woodcocks. I do know,	115
	When the blood burns, how prodigal the soul *passion maker*	
	Lends the tongue vows. These blazes, daughter, *promises*	
	Giving more light than heat, extinct in both *unreliable love*	
	Even in their promise, as it is a-making,	
	You must not take for fire. From this time	120
	Be something scanter of your maiden presence.	
	Set your entreatments at a higher rate	
	Than a command to parley. For Lord Hamlet,	
	Believe so much in him, that he is young,	
	And with a larger tether may he walk	125
	Than may be given you. In few, Ophelia,	

112. **fashion:** manner typical of a naive girl. [EDS.]—**Go to:** Literally, "Go on!" An old idiom of reproof and impatience, often intended to stop discussion, [as in "that's enough!" EDS.]. 113. **countenance:** confirmation. 115. **springes:** snares. The woodcock served as a proverbial synonym for credulous foolishness, some people believing that it actually had no brain. 116. **prodigal:** superabundantly. 117–19. **These blazes...a-making:** Proverbial, "Hot love soon cold": Such flashes of youthful fancy, more show than substance, die out even while the promise is being uttered. 122-3. **Set...parley:** When a besieger appears before the castle of your heart and summons you to a parley, do not immediately enter into negotiations (*entreatments*) for surrender. The metaphor by which a woman or a woman's heart is identified with a castle or walled town was well established long before Shakespeare's time.

Do not believe his vows; for they are brokers,
Not of that dye which their investments show,
But mere implorators of unholy suits,
Breathing like sanctified and pious bawds,
The better to beguile. This is for all:
I would not, in plain terms, from this time forth
Have you so slander any moment leisure†
As to give words or talk with the Lord Hamlet.
Look to't, I charge you. Come your ways.   135

interior/exterior

Hamlet as a false priest — holy suits that are in fact unholy   130

OPHELIA   I shall obey, my lord.   *Exeunt.*

SCENE IV. [*Elsinore. The platform before the Castle.*]

Enter Hamlet, Horatio, and Marcellus.

HAMLET   The air bites shrewdly; it is very cold.

HORATIO   It is a nipping and an eager air.

HAMLET   What hour now?

HORATIO   I think it lacks of twelve.

MARCELLUS   No, it is struck.

HORATIO   Indeed? I heard it not. It then draws near the season   5
          Wherein the spirit held his wont to walk.
                    A flourish of trumpets, and two pieces go off.
          What does this mean, my lord?

HAMLET   The King doth wake tonight and takes his rouse,
          Keeps wassail, and the swagg'ring upspring reels,
          And, as he drains his draughts of Rhenish down,   10
          The kettledrum and trumpet thus bray out

---

126. **In few:** in brief. 127. **brokers:** pimps. [EDS.] 128. **Not...show:** Ophelia has described Hamlet's vows as "holy" (line 114). Polonius retorts that their holiness is mere disguise.—**investments:** clothing [outward appearance. EDS.]. 129. **mere:** out-and-out. 130. **Breathing...bawds:** speaking in soft and persuasive accents, like hypocritical tempters [that is, pimps. EDS.]. 133. **slander:** disgrace; spend discreditably.—**moment:** momentary. 135. **Come your ways:** Come along.

SCENE IV
1. **shrewdly:** Literally, "cursedly" [thus, bitterly. EDS.]. 2. **eager:** sharp. 6. **the spirit:** Hamlet does not commit himself as to whether or not the apparition is his father's ghost.—**pieces:** weapons. 8. **doth... rouse:** sits up late and drinks deep. 9. **upspring:** The *upspring* was a wild "swaggering" dance. 12. **The**

---

†   In Almereyda's version, father and daughter sit together, and at the word **slander** he picks up her foot and ties her shoelaces, treating his daughter like a child. She does not answer, does not agree (no line 136). Similarly Scott's strong Ophelia does not acquiesce.

The triumph of his pledge.

HORATIO   Is it a custom?

HAMLET   Ay, marry, is't;
But to my mind, though I am native here
And to the manner born, it is a custom   15
More honored in the breach than the observance.
This heavy-headed revel east and west
Makes us traduced and taxed of other nations;
They clip us drunkards and with swinish phrase
Soil our addition; and indeed it takes   20
From our achievements, though performed at height,
The pith and marrow of our attribute.
So oft‡ it chances in particular men
That, for some vicious mole of nature in them,
As in their birth, — wherein they are not guilty,   25
Since nature cannot choose his origin, —
By the o'ergrowth of some complexion,
Oft breaking down the pales and forts of reason,
Or by some habit that too much o'erleavens
The form of plausive manners, that these men   30
Carrying, I say, the stamp of one defect,
Being nature's livery, or fortune's star,

---

triumph of his pledge: the feat of health-drinking, in which one drains the cup all at once.—**Is it a custom?** The King is holding a drinking bout, for which Germanic nations were once famous, and, in Shakespeare's day, the Danes especially so. This custom is distasteful to Hamlet. [Horatio, who knows so much about King Hamlet's combat history, does not know the court customs. EDS.] 13. **Ay, marry, is't:** Yes indeed it is. *Marry,* originally an oath "by the Virgin Mary" is by this time a mild swear word. 16. **More...observance:** more honorable to break than to observe. 17. **east and west:** far and wide. The Folio omits "This...scandal" (lines 17–38) [perhaps because lines that criticize Danes might be considered an insult to Anne of Denmark and her husband King James of Scotland. He was, at the time *Hamlet* was written, the likely heir to the English throne (and became king of England in 1603 after Queen Elizabeth died). [EDS.]. 18. **taxed:** blamed.—**of:** by. 19. **clip:** call—**with swinish phrase:** by calling us pigs. 20. **Soil our addition:** sully our reputation.—**indeed:** "in point of fact." 21. **at height:** at the full height of possible achievement. 22. **attribute:** reputation. 23. **in particular men:** in the case of *individuals.* 24. **some vicious mole of nature in them:** some natural fault which is a blemish. In what follows, three ways are mentioned in which this blemish may originate: (1) inherited by birth; (2) acquired by habit; (3) contracted accidentally or thoughtlessly. 26. **his:** its. 27. **the o'er-growth of some complexion:** the over-development of some part of one's constitution. One's *complexion* (temperament) was thought to be determined by the balance of four humors constituting one's physical make-up: blood, phlegm, red bile (or choler), and black bile (or melancholy). Depending upon which humor predominated, a person was sanguine, phlegmatic, choleric, or melancholic. If one *humor* increased excessively, a fault might result—rashness, sloth, irascibility, or moroseness. 29. **o'erleavens:** modifies (as leaven changes dough). 30. **plausive:** agreeable. 32. **nature's livery:** something by which one is marked by nature: either inherited because of temperament or resulting from the development of an excessive *complexion.*—**fortune's star:** determined by chance, the accidental forming of "some habit."

---

‡   Scott's Hamlet breaks off after the second word, seeing the Ghost.

Their virtues else — be they as pure as grace,
As infinite as man may undergo —
Shall in the general censure take corruption   35
From that particular fault. The dram of e'il
Doth all the noble substance often dout
To his own scandal.

Enter Ghost

HORATIO   Look, my lord, it comes.

HAMLET   Angels and ministers of grace defend us.[†]
               Be thou a spirit of health or goblin damned,   40
               Bring with thee airs from heaven or blasts from hell,
               Be thy intents wicked or charitable,
               Thou com'st in such a questionable shape
               That I will speak to thee. I'll call thee Hamlet,
               King, father, royal Dane. O, answer me.   45
               Let me not burst in ignorance, but tell
               Why thy canonized bones, hearsed in death,
               Have burst their cerements; why the sepulcher

---

33. **Their virtues else:** all their other qualities, however excellent.—**grace:** holiness. 34. **may undergo:** can sustain or support. Human nature is incapable of infinite goodness, but the virtues of these individuals come as near perfection as possible. 35. **Shall:** will inevitably.—**take corruption:** be infected. The world will see only their one fault and overlook their many virtues. 36. **dram:** small amount.—**e'il:** evil. 37. **often:** an emendation of "of a" from the Second Quarto.—**dout:** nullify (literally, put out). 38. **To his own scandal:** to one's utter disgrace. To summarize: "A small of evil often nullifies (in the world's opinion) all that is good in a man's nature." 39-49. Hamlet, like Horatio, is a scholar and knows how an apparition should be addressed. He too understands the danger of speaking to a spirit and the possibility that this may be a demon disguised as his father. Thus he begins by invoking the angels and good spirits to protect them all; then, calling the apparition by his father's name, he entreats it to tell its errand. [Hamlet's belief in the Ghost's honesty is confirmed finally when he sees the king react to the play-within-the-play (3.2.297-8); then when the Ghost again appears, in his mother's closet, Hamlet respectfully addresses him as "your gracious figure" and as "he" rather than "it" (81). Hamlet never considers, however, that a diabolical ghost could tell him the truth to move him to take action that might damn him (see *Macbeth* 1.3.138-41). EDS.] 40. **health:** salvation. A *spirit of health* is, then, a good spirit, as opposed to a demon or *goblin damned*. The antithesis is carried out in the next two lines. Hamlet does not raise the question whether his father's soul is saved or lost, but whether this apparition is a spirit of good or of evil. If it is the ghost of his father, then he assumes that it has come with good intent. 42. **charitable:** good, benevolent. 43. **questionable shape:** a shape (that of my father) which encourages me to question thee [while at the same time, its origin is dubious. EDS.]. 44-5. **Hamlet...Dane:** Hamlet the scholar knows that a supernatural being should be called upon by all known names that may belong to it. The theory was that the right name would force or induce it to speak.—**royal Dane:** Hamlet pauses for a moment after these words; but the Ghost says nothing, and so he calls upon it passionately for an answer. 47. **canónized:** sanctified, i.e., buried with all sacred rites.—**hearséd:** entombed. *Hearse* in Elizabethan English could mean "bier," "monument," or "tomb." 48. **cerements:** the waxed cloth in which the body was wrapped.

---

†   Zeffirelli's Hamlet makes the sign of the cross, a natural response for a Catholic but perhaps out
     of character for a student returning from Protestant Wittenberg. Many Hamlets hold up a sword
     displaying the cross-like hilt.

questioning why this is happening
Wherein we saw thee quietly inurned,
Hath oped his ponderous and marble jaws   50
To cast thee up again. What may this mean
That thou, dead corse, again in complete steel,
Revisits thus the glimpses of the moon,
Making night hideous, and we fools of nature
So horridly to shake our disposition   55
With thoughts beyond the reaches of our souls?
Say, why is this? wherefore? What should we do?

Ghost beckons Hamlet.

HORATIO   It beckons you to go away with it,
As if it some impartment did desire
To you alone.

MARCELLUS   Look with what courteous action   60
It waves you to a more removed ground.
But do not go with it.

HORATIO   No, by no means.

HAMLET   It will not speak. Then will I follow it.

HORATIO   Do not, my lord.

HAMLET   Why, what should be the fear?
I do not set my life at a pin's fee;   65
And for my soul, what can it do to that,
Being a thing immortal as itself?
It waves me forth again. I'll follow it.

HORATIO   What if it tempt you toward the flood, my lord,
Or to the dreadful summit of the cliff   70
That beetles o'er his base into the sea,
And there assume some other, horrible form
Which might deprive your sovereignty of reason
And draw you into madness? Think of it.
The very place puts toys of desperation,   75

---

51. **may:** can. 53. **fools of nature...souls:** and causing us (who are, in such a case, reduced to the condition of fools by our weak human nature) to agitate our minds with thoughts which grasp at more than our souls can comprehend. 57. **do:** Hamlet (like Horatio) thinks that the Ghost has come back to impose some duty on those who survive. 59. **impartment:** communication. 61. **removed:** distant. 62. **No, by no means:** Hamlet's friends still fear that the apparition is a demon. Hamlet knows the danger but is determined to take the risk: he cares nothing for his *life*; and no demon can hurt his *soul*. [Hamlet is one of Shakespeare's most religious characters. EDS.] 65. **a pin's fee:** the value of a pin. 72. **assume...form:** change its shape to some horrible form and then drive Hamlet to suicide. 73. **deprive your sovereignty of reason:** take away your reason. 75–8. **The very place...beneath:** The lack of Elizabethan stage scenery made such descriptive passages necessary. 75. **toys of desperation:** reckless or dangerous impulses, such as an impulse to throw one's self down from a dizzying height.

"Whither wilt thou lead me? Speak. I'll go no further" (1.5.1). Olivier's Hamlet holds his sword out to form a cross for protection, in case the Ghost is a demon.

	Without more motive, into every brain	
	That looks so many fadoms to the sea	
	And hears it roar beneath.	
HAMLET	It waves me still.	
	Go on. I'll follow thee.	
MARCELLUS	You shall not go, my lord.	
HAMLET	Hold off your hands.	80
HORATIO	Be ruled. You shall not go.	
HAMLET	My fate cries out	
	And makes each petty artire in this body	
	As hardy as the Nemean lion's nerve.	

[Ghost beckons.]

	Still am I called. Unhand me, gentlemen.	
	By heaven, I'll make a ghost of him that lets me.—	85
	I say, away. — Go on. I'll follow thee.	

Exeunt Ghost and Hamlet.

HORATIO	He waxes desperate with imagination.	
MARCELLUS	Let's follow. 'tis not fit thus to obey him.	

---

76. **motive:** cause. 77. **fadoms:** fathoms. 78. **waves:** beckons. 81. **My fate cries out:** Hamlet feels instinctively that this is the supreme moment of his life—his destiny. 82. **artire:** artery or sinew. 83. **Némean:** To kill the lion of Nemea (a valley in Greece) and fetch his skin was one of the Twelve Labors of Hercules. [Here Hamlet compares himself favorably to Hercules, but earlier he had disclaimed any likeness to that hero (1.2.153). EDS.] —**nerve:** sinew [or tendon. EDS.]. 85. **lets:** hinders.

HORATIO	Have after. To what issue will this come?
MARCELLUS	Something is rotten in the state of Denmark.	90
HORATIO	Heaven will direct it.
MARCELLUS	Nay, let's follow him. *Exeunt.*

SCENE V. [*Elsinore. The Castle. Another part of the fortifications.*]

Enter Ghost and Hamlet.

HAMLET	Whither wilt thou lead me? Speak. I'll go no further.†
GHOST	Mark me.
HAMLET	I will.
GHOST	My hour is almost come, When I to sulph'rous and tormenting flames Must render up myself.
HAMLET	Alas, poor ghost.
GHOST	Pity me not, but lend thy serious hearing 5 To what I shall unfold.
HAMLET	Speak. I am bound to hear.
GHOST	So art thou to revenge, when thou shalt hear.
HAMLET	What?
GHOST	I am thy father's spirit, Doomed for a certain term to walk the night, 10 And for the day confined to fast in fires, Till the foul crimes done in my days of nature

---

89. **Have after:** Come on, let's follow. [It seems that Horatio needs urging to follow the apparition. EDS.] 90. **state:** government, administration.

SCENE V
The ghost, followed by Hamlet, leaves the stage by one door; Horatio and his companions follow, and the stage is left empty for a moment. Then the ghost and Hamlet re-enter by the other door. Horatio and Marcellus are heard calling from behind the door (line 113), and they then enter by the same door by which Hamlet and the ghost had re-entered. 1. **no further:** Hamlet is still uncertain whether the apparition is a ghost or a demon. 3. **flames:** not of hell, but of purgatory (lines 10-13). 6. **bound:** obliged. 7. **revenge:** The ghost asks Hamlet to execute revenge but is explicit only about the fouling of the royal bed (82-3). [EDS.] 12. **foul crimes:** *Crime* means "fault" or "sin." [Though Hamlet idealizes his father, there is a hint here of his less-than-perfect humanity. EDS.]

---

†   Although Zeffirelli's Hamlet is at first startled by the apparition's appearance (in the previous scene), his Ghost, Paul Scofield—sad, tired, and seated against the battlements—appears gentle and fatherly, in contrast to Branagh's wild-eyed and hellacious Ghost. Branagh's camera tracks Hamlet running through a wood marked by fiery explosions emanating it seems from hell. Scott's Ghost leads Hamlet to a wild beach.

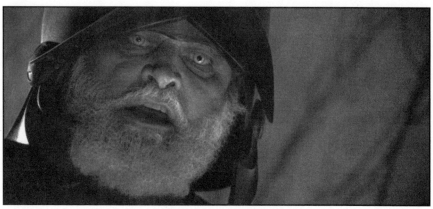

"Doomed for a certain term to walk the night" (1.5.10). Flames leap up and the earth rumbles just before Branagh's fearsome Ghost (Brian Blessed) hurls Hamlet to the ground.

Are burnt and purged away. But that I am forbid
To tell the secrets of my prison house,
I could a tale unfold whose lightest word   15
Would harrow up thy soul, freeze thy young blood,
Make thy two eyes, like stars, start from their spheres,
Thy knotted and combined locks to part,
And each particular hair to stand an end
Like quills upon the fretful porpentine.   20
But this eternal blazon must not be
To ears of flesh and blood. List, list, O, list.
If thou didst ever thy dear father love —

HAMLET   O God!

GHOST   Revenge his foul and most unnatural murther.   25

HAMLET   Murther?

GHOST   Murther most foul, as in the best it is;
              But this most foul, strange, and unnatural.

HAMLET   Haste me to know't, that I, with wings as swift
              As meditation or the thoughts of love,   30

---

16. **young blood:** Another indication of Hamlet's youth. 17. **like stars…spheres:** Each planet (according to the Ptolemaic astronomy) was fixed in a hollow sphere concentric with the earth and revolving about it as a center. 20. **porpentine:** porcupine: [a detailed description of the purgation of sins would make Hamlet's hair stand up like the quills on a porcupine. EDS.]. 21. **this eternal blazon:** the secrets of the world beyond the grave. 23. **If thou didst…love:** This adjuration, with Hamlet's reply, suggests the tender affection which existed between father and son. 25. **murther:** murder. 26. **Murther?** In the Quartos, the word ends with a period, which can mean the Ghost, hurrying to continue, interrupted Hamlet's speech. The Folios end the word with a question mark, a signal of surprise or horror. [EDS.] 30. **meditation:** thought.

"I am thy Father's spirit" (1.5.9). Unlike some others, Zeffirelli's Ghost (Paul Scofield) is gentle and fatherly, his eyes filling with tears as he ends his speech, charging Hamlet "Remember me" (91).

	May sweep to my revenge.	
GHOST	I find thee apt;	
	And duller shouldst thou be than the fat weed	
	That rots itself in ease on Lethe wharf,	
	Wouldst thou not stir in this. Now, Hamlet, hear.†	
	'Tis given out that, sleeping in my orchard,	35
	A serpent stung me. So the whole ear of Denmark	
	Is by a forged process of my death	
	Rankly abused. But know, thou noble youth,	
	The serpent that did sting thy father's life	
	Now wears his crown.	
HAMLET	O my prophetic soul.	40
	My uncle?‡	
GHOST	Ay, that incestuous, that adulterate beast,	

31. **apt:** ready, prompt. 32. **shouldst thou be:** you would surely be. 33. **rots:** the Quartos read "rootes"; the Folios' *rots* is better because the essence of the slimy water-weed seems to be decay; it thrives in corruption and "rots itself" through its lazy, stagnant life [growing on the banks of Lethe, the river of forgetfulness, in Hades. EDS.]. 35. **my orchard:** i.e., the palace garden.—**process:** account.—**abused:** deceived. 40. **O my prophetic soul:** [I have always hated my uncle; now I have a legitimate reason for doing so. EDS.] 42. **adulterate:** adulterous. [Claudius was adulterous in desiring his brother's wife, which is one of the reasons he murdered his brother (3.3.55). Whether he and the Queen were guilty literally of adultery is not clear. The play-within-the-play, which Hamlet designed to be modeled on the king's crime, does not include the player-queen's adultery. EDS.]

† Several films show the murder and King Hamlet's recognition of his murderer. In Branagh's version, the murderer looks almost as aghast at his deed as the victim. Scott's Hamlet experiences the pain of the poisoning; blood even flows from his ear while the Ghost holds power over him.

‡ Another of Branagh's flashcuts has Hamlet's image of someone, Claudius perhaps, unlacing the Queen's corset. It's what the Ghost's words make Hamlet think.

With witchcraft of his wit, with traitorous gifts —
O wicked wit and gifts, that have the power
So to seduce. — won to his shameful lust   45
The will of my most seeming-virtuous Queen
O Hamlet, what a falling-off was there,
From me, whose love was of that dignity
That it went hand in hand even with the vow
I made to her in marriage, and to decline   50
Upon a wretch whose natural gifts were poor
To those of mine.

Gertrude But virtue, as it never will be moved,
Though lewdness court it in a shape of heaven,
So lust, though to a radiant angel linked,   55
Will sate itself in a celestial bed
And prey on garbage.
But soft. methinks I scent the morning air.
Brief let me be. Sleeping within my orchard,
My custom always of the afternoon,   60
Upon my secure hour thy uncle stole,
With juice of cursed hebona in a vial,
And in the porches of my ears did pour   *poisoned through*
The leperous distilment; whose effect   *the ear*
Holds such an enmity with blood of man   65
That swift as quicksilver it courses through
The natural gates and alleys of the body,
And with a sudden vigor it doth posset
And curd, like eager droppings into milk,
The thin and wholesome blood. So did it mine;   70
And a most instant tetter barked about,
Most lazar-like, with vile and loathsome crust
All my smooth body.
Thus was I, sleeping, by a brother's hand
Of life, of crown, of queen, at once dispatched;   75

---

43. **witchcraft of his wit:** Claudius' intellect (*wit*) and powers of seduction have bewitched the Queen; [the extent of her guilt is a problem of the play for performances to resolve. EDS.]. 50. **decline:** fall back. 54. **a shape of heaven:** a heavenly [disguise. EDS.]. 61 **sécure:** free from anxiety and suspicion [perhaps overly confident. EDS.]. 62. **hebona:** ebony (in Latin *Hebenus*), the sap of which was thought to be deadly poison; [hebona or hebenon, has been identified also as henbane and also sometimes as yew. EDS.]. 63. **ears:** Ears were believed to be an entrance to the soul. Thus Claudius pours not only the literal poison into his brother's ears but also metaphorical poison, deceptive rhetoric, into the ears of his Court and his Queen. [EDS.] 64. **leperous** causing the symptoms of leprosy. [EDS.] 68. **posset:** coagulate. A posset was a curdled drink made of wine, ale, or hot milk, thick enough to be eaten—**eager:** sour. 71. **tetter:** skin eruption. **barked:** covered (as with the bark of a tree). 72. **lazar-like:** like a leper. The word is derived from *Lazarus*, the beggar (*Luke* 16. 20). 75. **queen:** *Queen* is the culmination of the sequence, as in the King's soliloquy (3.3.55).—**at once:** all at the same time.—**dispatched:** instantly deprived.

Cut off even in the blossoms of my sin,
Unhousled, disappointed, unaneled,
No reck'ning made, but sent to my account
With all my imperfections on my head.

HAMLET   O, horrible. O, horrible. most horrible.   80

GHOST   If thou hast nature in thee, bear it not.
Let not the royal bed of Denmark be
A couch for luxury and damned incest.
But, howsoever thou pursuest this act,
Taint not thy mind, nor let thy soul contrive   85
Against thy mother aught. Leave her to heaven,
And to those thorns that in her bosom lodge
To prick and sting her. Fare thee well at once.
The glowworm shows the matin to be near
And gins to pale his uneffectual fire.   90
Adieu, adieu, adieu. Remember me. *Exit.*

HAMLET   O all you host of heaven. O earth.
What else? And shall I couple hell? Hold, hold, my heart.
And you, my sinews, grow not instant old,
But bear me stiffly up. Remember thee?   95
Ay, thou poor ghost, while memory holds a seat
In this distracted globe. Remember thee?
Yea, from the table of my memory
I'll wipe away all trivial fond records,
All saws of books, all forms, all pressures past   100
That youth and observation copied there,
And thy commandment all alone shall live
Within the book and volume of my brain,

---

76. **sin:** general sinfulness. 77. **Unhousled:** not having received the Eucharist, administered by the priest shortly before death [communion. EDS.].—**disappointed:** unprepared (for death), as by confession and absolution.—**unaneled:** without extreme unction [the last rites of anointing with oil. EDS.]. 80. **O, horrible:** Both the ghost and Hamlet are given to exclamations in triplet. [EDS.] 83. **luxury:** lustfulness.—**damnéd:** Dissyllabic. [The Ghost does not want his wife to go to her new husband's bed; this is the abstinence that Hamlet urges in 3.4.159-70. EDS.] 85-6. **Taint not...aught:** Whether or not the Queen is guilty of murder (and Shakespeare is ambiguous on this point) the Ghost does not want Hamlet to punish her. [EDS.] 89. **the matin:** the dawn, [by metonymy, the prayer said at dawn. EDS.]. 90. **his uneffectual fire:** its fire which gives no heat and which dies out entirely and becomes of no effect as soon as day dawns. 91. **Remember me:** Eamon Duffy demonstrates that a soul from purgatory would have requested "remembrance" in prayer for its deliverance; this is the ultimate request that the ghost makes, but Hamlet promises to remember only in the sense of recollecting, without reference to prayer (lines 95-104). [EDS.] 93. **hell?** Hamlet invokes all the powers of the universe to aid him in his revenge and thinks of calling even upon the hosts of hell, if they should be needed; [he does not mention purgatory. EDS.]. 97. **this distracted globe:** referring to his own head; [the audience surely would have noted also the pun upon the recently-opened Globe Theatre. EDS.]. 98. **table:** tablet. Small ivory tablets were used for memoranda. See lines 100-1. 107). 99. **fond:** foolish—**saws of books:** wise sayings from books.—**forms:** ideas.—**pressures:** impressions.

	Unmixed with baser matter. Yes, by heaven.	
	O most pernicious woman.	105
	O villain, villain, smiling, damned villain.	
	My tables. Meet it is I set it down	
	That one may smile, and smile, and be a villain;	
	At least I am sure it may be so in Denmark.	[*Writes.*]
	So, uncle, there you are. Now to my word:	110
	It is "Adieu, adieu. Remember me."	
	I have sworn't.	
HORATIO	(*within*) My lord, my lord!	

Enter Horatio and Marcellus.

MARCELLUS	Lord Hamlet!	
HORATIO	Heaven secure him!	
HAMLET	So be it.	
MARCELLUS	Illo, ho, ho, my lord!	115
HAMLET	Hillo, ho, ho, boy. Come, bird, come	
MARCELLUS	How is't, my noble lord?	
HORATIO	What news, my lord?	
HAMLET	O, wonderful.	
HORATIO	Good my lord, tell it.	
HAMLET	No, you will reveal it.	
HORATIO	Not I, my lord, by heaven.	
MARCELLUS	Nor I, my lord.	120
HAMLET	How say you then? Would heart of man once think it? But you'll be secret?	
BOTH	Ay, by heaven, my lord.	
HAMLET	There's ne'er a villain dwelling in all Denmark but he's an arrant knave.	
HORATIO	There needs no ghost, my lord, come from the grave To tell us this.	125

---

107. **My tables:** Hamlet may or may not write on an actual tablet. [EDS.] —**Meet:** proper. 110. **my word:** my motto; henceforth, the guiding principle of my life. 113. **Heaven secure him:** Horatio again expresses his fear that the apparition may be a demon. 114. **So be it:** "Amen." 116. **Hillo...come:** The halloo of Marcellus reminds Hamlet of the falconer's call in summoning a hawk. In what follows Hamlet speaks flippantly of the ghost and its errand.

HAMLET	Why, right. You are in the right.
	And so, without more circumstance at all,
	I hold it fit that we shake hands and part;
	You, as your business and desire shall point you,
	For every man hath business and desire, 130
	Such as it is; and for my own poor part, look you, I'll go pray.
HORATIO	These are but wild and whirling words, my lord.
HAMLET	I am sorry they offend you, heartily; yes, faith, heartily.
HORATIO	There's no offence, my lord. 135
HAMLET	Yes, by Saint Patrick, but there is, Horatio,
	And much offence too. Touching this vision here,
	It is an honest ghost, that let me tell you.
	For your desire to know what is between us,
	O'ermaster't as you may. And now, good friends, 140
	As you are friends, scholars, and soldiers,
	Give me one poor request.
HORATIO	What is't, my lord? We will.
HAMLET	Never make known what you have seen tonight.
BOTH	My lord, we will not.
HAMLET	Nay, but swear't.
HORATIO	In faith, 145
	My lord, not I.
MARCELLUS	Nor I, my lord — in faith.
HAMLET	Upon my sword.
MARCELLUS	We have sworn, my lord, already.
HAMLET	Indeed, upon my sword, indeed.

Ghost cries under the stage.

GHOST	Swear.
HAMLET	Aha boy, say'st thou so? Art thou there, truepenny? 150
	Come on. You hear this fellow in the cellarage.
	Consent to swear.

---

127. **circumstance:** Ceremonious talk. 136. **by Saint Patrick:** St. Patrick's Purgatory was a cave in Ireland supposed to provide an entrance to purgatory; the ghost's appearance as from purgatory may have inspired Hamlet's oath. [EDS.] 137. **offence:** Hamlet plays upon Horatio's word; he repeats it and applies it in a different sense. 138. **an honest ghost:** What he appears to be, not a disguised demon. 139. **what is between us:** Later, Hamlet confides the secret solely to Horatio (see 3.2.81-2). 140. **as you may:** as best you can. 147. **Upon my sword:** The hilt of his sword forms a cross [an appropriate symbol by which to swear. EDS.].—**sworn...already:** since "in faith" is an oath. 150. **truepenny:** honest old boy; [disrespectful. EDS.].

HORATIO	Propose the oath, my lord.	
HAMLET	Never to speak of this that you have seen.	
	Swear by my sword.	
GHOST	[*beneath*] Swear.	155
HAMLET	Hic et ubique? Then we'll shift our ground.	
	Come hither, gentlemen,	
	And lay your hands again upon my sword.	
	Never to speak of this that you have heard:	
	Swear by my sword.	160
GHOST	[*beneath*] Swear by his sword.	
HAMLET	Well said, old mole. Canst work i' th' earth so fast?	
	A worthy pioner. Once more remove, good friends.	
HORATIO	O day and night, but this is wondrous strange.	
HAMLET	And therefore as a stranger give it welcome.	165
	There are more things in heaven and earth, Horatio,	
	Than are dreamt of in your philosophy.	
	But come.	
	Here, as before, never, so help you mercy,	
	How strange or odd soe'er I bear myself	170
	(As I perchance hereafter shall think meet	
	To put an antic disposition on),	
	That you, at such times seeing me, never shall,	
	With arms encumb'red thus, or this headshake,	
	Or by pronouncing of some doubtful phrase,	175
	As "Well, well, we know," or "We could, an if we would,"	
	Or "If we list to speak," or "There be, an if they might,"	
	Or such ambiguous giving out, to note	
	That you know aught of me—this not to do,	
	So grace and mercy at your most need help you,	180

---

156. **Hic et ubique:** Here and everywhere. 161. **old mole:** "mole" suggests that the ghost's voice comes from below, which could mean hell or purgatory. [EDS.] 163. **pioner:** miner. Pioners or pioneers were foot-soldiers who dug trenches and mines. [Since demons were supposed to inhabit mines, Hamlet could allude here to its diabolical nature—though he has said it is "honest." EDS.] 165. **as a stranger give it welcome:** It was a point of good manners, when receiving strangers into one's house, not to question them about themselves. 167. **dreamt of:** even *dreamt* of.—**your philosophy:** Either the philosophy that people generally speak of (see, for example, 4.3.21, for this use of "your") or Horatio's philosophy specifically. Philosophy here implies Stoicism, presumably from Seneca, who taught that one should be guided by reason rather than emotion. [EDS.] 172. **put...on:** Pretend madness.—**antic:** fantastic. 173-9. **That you...to do:** Hamlet makes them swear that they will not indicate to others that they know more than they choose to tell. 180. **grace:** God's grace. An elaboration of "So help you God."

Swear.†

GHOST   [*beneath*] Swear.

                                              [*They swear.*]

HAMLET   Rest, rest, perturbed spirit. So, gentlemen,
                  With all my love I do commend me to you;
                  And what so poor a man as Hamlet is   185
                  May do t' express his love and friending to you,
                  God willing, shall not lack. Let us go in together;
                  And still your fingers on your lips, I pray.
                  The time is out of joint. O cursed spite
                  That ever I was born to set it right.   190
                  Nay, come, let's go together.   *Exeunt.*

ACT II

SCENE I. [*Elsinore. A room in the house of Polonius.*]

Enter Polonius and Reynaldo.

POLONIUS   Give him this money and these notes, Reynaldo.

REYNALDO   I will, my lord.

POLONIUS   You shall do marvell's wisely, good Reynaldo,
                  Before you visit him, to make inquire
                  Of his behavior.

REYNALDO   My lord, I did intend it.   5

---

184. **commend me to you:** protest my devotion to you. Literally, "hand myself over to you." 185. **so poor:** Hamlet alludes to his uncle's having obtained the election to the kingship, which would naturally have fallen to *him*. [He is thus left without power or money. EDS.] 188. **still:** always. 189. **O cursèd spite:** Hamlet has resolved to remember the ghost, but he may not know how to achieve what the ghost wants: The ghost has asked that his murder be avenged (without saying how: by regicide? by legal means?), and that his queen be left to heaven (yet Hamlet is not to allow the throne of Denmark to be soiled by incest). [EDS.] 191. **together:** i.e., as friends and equals. This is Hamlet's protest against the ceremonious respect that his companions want to pay him. They stand back to let him go first, but he insists on their walking by his side. [Shakespeare often buries such stage directions within the dialogue. EDS.]
ACT II. SCENE I.
1. **notes:** messages. 3. **marvell's:** marvelously.

---

†   Though the text does not call for it, Scott's Horatio and Marcellus mumble their oath as they
     grasp, with Hamlet, the hilt of the sword. As the Ghost echoes the word *swear,* his arm reaches
     through the sand to the sword, which he pulls down below, bloodying the hands of the men as he
     does so.

POLONIUS	Marry, well said, very well said. Look you, sir,
	Enquire me first what Danskers are in Paris;
	And how, and who, what means, and where they keep,
	What company, at what expense; and finding
	By this encompassment and drift of question	10
	That they do know my son, come you more nearer
	Than your particular demands will touch it.
	Take you, as 'twere, some distant knowledge of him;
	As thus, "I know his father and his friends,
	And in part him." Do you mark this, Reynaldo?	15
REYNALDO	Ay, very well, my lord.
POLONIUS	"And in part him, but," you may say, "not well.
	But if 't be he I mean, he's very wild
	Addicted so and so"; and there put on him
	What forgeries you please; marry, none so rank	20
	As may dishonor him — take heed of that;
	But, sir, such wanton, wild, and usual slips
	As are companions noted and most known
	To youth and liberty.
REYNALDO	As gaming, my lord.
POLONIUS	Ay, or drinking, fencing, swearing, quarrelling,	25
	Drabbing. You may go so far.
REYNALDO	My lord, that would dishonor him.
POLONIUS	Faith, no, as you may season it in the charge.
	You must not put another scandal on him,
	That he is open to incontinency.	30
	That's not my meaning. But breathe his faults so quaintly
	That they may seem the taints of liberty,
	The flash and outbreak of a fiery mind,

[handwritten margin note beside lines 27–29: "willing to ruin the honor/ image of his children"]

---

6. **Marry:** Indeed. 7. **Enquire me:** ask, on my behalf. [EDS.]—**Danskers:** Danes. 8. **how:** how they come to be there.—**who:** of what rank. —**means:** supply of money.—**keep:** reside. [EDS.] 9. **finding:** if you find. 10. **By this...question:** by this roundabout means of inquiry. 11-12. **come...it:** then you will come closer than you would by direct questioning. [EDS.] Polonius then shows how this may be done by making remarks that tempt the hearer to tell what he may have observed. 19. **put on him** accuse him of. [EDS.] 20. **forgeries:** imaginary faults.—**rank:** unrestrained. [EDS.] 22. **wanton:** practically synonymous with the next word, *wild*. 23. **slips:** mistakes associated with youth. [EDS.] 24: **liberty:** freedom from restraint. 25. **fencing:** Though fencing was a valued and respected accomplishment, fencing schools sometimes attracted a wild crowd, so that spending too much time there might harm one's reputation. 26. **Drabbing:** seeking prostitutes. [EDS.] 28. **season it in the charge:** soften the accusation in the very act of bringing it. 30. **incontinency:** immoderate indulgence. [Polonius does not mind a little drabbing. EDS.] 31. **breathe...quaintly:** suggest his faults so subtly. 32. **taints of liberty:** faults related to his freedom from restraint; see line 24.

	A savageness in unreclaimed blood,	
	Of general assault.	
REYNALDO	But, my good lord —	35
POLONIUS	Wherefore should you do this?	
REYNALDO	Ay, my lord,	
	I would know that.	
POLONIUS	Marry, sir, here's my drift,	
	And I believe it is a fetch of warrant.	
	You laying these slight sullies on my son	
	As 'twere a thing a little soiled i' th' working,	40
	Mark you,	
	Your party in converse, him you would sound,	
	Having ever seen in the prenominate crimes	
	The youth you breathe of guilty, be assured	
	He closes with you in this consequence:	45
	"Good sir," or so, or "friend," or "gentleman" —	
	According to the phrase or the addition	
	Of man and country —	
REYNALDO	Very good, my lord.	
POLONIUS	And then, sir, does 'a this — 'a does — What was I about	
	to say? By the mass†, I was about to say something. Where	50
	did I leave?	
REYNALDO	At "closes in the consequence," at "friend or so,"	
	and "gentleman."	
POLONIUS	At "closes in the consequence" — Ay, marry.	
	He closes thus: "I know the gentleman.	55
	I saw him yesterday, or t'other day,	
	Or then, or then, with such or such; and, as you say,	
	There was 'a gaming; there o'ertook in's rouse;	

---

34. **unreclaimed:** untamed by age and experience.—**Of general assault:** affecting everybody in Laertes's position. 37. **my drift:** my meaning. 48. **a fetch of warrant:** a justifiable, clever device to find out what you need to know. [EDS.] 39. **Sullies:** faults. [EDS.] 40. **soiled i' th' working:** [sullied by the process of growing to manhood. EDS.] The image comes from the marks that a worker's hands may leave on delicate material. 43. **Having ever seen:** if he has ever seen.—**prenominate:** previously mentioned. [EDS.] —**crimes:** faults. 44. **breathe of:** make these suggestions about. 45. **He closes...consequence:** He will be sure to agree with you, following up your remark as follows. 47. **addition:** mode of address. 49. **'a:** he. 50. Polonius, amplifying with comic verbosity the supposed titles Reynaldo's hearer will use in addressing him, loses the thread of his discourse here. 58. **o'ertook in's rouse:** overcome (by intoxication) in his drinking.

---

† Scott's dignified Polonius does not lose the thread of his argument; Scott omits these lines as incompatible with this Polonius.

	There falling out at tennis"; or perchance,	
	"I saw him enter such a house of sale,"	60
	Videlicet, a brothel, or so forth.	
	See you now —	
	Your bait of falsehood takes this carp of truth;	
	And thus do we of wisdom and of reach,	
	With windlasses and with assays of bias,	65
	By indirections find directions out.	
	So, by my former lecture and advice,	
	Shall you my son. You have me, have you not?	

REYNALDO   My lord, I have.

POLONIUS   God b' wi' ye, fare ye well.

REYNALDO   Good my lord.   [*Going.*] 70

POLONIUS   Observe his inclination in yourself.

REYNALDO   I shall, my lord.

POLONIUS   And let him ply his music.

REYNALDO   Well, my lord.

POLONIUS   Farewell.   *Exit Reynaldo.*

                              Enter Ophelia.

                 How now, Ophelia? What's the matter?

OPHELIA   O my lord, my lord, I have been so affrighted.   75

POLONIUS   With what, i' th' name of God?

OPHELIA   My lord, as I was sewing in my closet,

---

59. **falling out:** quarrelling. 61. **Videlicet:** Latin. "that is," introducing "a brothel" as an example of a "house of sale." [EDS.] 63. **bait…carp:** worm to catch the truth. [EDS.] 64. **we of wisdom and of reach:** we wise persons. 65. **windlasses:** roundabout ways.—**assays of bias:** indirect attempts. A figure from bowling. The *bias* is the curve which the bowl makes in reaching its goal—like a "curve" in baseball. 66. **by…out:** by indirect means discover truths. 67. **lecture and advice:** lesson and instructions. 68. **You have me:** You catch my meaning, "You get me?" 70. **Good my lord:** Merely a polite phrase, used upon leaving, accompanied by a bow. 71. **in yourself:** by yourself. [Reynaldo is to be observant himself and not depend on rumors alone. Or, if Reynaldo is played as a young man, Polonius may urge him to watch his own behavior. EDS.] 73. **And let him ply his music:** See that Laertes does not neglect his practice of music, [possibly literally urging Reynaldo to encourage Laertes's musical practice; or Polonius says this figuratively, "Let him behave as he usually would," perhaps so as to enable Reynaldo to inform Polonius of what Laertes is usually up to when on his own. EDS.] 77. **closet:** private sitting room.

Lord Hamlet, with his doublet all unbraced,
No hat upon his head, his stockings fouled,
Ungartered, and down-gyved to his ankle;   80
Pale as his shirt, his knees knocking each other,
And with a look so piteous in purport
As if he had been loosed out of hell
To speak of horrors — he comes before me.

POLONIUS   Mad for thy love?

OPHELIA   My lord, I do not know,   85
But truly I do fear it.

POLONIUS   What said he?

OPHELIA   He took me by the wrist and held me hard;
Then goes he to the length of all his arm,
And, with his other hand thus o'er his brow,
He falls to such perusal of my face   90
As he would draw it. Long stayed he so.
At last, a little shaking of mine arm,
And thrice his head thus waving up and down,
He raised a sigh so piteous and profound
As it did seem to shatter all his bulk   95
And end his being. That done, he lets me go,
And with his head over his shoulder turned
He seemed to find his way without his eyes,
For out o' doors he went without their help
And to the last bended their light on me.   100

POLONIUS   Come, go with me. I will go seek the King.
This is the very ecstasy of love,   self destructive nature
Whose violent property fordoes itself   of love
And leads the will to desperate undertakings

78-100. **Lord Hamlet...on me:** (1) Hamlet may be pretending madness, as he had announced in 1.5 he planned to do; (2) he may not be pretending but exhibiting true mental instability (which need not be apparent at all times); (3) he may be puzzling over whether or not and to what degree Ophelia can be trusted; (4) he may be saying his farewell to her, knowing that he cannot continue the relationship in the face of her rejection of him (lines 109-10) or knowing that she cannot follow him where he needs to go to enact his revenge. Since textually the audience hears about the scene only from Ophelia's perspective, it is difficult to assess his reasons. [EDS.] 78. **doublet:** a close-fitting jacket. Doublet and hose (breeches) were the regular essentials of masculine attire.—**unbraced:** unlaced. The doublet was laced or buttoned from the bottom nearly to the top. At the top it was left open for a short distance, so as to show the shirt. To leave it "*all*" unbraced" was sloppy. 79. **No hat:** hats were commonly worn indoors as well as out. [EDS.]—**fouled:** soiled [or wrinkled. EDS.]. 80. **down-gyved:** falling like chains round his ankles. 85. **Mad:** Hamlet had already begun to "put an antic disposition on" (1.5.172), and Polonius, like the King and Queen, was concerned to discover the cause. Now he thinks he has it. 91. **As:** as if. 92. **shaking of mine arm:** shaking my arm. 95. **As:** that.—**his bulk:** his whole body. 102. **ecstasy:** madness. 103. **Whose...itself:** which has this trait when it is violent—and is thus self-destructive.

As oft as any passion under heaven   105
That does afflict our natures. I am sorry.
What, have you given him any hard words of late?

OPHELIA   No, my good lord; but, as you did command,
I did repel his letters and denied His access to me.

POLONIUS   That hath made him mad.   110
I am sorry that with better heed and judgment
I had not quoted him. I feared he did but trifle
And meant to wrack thee; but beshrew my jealousy.
By heaven, it is as proper to our age
To cast beyond ourselves in our opinions   115
As it is common for the younger sort
To lack discretion.
Come, go we to the King.
This must be known; which, being kept close, might move
More grief to hide than hate to utter love.   119
Come.   *Exeunt.*

SCENE II. [*Elsinore. A room in the Castle.*]

Flourish. Enter King and Queen, Rosencrantz, and Guildenstern, cum aliis.

KING   Welcome, dear Rosencrantz and Guildenstern.
Moreover that we much did long to see you,
The need we have to use you did provoke
Our hasty sending. Something have you heard
Of Hamlet's transformation. So I call it,   5
Sith nor th' exterior nor the inward man
Resembles that it was. What it should be,
More than his father's death, that thus hath put him
So much from th' understanding of himself,
I cannot dream of. I entreat you both   10

---

112. **quoted:** observed. 113. **beshrew:** literally "curse." 114. **proper to:** characteristic of. 115. **To cast beyond ourselves:** to err by going too far. It is sometimes characteristic of the young not to see all there is in a matter; of the old, to see more than there is in it. 118-19. **which...love:** To conceal it might cause more sorrow than to reveal it. Polonius, though of high rank, believes that the King and Queen will disapprove Hamlet's marrying Ophelia. Before the nunnery scene (3.1.40-2) and at the graveside (5.1.267), the Queen's words suggest she would not object to their marriage. 118. **close:** secret.
SCENE II.
cum aliis: with others. 2. **Moreover that:** besides the fact that. 5–10. The King's language suggests that Hamlet's appearance and behavior, since he has begun to play the madman, are quite different from what they were in 1.2. Then he was merely sorrowful; now he looks and acts like a lunatic. 6. **Sith:** since. 7. **that:** what.

That, being of so young days brought up with him,   *childhood friends*
And since so neighbored to his youth and havior,
That you vouchsafe your rest here in our court
Some little time; so by your companies
To draw him on to pleasures, and to gather   15
So much as from occasion you may glean,
Whether aught to us unknown afflicts him thus
That, opened, lies within our remedy.

QUEEN   Good gentlemen, he hath much talked of you,
And sure I am two men there are not living   20
To whom he more adheres. If it will please you
To show us so much gentry and good will
As to expend your time with us awhile
For the supply and profit of our hope,
Your visitation shall receive such thanks   25
As fits a king's remembrance.

ROSENCRANTZ   Both your Majesties
Might, by the sovereign power you have of us,
Put your dread pleasures more into command
Than to entreaty.

GUILDENSTERN   But we both obey,
And here give up ourselves, in the full bent,   30
To lay our service freely at your feet,
To be commanded.

KING   Thanks, Rosencrantz and gentle Guildenstern.
QUEEN   Thanks, Guildenstern and gentle Rosencrantz.   *one + same*
And I beseech you instantly to visit   35
My too much changed son. — Go, some of you,
And bring these gentlemen where Hamlet is.

GUILDENSTERN   Heavens make our presence and our practices
Pleasant and helpful to him.

QUEEN   Ay, amen.   *Exeunt Rosencrantz and Guildenstern,*
                                          [*with some Attendants*].

                          Enter Polonius.

11-12. **being...havior:** Rosencrantz and Guildenstern had been selected, as the custom was, to be Hamlet's playfellows when he and they were young. 11. **of:** from. 13. **vouchsafe your rest:** consent to remain. 16. **occasion:** opportunity. 21. **more adheres:** is more attached. 22. **gentry:** courtesy. 24. **the supply and profit:** the fulfillment and furtherance. 26–34. Shakespeare has made Rosencrantz and Guildenstern nearly indistinguishable in character, manners, and language. 27. **of:** over. 28. **your dread pleasures:** your wishes as our revered sovereigns.—**into:** into the form of. 30. **in the full bent:** with full intention. The figure comes from the bending of a bow when one takes aim.

POLONIUS	Th' ambassadors from Norway, my good lord,	40
	Are joyfully returned.	
KING	Thou still hast been the father of good news.	
POLONIUS	Have I, my lord? Assure you, my good liege,	
	I hold my duty as I hold my soul,	
	Both to my God and to my gracious king;	45
	And I do think — or else this brain of mine	
	Hunts not the trail of policy so sure	
	As it hath used to do — that I have found	
	The very cause of Hamlet's lunacy.	
KING	O, speak of that. That do I long to hear.	50
POLONIUS	Give first admittance to th' ambassadors.	
	My news shall be the fruit to that great feast.	
KING	Thyself do grace to them, and bring them in.	

[Exit Polonius.]

	He tells me, my dear Gertrude, he hath found	
	The head and source of all your son's distemper.	55
QUEEN	I doubt it is no other but the main,	
	His father's death and our o'erhasty marriage.	
KING	Well, we shall sift him.	

Enter Polonius, Voltemand, and Cornelius.

	Welcome, my good friends.	
	Say, Voltemand, what from our brother Norway?	
VOLTEMAND	Most fair return of greetings and desires.	60
	Upon our first, he sent out to suppress	

---

42. **Thou...news:** This speech shows the same style of friendly compliment in which the King habitually addresses Polonius, who is an important person at court. Both the King and the Queen are fond of "the good old man" (as the Queen calls him, in 4.1.12). *Thou* (instead of *you*) expresses the warmth of their feeling. [*Thou* was used by someone speaking to a social inferior; the person spoken to would reply respectfully by using *you*. Compare the dialogue of the King and Laertes in 1.2.42 ff. EDS.]—**still:** always. 43. **Assure you:** rest assured.—**liege:** sovereign. 44-5. **I hold...king:** I regard my duty both to God and to my king as highly as I value my soul. 47. **policy:** statesmanship. 49. **lunacy:** Hamlet had begun to play the madman after his interview with the Ghost. His behavior with Ophelia furnished Polonius with an explanation for Hamlet's supposed madness. [Love sickness might cause lovers to behave strangely, exhibiting symptoms akin to those of melancholia—i.e. mood swings, mental distraction, slovenliness, etc. EDS.] 52. **the fruit:** the dessert. 53. **grace:** honor [also the prayer said before a meal, building on the meal imagery in 52. EDS]. 54-5. **He tells me...distemper:** The King, throughout the first part of the play, confides immediately to his wife anything that he learns about Hamlet. [Note that he uses the milder word *distemper*, not *lunacy* or *madness*. EDS.] 55. **head:** origin. 56. **doubt:** suspect. 56-7. **it is...o'erhasty marriage:** The queen understands what ails him; she knows her marriage has been hasty. [EDS.] 59. **Norway:** the King of Norway. 60. **greetings and desires:** i.e., the good wishes with which the Danish missive began. 61. **Upon our first:** as soon as we made known our business.

His nephew's levies; which to him appeared
To be a preparation 'gainst the Polack,
But better looked into, he truly found
It was against your Highness; whereat grieved,   65
That so his sickness, age, and impotence
Was falsely borne in hand, sends out arrests
On Fortinbras; which he, in brief, obeys,
Receives rebuke from Norway, and, in fine,
Makes vow before his uncle never more   70
To give th' assay of arms against your Majesty.
Whereon old Norway, overcome with joy,
Gives him three thousand crowns in annual fee
And his commission to employ those soldiers,
So levied as before, against the Polack;   75
With an entreaty, herein further shown,

                                            [*Gives a paper.*]

That it might please you to give quiet pass
Through your dominions for this enterprise,
On such regards of safety and allowance
As therein are set down.

KING   It likes us well;   80
And at our more considered time we'll read,
Answer, and think upon this business.
Meantime we thank you for your well-took labor.
Go to your rest; at night we'll feast together.
Most welcome home.   *Exeunt Ambassadors.*

POLONIUS   This business is well ended.   85
My liege, and madam, to expostulate
What, majesty should be, what duty is,
Why day is day, night night, and time is time,
Were nothing but to waste night, day, and time.
Therefore, since brevity is the soul of wit,   90
And tediousness the limbs and outward flourishes,

---

65. **grieved:** indignant. 66. **impotence:** feeble health. 67. **borne in hand:** The phrase implies not merely a single act, but a systematic course of deception.—**arrests:** writs of arrest [stopping him in what he was doing. EDS.], summoning him to the King's presence. 69. **in fine:** in conclusion. [EDS.] 70-1. **Never... arms:** never to bring the question to the test of warfare. 73. **fee:** income. 79-80. **On...set down:** on such conditions as are submitted for your approval. 80. **likes:** pleases. 81. **at our more considered time:** when we have more time. [EDS.] 86-105. **My liege...Perpend:** Instead of coming to the point, Polonius begins his speech with a windy introduction. 86. **expostulate:** discuss. 88-9. **Why day is day...and time:** Polonius declares that to explain what kings are owed and the duties of subjects to their kings would be as superfluous as to define day or night. 90-1. **brevity...flourishes:** *Wit* here signifies "wisdom." The whole remark means: "The wise or instructive part of every speech may be expressed in a few words; and wisdom adorned with superfluous words becomes tedious."

I will be brief. Your noble son is mad.
Mad call I it; for, to define true madness,
What is't but to be nothing else but mad?
But let that go.

QUEEN More matter, with less art.   95

POLONIUS Madam, I swear I use no art at all.
That he is mad, 'tis true: 'tis true 'tis pity;
And pity 'tis 'tis true. A foolish figure.
But farewell it, for I will use no art.
Mad let us grant him then. And now remains   100
That we find out the cause of this effect —
Or rather say, the cause of this defect,
For this effect defective comes by cause.
Thus it remains, and the remainder thus.
Perpend.   105
I have a daughter (have while she is mine),
Who in her duty and obedience, mark,
Hath given me this. Now gather, and surmise.
                        [*Reads*] *the letter.*

"To the celestial, and my soul's idol, the most beautified
Ophelia," —

That's an ill phrase, a vile phrase; "beautified' is a vile phrase.
But you shall hear. Thus: [*Reads.*]

"In her excellent white bosom, these," &c.

QUEEN Came this from Hamlet to her?

POLONIUS Good madam, stay awhile. I will be faithful.   [*Reads.*] 115
"Doubt thou the stars are fire;
    Doubt that the sun doth move;
Doubt truth to be a liar;
    But never doubt I love.

"O dear Ophelia, I am ill at these numbers; I have not art to
reckon my groans; but that I love thee best, O most best,
believe it. Adieu.

---

95. **More matter, with less art:** Get to the point. [EDS.] 104. **Thus...thus:** Polonius cannot help playing on words; he is constitutionally unable to get to the point. [EDS.] 105. **Perpend:** Consider. 116. **Doubt... fire:** Hamlet's poetry is poor, as he himself confesses in line 120; but it was expected that every lover should show his devotion in verse. 117. **that the sun doth move:** i.e., about the earth—the center of the system according to the old (Ptolemaic) astronomy. 118. **Doubt:** suspect. 120. **ill at these numbers:** a poor hand at this verse-making. 121. **to reckon my groans:** to express my love pains in the set forms of verse; [*groans* may also have a sexual connotation. EDS.].

"Thine evermore, most dear lady, whilst this machine is to
                                        him, HAMLET."

This, in obedience, hath my daughter shown me;[†]   125
And more above, hath his solicitings,
As they fell out by time, by means, and place,
All given to mine ear.

KING   But how hath she
                   Received his love?

POLONIUS   What do you think of me? *turns back on himself*

KING   As of a man faithful and honorable.   130

POLONIUS   I would fain prove so. But what might you think,
                   When I had seen this hot love on the wing
                   (As I perceived it, I must tell you that,
                   Before my daughter told me), what might you,
                   Or my dear Majesty your queen here, think,   135
                   If I had played the desk or table book,
                   Or given my heart a winking, mute and dumb,
                   Or looked upon this love with idle sight?
                   What might you think? No, I went round to work
                   And my young mistress thus I did bespeak: 140
                   "Lord Hamlet is a prince, out of thy star.
                   This must not be." And then I prescripts gave her,[‡]
                   That she should lock herself from his resort,
                   Admit no messengers, receive no tokens.
                   Which done, she took the fruits of my advice,   145
                   And he, repulsed, a short tale to make,
                   Fell into a sadness, then into a fast,

123-4. **whilst...him:** as long as this body remains his; as long as he lives. Hamlet thinks of his body as a complicated piece of mechanism to which his soul supplies the driving power. 126. **above:** besides. 131. **might:** would. 133. **As I perceived it:** Polonius (as he has told Ophelia, in 1.3.91–5) had been informed of Hamlet's wooing by others. By this time, however, the old man has come to believe that he discovered it for himself. 136. **played...table book:** stored the matter away in my own mind, as one locks up letters in a desk or makes an entry in one's "tables" or note-book. [In other words, kept it to himself. EDS.] 137. **given...winking:** forced my heart to shut its eyes to what was going on. 138. **with idle sight:** with unintelligent or unperceiving eyes. 139. **What might you think?** Polonius implies that they could then have supposed him capable of intriguing to obtain a royal marriage for his daughter.—**round:** directly, without mincing matters. 140. **my young mistress:** this young lady.—**be-speak:** address. 141. **out of thy star:** above your social status; a reference to the common belief in astrology and to what is fated by the stars. [EDS.] 142. **prescripts:** definite orders. 145. **she...advice:** she carried out my advice. Good advice "bears fruit" when it is carried out in action.

---

†   Almereyda's Polonius lies when he says this line; Ophelia had not willingly given him Hamlet's poem, and she tries to get it back. She suffers visibly as Polonius tells the King and Queen, lounging by a pool, about Hamlet's love for her.

‡   Almereyda's Ophelia imagines herself jumping into the pool.

Thence to a watch, thence into a weakness,
Thence to a lightness, and, by this declension,
Into the madness wherein now he raves,   150
And all we mourn for.

KING   Do you think 'tis this?

QUEEN   It may be, very like.

POLONIUS   Hath there been such a time — I would fain know that —
That I have positively said "'Tis so,"
When it proved otherwise?

KING   Not that I know.   155

POLONIUS   [points to his head and shoulder] Take this from this, if
this be otherwise.
If circumstances lead me, I will find
Where truth is hid, though it were hid indeed
Within the center.

KING   How may we try it further?

POLONIUS   You know sometimes he walks four hours together   160
Here in the lobby.

QUEEN   So he does indeed.

POLONIUS   At such a time I'll loose my daughter to him.
Be you and I behind an arras then.
Mark the encounter. If he love her not,
And be not from his reason fall'n thereon,   165
Let me be no assistant for a state,
But keep a farm and carters.

KING   We will try it.

Enter Hamlet, reading on a book.

QUEEN   But look where sadly the poor wretch comes reading.

---

148. **watch:** sleeplessness. 149. **declension:** downward course (from bad to worse). 150. **raves:** This is another clear distinction between Hamlet's melancholy in the first court scene and his present supposed lunacy. [In the *Anatomy of Melancholy* (1632), Robert Burton describes a form of madness in which lovers become so deeply depressed and distracted that they cannot eat or sleep. EDS.] 159. **the center:** the earth's center, which was also the center of the universe according to the Ptolemaic astronomy. 160. **four hours:** *Four* was used for an indefinite number, as we say "three or four." 161. **loose my daughter:** Has an unpleasant connotation of treating her as sexual bait. [EDS.] 163. **arras:** tapestry hanging on a frame at a little distance from the wall. 165. **thereon:** on that account. 166-7. **Let me...carters:** Let me lose my position and become a farmer. [EDS.]

POLONIUS	Away, I do beseech you, both away.
	I'll board him presently. O, give me leave.* 170
	Exeunt King and Queen, [with Attendants].
	How does my good Lord Hamlet?
HAMLET	Well, God-a-mercy.
POLONIUS	Do you know me, my lord?
HAMLET	Excellent well. You are a fishmonger.
POLONIUS	Not I, my lord. 175
HAMLET	Then I would you were so honest a man.
POLONIUS	Honest, my lord?
HAMLET	Ay, sir. To be honest, as this world goes, is to be
	one man picked out of ten thousand.
POLONIUS	That's very true, my lord. 180
HAMLET	For if the sun breed maggots in a dead dog, being
	a god kissing carrion — Have you a daughter?
POLONIUS	I have, my lord. 184
HAMLET	Let her not walk i' th' sun. Conception is a blessing,
	but not as your daughter may conceive. Friend, look to't.
POLONIUS	[*aside*] How say you by that? Still harping on my
	daughter. Yet he knew me not at first. He said I was a
	fishmonger. He is far gone, far gone. And truly in my youth

Handwritten annotations: "King" above "sun" (line 181); "Echo of Queen → Hamlet" above "Let her not walk i' th' sun."

---

170. **board:** approach.—**presently:** without delay.—**give me leave:** A courteous request for privacy: "permit me to be alone." 171-3. Speeches are prose in this section, except when the player recites Aeneas' story to Dido, which is a verse-form more formal and stilted than Shakespeare's usual iambic verse. [EDS.] 172. **God-a-mercy:** thank you. The phrase originally meant "God have mercy." 174. **You are a fishmonger:** Many attempts have been made to make sense out of this speech. Coleridge thought that Hamlet means "You are sent to fish out the secret." Perhaps the remark is merely a bit of Hamlet's pretended insanity. [Or since *fishmonger* was slang for a prostitute's "procurer" or pimp, the label implies Hamlet has overheard Polonius and the King's plan to use Ophelia as bait while they are spying from behind the arras. EDS.] 181. **sun:** a royal symbol, standing for a king; Helios was the mythical sun god, as was Apollo. Hamlet has punned on *son/sun* before (1.2.67) and could be taunting Polonius for his suspicions that led him to tell Ophelia to deny his access to her. [EDS.] 182. **a god kissing carrion:** the sun, shining on Earth, seems to kiss it, producing spontaneous generation: i.e., maggots were thought to be generated by sunshine. [EDS.] 185. **Let her...sun:** Keep her at home, away from him.— **conception:** pun: (1) *conception* of a child, a bad outcome for an unmarried woman; (2) *conception* of an idea, the sense being, while knowledge is generally good, what Ophelia might learn might hurt her. [EDS.] 187. **How say you by that?** "What do you say to that?" "I told you so!"—**Still:** always.

---

*   Scott provides the information that Hamlet is unhinged by showing that when he thinks he is alone he cannot concentrate; he throws books around; he hears voices, particularly the Ghost's. He breaks his glasses and tries to use the lens to harm himself. Scott cuts here to 3.1.56. "To be or not to be." Polonius rather than Ophelia interrupts him.

I suffered much extremity for love — very near this. I'll speak to him again. — What do you read, my lord?

HAMLET   Words, words, words.

POLONIUS   What is the matter, my lord?   195

HAMLET   Between who?

POLONIUS   I mean, the matter that you read, my lord.

HAMLET   Slanders, sir; for the satirical rogue says here that old men have grey beards; that their faces are wrinkled; their eyes purging thick amber and plum-tree gum; and that they have a plentiful lack of wit, together with most weak hams. All which, sir, though I most powerfully and potently believe, yet I hold it not honesty to have it thus set down; for you yourself, sir, should be old as I am if, like a crab, you could go backward.

POLONIUS   [aside] Though this be madness, yet there is method in't. — Will you walk out of the air, my lord?

HAMLET   Into my grave?   210

POLONIUS   Indeed, that is out o' th' air. [Aside] How pregnant sometimes his replies are. A happiness that often madness hits on, which reason and sanity could not so prosperously be delivered of. I will leave him and suddenly contrive the means of meeting between him and my daughter. — My honorable lord, I will most humbly take my leave of you.   218

HAMLET   You cannot, sir, take from me anything that I will more willingly part withal — except my life, except my life, except my life.

Enter Rosencrantz and Guildenstern.

POLONIUS   Fare you well, my lord.

HAMLET   These tedious old fools.

POLONIUS   You go to seek the Lord Hamlet. There he is.

---

195. **the matter:** Polonius means, "What is the *subject matter* of the book?" But Hamlet chooses to take *matter* as "the subject of a quarrel," as if Polonius had said "What's the fight?" The joke was an old one in Elizabethan times and thus seems all the madder since Hamlet doesn't seem to have been prone to stale witticisms. 204. **honesty:** honorable conduct. Hamlet means that, although these things are facts, it isn't fair to mention them in satirizing old men, since the elderly are not to blame for their age. 203-5. **for you...backward:** If you could "walk backward," you would quickly return to youth and be no older than I am. 204. **should be:** would undoubtedly be. 211. **pregnant:** quick-witted, [meaningful. EDS.]. 212. **happiness:** cleverness. 220. **withal:** with. 223. **These...fools:** This insult may or may not be heard by Polonius, who is leaving.

ROSENCRANTZ	[*to Polonius*] God save you, sir.	225

Exit [Polonius].

GUILDENSTERN	My honored lord.
ROSENCRANTZ	My most dear lord.
HAMLET	My excellent good friends! How dost thou, Guildenstern?
	Ah, Rosencrantz. Good lads, how do ye both? 230
ROSENCRANTZ	As the indifferent children of the earth.
GUILDENSTERN	Happy in that we are not over-happy.
	On Fortune's cap we are not the very button.
HAMLET	Nor the soles of her shoe?
ROSENCRANTZ	Neither, my lord. 235
HAMLET	Then you live about her waist, or in the middle of her favors?
GUILDENSTERN	Faith, her privates we.
HAMLET	In the secret parts of Fortune? O, most true. she is *— fortune in many mens*
	a strumpet. What news?
ROSENCRANTZ	None, my lord, but that the world's grown honest.
HAMLET	Then is doomsday near. But your news is not true.
	Let me question more in particular. What have you, my good
	friends, deserved at the hands of Fortune that she sends you
	to prison hither?
GUILDENSTERN	Prison, my lord?
HAMLET	Denmark's a prison.
ROSENCRANTZ	Then is the world one. 250
HAMLET	A goodly one; in which there are many confines,
	wards, and dungeons, Denmark being one o' th' worst.
ROSENCRANTZ	We think not so, my lord. 254
HAMLET	Why, then 'tis none to you; for there is nothing
	either good or bad but thinking makes it so. To me it is a
	prison.
ROSENCRANTZ	Why, then your ambition makes it one. *disappoinment in not inheriting the throne*

---

231. **As…earth:** like the general run of mortals. 235. **Neither:** not that either. 240. **strumpet:** [whore. EDS.] Fortune is so called proverbially, because she grants favors to all men and is constant to none. See also line 515. 258. **your ambition:** They suspect that Hamlet's secret trouble is disappointment at not having inherited the throne, and on this matter they insist on sounding him throughout the interview. Hamlet soon discovers their theory, and he teases them by giving them some ground for thinking they are right, but he gives no clear evidence. [Their insistence and their disinclination to listen to him, makes him believe they are no longer his friends. For example, he says that he has had bad dreams, but that personal point does not interest them. EDS.]

	Tis too narrow for your mind.	*out wits them* *misleads them* 259
HAMLET	O God, I could be bounded in a nutshell and count myself a king of infinite space, were it not that I have bad dreams.	
GUILDENSTERN	Which dreams indeed are ambition; for the very substance of the ambitious is merely the shadow of a dream.	265
HAMLET	A dream itself is but a shadow.	
ROSENCRANTZ	Truly, and I hold ambition of so airy and light a quality that it is but a shadow's shadow.	
HAMLET	Then are our beggars bodies, and our monarchs and outstretched heroes the beggars' shadows. Shall we to th' court? for, by my fay, I cannot reason.	272
BOTH	We'll wait upon you.	
HAMLET	No such matter. 1 will not sort you with the rest of my servants; for, to speak to you like an honest man, I am most dreadfully attended. But in the beaten way of friendship, what make you at Elsinore?	
ROSENCRANTZ	To visit you, my lord; no other occasion.	279
HAMLET	Beggar that I am, I am even poor in thanks; but I thank you; and sure, dear friends, my thanks are too dear a halfpenny. Were you not sent for? Is it your own inclining? Is it a free visitation? Come, deal justly with me. Come, come. Nay, speak.	285
GUILDENSTERN	What should we say, my lord?	

264-72 **Which dreams...cannot reason:** Hamlet has intentionally wandered from the point which Rosencrantz is trying to investigate, and Guildenstern brings him back to it. But the result is simply a quibbling dialogue on the subject of ambition. Thus Hamlet outwits his cross-examiners. 270-1. **Then...shadows:** This is an instance of that paradoxical reasoning in which the wits of Shakespeare's time delighted. Guildenstern has said, in effect, that ambition is merely a shadow; Hamlet argues as follows: "If ambition is a shadow, our monarchs and heroes, who are entirely composed of ambition, must be shadows, and our beggars, the only persons in the world who have no ambition, must alone be composed of real substance. If, now, the beggars are the only real bodies, and the monarchs and heroes are shadows, then the monarchs and heroes must be the shadows of the beggars, since there cannot be a shadow without a real body to cast it." 270. **Outstretched:** suggests the fantastic length of a man's shadow. The hero seems very tall, but he is in fact only the ludicrously elongated shadow of some quite ordinary beggar. 272. **fay:** faith. 273. **wait upon you:** serve you. [EDS.] 274. **No such matter:** Not at all. As usual, Hamlet declines to allow his friends to call themselves his servants.—**sort you with:** associate you with, as in the same social class. 275-6. **I am most dreadfully attended:** My attendants are a very poor lot. [Or he is accompanied by thoughts that he wishes he did not have. EDS.] 278. **what make you?** what are you doing? 280-2. **Beggar that I am:** This comment is similar to that in 1.5.185-7. [EDS.]—**too dear a halfpenny:** too dear at the price of a halfpenny. His thanks are worthless, he implies, since he has no power in the state. 284. **justly:** honestly. 286. **What should we say?** Being unprepared for Hamlet's questioning, they betray themselves at once by their hesitation.

HAMLET	Why, anything — but to th' purpose. You were sent for; and there is a kind of confession in your looks, which your modesties have not craft enough to color. I know the good King and Queen have sent for you.

291

ROSENCRANTZ	To what end, my lord?

HAMLET	That you must teach me. But let me conjure you by the rights of our fellowship, by the consonancy of our youth, by the obligation of our ever-preserved love, and by what more dear a better proposer could charge you withal, be even and direct with me, whether you were sent for or no.

299

ROSENCRANTZ	[aside to Guildenstern] What say you?

HAMLET	[aside] Nay then, I have an eye of you. — If you love me, hold not off.

GUILDENSTERN	My lord, we were sent for.

303

HAMLET	I will tell you why. So shall my anticipation prevent your discovery, and your secrecy to the King and Queen molt no feather. I have of late — but wherefore I know not — lost all my mirth, forgone all custom of exercises; and indeed, it goes so heavily with my disposition that this goodly frame, the earth, seems to me a sterile promontory; this most excellent canopy, the air, look you, this brave o'erhanging firmament, this majestical roof fretted with golden fire — why, it appeareth no other thing to me than a foul and pestilent congregation of vapors. What a piece of work is a man! how noble in reason! how infinite in faculties! in form and moving how express and admirable! in action how like an angel! in apprehension how like a god! the beauty of the world, the paragon of animals. And yet to me what is this quintessence of dust? Man delights not me — no, nor woman neither, though by your smiling you seem to say so.

reason — apprehension
moving — action

ROSENCRANTZ	My lord, there was no such stuff in my thoughts.

323

---

292. **To what end?** Why should we be sent for?. 293. **consonancy:** harmony. 297. **by what...withal:** by anything even more sacred that a better talker might urge in appealing to you.—**withal:** with.—**even:** frank. 301. **of you:** on you. 304–6. **So...feather:** Thus my answering my own question in advance will head off your confession, and so your promise of secrecy will not be broken in the least. *Prevent* in the sense of "forestall" and *discovery* in the sense of "disclosure" are both common. 307. **mirth:** cheerfulness. 308. **frame:** structure. 309. **a sterile promontory:** a barren rocky point jutting out into the sea of eternity. 310. **brave:** splendid. 311. **fretted:** adorned with fretwork, like the ceiling of a magnificent hall. 313. **a man:** Hamlet's meaning is not "What a masterpiece is *mankind*," but "Look at *a man*, and see what a masterpiece he is." It is the individual, not the race, that is in his mind, as the rest of the sentence proves. 314. **express:** precisely adapted to its purpose—like a delicately adjusted piece of mechanism. 317. **this quintessence of dust:** this finest extract or sublimation of dust.

HAMLET   Why did you laugh then, when I said 'Man delights not me'?

ROSENCRANTZ To think, my lord, if you delight not in man, what
            lenten entertainment the players shall receive from you. We
            coted them on the way, and hither are they coming to offer
            you service.   331

HAMLET   He that plays the king shall be welcome — his Majesty
            shall have tribute of me; the adventurous knight shall use his
            foil and target; the lover shall not sigh gratis; the humorous
            man shall end his part in peace; the clown shall make those
            laugh whose lungs are tickle o' th' sere; and the lady shall say
            her mind freely, or the blank verse shall halt for't. What
            players are they?   340

ROSENCRANTZ Even those you were wont to take such delight in, the
            tragedians of the city.

HAMLET   How chances it they travel? Their residence, both
            in reputation and profit, was better both ways.   345

ROSENCRANTZ I think their inhibition comes by the means of the late
            innovation.

HAMLET   Do they hold the same estimation they did when I
            was in the city? Are they so followed?   350

ROSENCRANTZ No indeed are they not.

HAMLET   How comes it? Do they grow rusty?

ROSENCRANTZ Nay, their endeavor keeps in the wonted pace; but
            there is, sir, an eyrie of children, little eyases, that cry out on
            the top of question and are most tyrannically clapped for't.
            These are now the fashion, and so berattle the common stages

---

328–9. **what lenten entertainment:** what a poor reception. 330. **coted:** passed. 332. **He...king:** In the
next several lines, Hamlet mentions the types of characters who might appear in a play. [EDS.] 333. **the
adventurous knight:** the knight errant, wandering in search of adventures. He was a common figure
in certain Elizabethan dramas of an old-fashioned type which were the lineal descendants of medieval
romances. 334. **target:** a small shield.—**the humorous man:** the man with a dominant humor, another
stock character in Elizabethan plays. 338. **whose lungs...sere:** [People all too ready to laugh at anything.
EDS.] The *sere* or *sear* is a part of the mechanism of a gun-lock; if it is *tickle* (delicately adjusted), the gun
goes off at a touch. The lungs are often mentioned as the instruments of laughter. 338-9. **the lady...
for't:** The lady shall speak her mind freely, even if that should spoil the regularity of the meter. 339.
halt: limp, [be imperfect metrically. EDS.]. 344. **Their residence:** their remaining at the capital as a
resident company. 346-7. **their inhibition...innovation:** The new fashion hinders the actors (from
remaining at the capital). Hamlet, having been away from Denmark, at the university in Wittenberg,
does not know what this new fashion is, as his next speech proves, and so Rosencrantz explains: the
novelty consists in having companies of boys act in public. 354. **an eyrie:** a nest or brood.—**eyases:**
young or nestling hawks. 354-5. **cry...question:** shriek out their speeches in a key above that of natural
talk, referring to the "childish treble" of the youngsters' voices. 355. **tyrannically:** The stage tyrant
was a noisy and violent character. 356. **berattle...stages:** In their plays these children berate the adult
theaters, which they style contemptuously "the common stages."

(so they call them) that many wearing rapiers are afraid of
goose-quills and dare scarce come thither.   360

HAMLET   What, are they children? Who maintains 'em? How
are they escoted? Will they pursue the quality no longer than
they can sing? Will they not say afterwards, if they should
grow themselves to common players (as it is most like, if their
means are no better), their writers do them wrong to make
them exclaim against their own succession.   368

ROSENCRANTZ   Faith, there has been much to do on both sides; and
the nation holds it no sin to tarre them to controversy. There was,
for a while, no money bid for argument unless the poet
and the player went to cuffs in the question.

HAMLET   Is't possible?   374

GUILDENSTERN   O, there has been much throwing about of brains.

HAMLET   Do the boys carry it away?

ROSENCRANTZ   Ay, that they do, my lord — Hercules and his load too.   379

HAMLET   It is not very strange; for my uncle is King of Denmark,
and those that would make mows at him while my
father lived give twenty, forty, fifty, a hundred ducats apiece
for his picture in little. 'Sblood, there is something in this more
than natural, if philosophy could find it out.   385

Flourish for the Players.

GUILDENSTERN   There are the players.

359-60. **many...thither:** many gentlemen are so much afraid of satirical pens that they hardly dare
visit an ordinary theater lest the world think them behind the times. The *goose-quills* are the pens of the
poets who, in writing plays for the child actors, insert speeches berating "common stages" as unfit to be
patronized by any person of taste. 362. **escoted:** supported (financially). 362-5. **Will they pursue...
succession:** Will they give up the stage when their voices change? If not, they must become "common
players" in course of time, and then they may well blame their authors for having put into their mouths
satirical attacks on their own *succession,* i.e., on what they themselves are going to be by-and-by. 362.
the quality: the (actor's) profession. 369. **much to do:** a great hubbub.—**on both sides:** The grown-up
players had retorted by satirizing the child actors. 370. **tarre:** egg on, incite. 371. **argument:** plot. 373.
question: dialogue. For a time no play was saleable unless it embodied a quarrelsome dialogue between
a Poet and a Player (on the subject of the grown-up actors and the children's companies). 376. **carry it
away:** get the victory. 379. **Hercules and his load too:** The load of Hercules is the globe, which he bore
upon his shoulders to relieve Atlas while Atlas fetched the apples of the Hesperides. The meaning is that
the boys "have won the whole world of playgoers," "they carry all before them"; but there may be an
allusion to the Globe Theatre and its sign, which is said to have been Hercules with his load (the globe)
on his shoulders. 380-3. **my uncle...little:** Hamlet lets his animosity against the King show, and the
response of Rosencrantz and Guildenstern would further distance him from them. [EDS.] 381. **mows:**
faces. 384. **his picture in little:** a miniature of him.—**'Sblood:** by God's blood. A rather rough oath.
385. **philosophy:** rational thought. [EDS.]

HAMLET	Gentlemen, you are welcome to Elsinore. Your hands, come. Th' appurtenance of welcome is fashion and ceremony. Let me comply with you in this garb, lest my extent to the players (which I tell you must show fairly outwards) should more appear like entertainment than yours. You are welcome. But my uncle-father and aunt-mother are deceived.
GUILDENSTERN	In what, my dear lord? 395
HAMLET	I am but mad north-north-west. When the wind is southerly I know a hawk from a handsaw. *– cleverly disguised language*

Enter Polonius.

POLONIUS	Well be with you, gentlemen.
HAMLET	Hark you, Guildenstern — and you too — at each ear a hearer. That great baby you see there is not yet out of his swaddling clouts. 401
ROSENCRANTZ	Happily he's the second time come to them; for they say an old man is twice a child.
HAMLET	I will prophesy he comes to tell me of the players. Mark it. — You say right, sir; a Monday morning; 'twas so indeed.
POLONIUS	My lord, I have news to tell you,
HAMLET	My lord, I have news to tell you. When Roscius was an actor in Rome — 410
POLONIUS	The actors are come hither, my lord.
HAMLET	Buzz, buzz.

387-92. **Your...yours:** Hamlet makes a show of warmth to Rosencrantz and Guildenstern, warning them that he may be forced to show more cordiality to the players than he has to them. [EDS.] 389. **comply...garb:** use compliments (or ceremony) with you in this style. 389-90. **my extent:** my display of cordiality. 390. **show:** appear. 391. **entertainment:** welcome. 395. **In what?** Spoken eagerly, for now at last Guildenstern thinks Hamlet is about to tell what ails him; but the next speech is as baffling to the cross-questioners as ever. 397. **I know a hawk from a handsaw:** A proverb: "I can distinguish between things that do not resemble each other at all"; "I have some little common sense and discrimination." The speech sounds to Rosencrantz and Guildenstern like mere raving, but the audience understands Hamlet's hidden meaning: he is sane enough when the circumstances are suitable. He has, in fact, given few signs of insanity in the preceding dialogue, but as soon as Polonius enters he talks as wildly as in his previous conversation with the old courtier (2.2.172 ff.). 399-400. **at each ear...a hearer:** Hamlet asks the two men to bend to hear him [so as to pretend to Polonius they are deep in conversation. EDS.]. 402. **Happily:** haply, perhaps. 403. **an old man...child:** well-known proverb. [EDS.] 406-7. **You say right...indeed:** Addressed to Rosencrantz, in order to seem to be in the midst of a conversation when Polonius comes up. 409. **I...you:** Hamlet repeats the words of Polonius, mimicking his tone. 409-10. **When Roscius...Rome:** Since Roscius lived in Cicero's time, the remark might well inform Polonius that his news is stale news; but the old man takes it as mere madness and goes on with the speech which Hamlet has interrupted. 412. **Buzz:** A rude exclamation signifying that Hamlet takes no interest in what Polonius says.

POLONIUS	Upon my honor —
HAMLET	Then came each actor on his ass —
POLONIUS[†]	The best actors in the world, either for tragedy, comedy, history, pastoral, pastoral-comical, historical-pastoral, tragical-historical, tragical-comical-historical-pastoral; scene individable, or poem unlimited.[‡] Seneca cannot be too heavy, nor Plautus too light. For the law of writ and the liberty, these are the only men.
HAMLET	O Jephthah, judge of Israel, what a treasure hadst thou.
POLONIUS	What treasure had he, my lord?
HAMLET	Why, 425

> "One fair daughter, and no more,
> The which he loved passing well."

POLONIUS	[*aside*] Still on my daughter.
HAMLET	Am I not i' th' right, old Jephthah?
POLONIUS	If you call me Jephthah, my lord, I have a daughter that I love passing well. 431

---

414. **Then...ass:** Spoken, or chanted, as if it were a line from a song. 415-18 **tragedy, comedy...poem unlimited:** Polonius's first five terms distinguishes pure pastoral from such plays as Shakespeare's *As You Like It*, which are comedies with a pastoral admixture. *Tragical-historical*, too, is an acceptable term for what we call "historical tragedy" (like *Macbeth* or *Julius Caesar*), as distinguished from "history" plays (like *King John* or *Henry IV*). But the old man's tongue runs faster than his thoughts, and he ends his catalogue with a preposterous four-story adjective that never fails to bring down the house. 417-18. **scene...unlimited:** dramas that observe the unities of place and time and also those that give no heed to such limitations. [See note 421. EDS.] Elizabethan critics were inclined to judge drama by its adherence to strict Aristotelian rules about place (requiring a single space for action) and time (over the course of at most a day). Shakespeare almost always bent the rules, but he was well aware of them and knew how to construct such plays if he so chose, as in *The Comedy of Errors* and *The Tempest*. 418. **Seneca:** The favorite classical tragedian in Shakespeare's time. Latin classical plays were often taught in the original and in translation and performed at public schools and universities. Polonius, like Hamlet, was a "university man" (see 3.2.104). 421. **Plautus:** Roman writer of comedies. [EDS.]—**the law of writ:** plays composed according to the rules of writing, that is, those that observe the three unities (of time, place, and action).—**the liberty:** plays which show complete freedom from such restrictions. Polonius is repeating what he has already said. 422. **only:** uniquely excellent. 423. **Jephthah:** See *Judges* 11.30-40. [After winning a victory, Jephthah vowed to sacrifice the first being that he saw upon arriving home; he thus sacrificed his daughter, a virgin. Hamlet implies that Polonius sacrifices his daughter for his own purposes. EDS.] **What treasure had he?** Polonius seems to be or pretends to be ignorant of the Bible. [EDS.] 427. **passing:** surpassingly. 428. **Still:** always.

---

†   Zeffirelli moves Polonius's news of the actors and commentary on dramatic genre, using those lines to introduce the play the within the play (3.2); his Polonius delivers the speech to the entire court, making it intentionally comic, much to the amusement of everyone present, including the King and Queen.

‡   Branagh reduces the potential for laughter at Polonius by having him read the genres from the players' playbill.

HAMLET	Nay, that follows not.
POLONIUS	What follows then, my lord?
HAMLET	Why,

       "As by lot, God wot,"   435

and then, you know,

       "It came to pass, as most like it was."

The first row of the pious chanson will show you more; for
look where my abridgment comes   439

Enter four or five Players.

You are welcome, masters; welcome, all. — I am glad to see
thee well. —Welcome, good friends. — O, my old friend?
Why, thy face is valanced since I saw thee last. Com'st thou
to beard me in Denmark? — What, my young lady and
mistress? By'r Lady, your ladyship is nearer to heaven than
when I saw you last by the altitude of a chopine. Pray God
your voice, like a piece of uncurrent gold, be not cracked within
the ring. — Masters, you are all welcome. We'll e'en to't like
French falconers, fly at anything we see. We'll have a speech
straight. Come, give us a taste of your quality. Come, a
passionate speech.

1. PLAYER	What speech, my good lord?
HAMLET	I heard thee speak me a speech once, but it was never

acted; or if it was, not above once; for the play, I remember,
pleased not the million, 'twas caviary to the general; but it
was (as I received it, and others, whose judgments in such

---

432. **that follows not:** [Polonius, Hamlet says, has not shown love for his daughter. EDS.], but Polonius
takes the remark for mere insanity. 438. **row:** stanza. 439. **my abridgment:** (1) the players, who cut
short my quotation [and (2) who provide entertainment and thus shorten the time. EDS.].—**chanson:**
French word for song. [EDS.] 440. **masters:** gentlemen. 442. **valanced:** fringed with a beard. 443. **to
beard me:** confront me; Hamlet plays on the meaning of *valanced*. [EDS.]—**lady:** said to the boy who
acted women's parts. No English actress appeared on a public stage in London until the revival of the
theaters, after the Restoration of the monarchy (1660). 444. **mistress:** madam. 445. **chopine:** a kind
of wooden stilt, sometimes a foot or eighteen inches in height, placed under the sole of a woman's shoe
to increase her stature. Chopines were much worn in the East and in Venice, and the fashion made
some progress in England in the seventeenth century. 446. **cracked:** A coin would not pass if it had a
crack extending from the edge to a point inside the circle that surrounded the monarch's head or other
device. Hamlet hopes that the boy's voice is not so cracked as to spoil its *ring*—that it is still "as clear
as a bell." [pun: As a boy reaches puberty, his voice cracks. EDS.] 447. **We'll e'en to't:** We'll just go at it.
448. **French falconers:** Famous for their skill and for the excellent training of their falcons.—**fly...see:**
let the hawk fly in quest of any bird in sight; literally, undertake anything, no matter how difficult. 450.
your quality: your professional ability. 451. **passionate:** emotional. 456. **caviary:** caviar, a Russian
delicacy made of sturgeon's eggs. It was a novelty in England in Shakespeare's time, and fondness for
it was and still is, an "acquired taste." — **caviary to the general:** The intellectual kind of play not
appreciated by the general run of playgoers.

matters cried in the top of mine) an excellent play, well
digested in the scenes, set down with as much modesty as cunning.
I remember one said there were no sallets in the lines
to make the matter savory, nor no matter in the phrase that
might indict the author of affectation; but called it an honest
method, as wholesome as sweet, and by very much more handsome
than fine. One speech in't I chiefly loved. 'Twas Æneas'
tale to Dido, and there about of it especially where he speaks of
Priam's slaughter. If it live in your memory, begin at this
line — let me see, let me see: 471

  "The rugged Pyrrhus, like th' Hyrcanian beast—"
'Tis not so; it begins with Pyrrhus: - *reveng̶e-ful son*

  "The rugged Pyrrhus, he whose sable arms,
  Black as his purpose, did the night resemble   475
  When he lay couched in the ominous horse,
  Hath now this dread and black complexion smeared
  With heraldry more dismal. Head to foot
  Now is he total gules, horridly tricked
  With blood of fathers, mothers, daughters, sons,   480
  Baked and impasted with the parching streets,
  That lend a tyrannous and a damned light
  To their lord's murther. Roasted in wrath and fire,
  And thus o'ersizsd with coagulate gore,
  With eyes like carbuncles, the hellish Pyrrhus
  Old grandsire Priam seeks."

So, proceed you.

POLONIUS   Fore God, my lord, well spoken, with good accent and good
discretion.

---

458. **cried in the top of mine:** were more authoritative than mine; literally, called out with a louder
voice than mine. 459. **set down:** written.—**modesty:** artistic restraint.—**cunning:** skill. 460. **sallets:**
[salad; side dish, sometimes spicy. EDS.]; hence, figuratively, spicy passages. 462. **honest:** in good taste.
463. **wholesome:** sound and clear.—**more handsome than fine:** elegant, but not gaudy. 470. **Priam's
slaughter:** [killing of King Priam, during the fall of Troy, told in Virgil's *Æneid*. EDS.] Whether the
passages recited are actually quotations from some lost tragedy is unknown, but there is a strong
resemblance between the style of the player's speech and the language in which Christopher Marlowe
tells the same story in his *Tragedy of Dido*. 472. **th' Hyrcanian beast:** Hyrcania was a wild region in
Asia, famous for tigers. 473. **Pyrrhus:** Greek hero in the Trojan War; Pyrrhus was Achilles' son, an
unrestrained, blood-thirsty revenger. But see lines 501-4. [EDS.] 474. **sable arms:** black armor. [EDS.]
476. **couched:** hidden.—**ominous:** deadly. [EDS.]—**horse:** The Greek army was concealed within an
enormous wooden horse, presented as a gift to the Trojans, who naively brought it into their city:
The trick led to the saying "Beware of Greeks bearing gifts." [EDS.] 478. **dismal:** ill-omened.—**gules:**
the heraldic term for "red."—**tricked:** adorned. 481. **Baked...parching:** The city was on fire. 482.
tyrannous: savage. 484. **o'ersized:** glued over.—**coagulate:** clotted. 485. **carbuncles:** garnets or
similar red stones, thought to emit light by their own nature.

1. PLAYER	"Anon he finds him,	490
	Striking too short at Greeks. His antique sword,	
	Rebellious to his arm, lies where it falls,	
	Repugnant to command. Unequal matched,	
	Pyrrhus at Priam drives, in rage strikes wide;	
	But with the whiff and wind of his fell sword	495
	Th' unnerved father falls. Then senseless Ilium,	
	Seeming to feel this blow, with flaming top	
	Stoops to his base, and with a hideous crash	
	Takes prisoner Pyrrhus' ear. For lo, his sword,	
	Which was declining on the milky head	500
	Of reverend Priam, seemed i' th' air to stick.	
	So, as a painted tyrant, Pyrrhus stood,	
	And, like a neutral to his will and matter,	
	Did nothing.	
	But, as we often see, against some storm,	505
	A silence in the heavens, the rack stand still,	
	The bold winds speechless, and the orb below	
	As hush as death — anon the dreadful thunder	
	Doth rend the region; so, after Pyrrhus' pause,	
	Aroused vengeance sets him new awork;	510
	And never did the Cyclops' hammers fall	
	On Mars's armor, forged for proof eterne,	
	With less remorse than Pyrrhus' bleeding sword	
	Now falls on Priam.	
	Out, out, thou strumpet Fortune. All you gods,	
	In general synod take away her power;	515
	Break all the spokes and fellies from her wheel.	
	And bowl the round nave down the hill of heaven,	
	As low as to the fiends."	
POLONIUS	This is too long.	520

---

491. **His antique sword:** the sword which he had wielded long ago in his youth. 495. **the whiff and wind:** gusty breeze. [EDS.]—**fell:** cruel. 496. **unnerved:** feeble in sinew.—**senseless:** having no feeling.—**Ilium:** Stronghold of Troy. 498. **his:** its. 503-4. **like...nothing:** Pyrrhus paused midway between his purpose and its fulfillment. 505. **against:** just before. 506. **rack:** clouds. 507. **the orb below:** this round earth. 509. **the region:** the air. 511. **Cyclops':** The Cyclops were the gigantic one-eyed workmen of Vulcan, the god of blacksmiths' work and the manufacture of armor. 512. **for proof eterne:** to stand the test forever. 513. **remorse:** pity. 515. **Out:** An interjection of contempt and abhorrence.—**strumpet Fortune:** See note 240. 517. **fellies:** the "rim" of Fortune's wheel.—**her wheel:** The allegory of Fortune's wheel represents Fortune as sitting by a wheel which she turns by means of a crank. On this wheel are mortals, who are therefore sometimes rising, sometimes at the summit, and sometimes declining or at the very bottom of their fate. 518. **nave:** the hub.

HAMLET	It shall to the barber's, with your beard. — Prithee say on. He's for a jig or a tale of bawdry, or he sleeps. Say on; come to Hecuba.
1. PLAYER	"But who, O who, had seen the mobled queen —"
HAMLET	"The mobled queen"? 526
POLONIUS	That's good. "Mobled queen" is good.

1. PLAYER   'Run barefoot up and down, threat'ning the flames
    With bisson rheum; a clout upon that head
    Where late the diadem stood, and for a robe,   530
    About her lank and all o'erteemed loins,
    A blanket, in the alarm of fear caught up —
    Who this had seen, with tongue in venom steeped
    'Gainst Fortune's state would treason have pronounced.
    But if the gods themselves did see her then,   535
    When she saw Pyrrhus make malicious sport
    In mincing with his sword her husband's limbs,
    The instant burst of clamor that she made
    (Unless things mortal move them not at all)
    Would have made milch the burning eyes of heaven   540
    And passion in the gods."

POLONIUS   Look, where he has not turned his color, and has tears[†] in's eyes. Prithee no more.

HAMLET   'Tis well. I'll have thee speak out the rest of this soon. — Good my lord, will you see the players well bestowed? Do you hear? Let them be well used; for they are the abstract and brief chronicles of the time. After your death you were better have a bad epitaph than their ill report while you live. 551

---

521. **It shall…beard:** Hamlet, irritated at Polonius's interruption and criticism, retorts sharply: "Too long? So is your beard! We'll send them both to the barber together." [Polonius responds by inserting a compliment to the player when he gets a chance; see line 527. EDS.] 522. **a jig:** a comic dialogue (or short farce) in song and dance. These were a favorite form of entertainment on the stage and often followed the performance of a play. 525. **mobled:** muffled. The word is unusual and Hamlet repeats it, perhaps considering its aptness. Polonius, however, admires or pretends to admire it. 529. **bisson rheum:** blinding tears.—**a clout:** a cloth. [Those critics who cared about the unities were upset about Shakespeare's use of such homely, low diction in a tragedy. EDS.] 531. **o'erteemed:** worn out by childbearing. 534. **state:** government of the world. 539. **Unless…at all:** unless the Epicurean doctrine be true, that the gods live in unruffled calm and are never disturbed by sympathy for mankind. 540. **milch:** flowing with tears; literally, yielding milk.—**eyes:** the stars. 541. **passion:** strong emotion. 542. **where:** a contraction of *whether*. [EDS.] 543. **in's:** in his. 545. **well bestowed:** lodged and otherwise well provided for. 546. **abstract:** summary. [EDS.] Always a noun in Shakespeare. 547. **you were better:** "It would be better *for you.*"

---

†   Scott's player and Hamlet are both tearful.

Polonius	My lord, I will use them according to their desert.
Hamlet	God's bodykins, man, much better. Use every man after his desert, and who should scape whipping? Use them after your own honor and dignity. The less they deserve, the more merit is in your bounty. Take them in.
Polonius	Come, sirs.
Hamlet	Follow him; friends. We'll hear a play tomorrow.

> *Exeunt Polonius and Players [except the First].*

Dost thou hear me, old friend? Can you play "The Murther of Gonzago"?

1. Player	Ay, my lord.	564
Hamlet	We'll ha't to-morrow night. You could, for a need, study a speech of some dozen or sixteen lines which I would set down and insert in't, could you not?	
1. Player	Ay, my lord.	569
Hamlet	Very well. Follow that lord — and look you mock him not. [*Exit First Player.*] My good friends, I'll leave you till night. You are welcome to Elsinore.	
Rosencrantz	Good my lord.	
Hamlet	Ay, so, God b' wi' ye.	

> *Exeunt [Rosencrantz and Guildenstern].*

Now I am alone.	575

O, what a rogue and peasant slave am I.
Is it not monstrous that this player here,
But in a fiction, in a dream of passion,

---

552. **I will…desert:** I will treat them as well as they deserve. 553. **God's bodykins:** A common oath. *Bodykins* means "little body," i.e., "the host" or "consecrated wafer."[The play does not show us enough of Hamlet before his pretended madness to tell if he would use such crude language, but Ophelia's description of him as a "noble mind" (3.1.158-68) suggests that he had not been accustomed to speak this way. On the other hand, see 2.2.603, where he uses similar language when he is alone. EDS.] —**much better:** Hamlet's standard of behavior is above that of Polonius: treat people better than they deserve. 553-4. **Use…whipping:** He has, however, a jaundiced view of human worth. [EDS.] 555. **after:** according to. 562. **The Murther of Gonzago:** No such drama is known, nor is it likely that it ever existed apart from the tragedy of *Hamlet.* Plays within plays, however, were common. 566. **dozen or sixteen lines:** Much ingenuity has been wasted in trying to identify Hamlet's dozen or sixteen lines, as if we were to suppose that Shakespeare wrote *The Murther of Gonzago* without them and then inserted them somewhere. [What Hamlet's request does tell us, perhaps, is that playtexts could be malleable, with additions and subtractions for the occasion. EDS.] 570. **mock him not:** This may be said ironically. Hamlet cannot believe that a poor traveling player would think of mocking a nobleman. [EDS.] 574. **Good my lord:** *my lord,* considered as one word, is preceded by the adjective; a courteous phrase of leave-taking. 576. **rogue:** wretched fellow. 578. **dream:** made-up emotion. [EDS.]—**passion:** strong emotion.

Could force his soul so to his own conceit
That, from her working, all his visage wanned,   580
Tears in his eyes, distraction in's aspect,
A broken voice, and his whole function suiting
With forms to his conceit? And all for nothing. For Hecuba.
What's Hecuba to him, or he to Hecuba,   585
That he should weep for her? What would he do,
Had he the motive and the cue for passion
That I have? He would drown the stage with tears
And cleave the general ear with horrid speech;
Make mad the guilty and appall the free,   590
Confound the ignorant, and amaze indeed
The very faculties of eyes and ears. Yet I,
A dull and muddy-mettled rascal, peak
Like John-a-dreams, unpregnant of my cause,   595
And can say nothing. No, not for a king,
Upon whose property and most dear life
A damned defeat was made. Am I a coward?
Who calls me villain? breaks my pate across?
Plucks off my beard and blows it in my face?   600
Tweaks me by th' nose? gives me the lie i' th' throat
As deep as to the lungs? Who does me this, ha?
'Swounds, I should take it. for it cannot be
But I am pigeon-livered and lack gall
To make oppression bitter, or ere this   605
I should have fatted all the region kites,

579-80. **Could...wanned:** could force his soul into such accord with his conception (of the part he played) that, by the operation of his soul (upon his bodily powers), his whole face grew pale. 582. **his whole function:** all the powers of his body—i.e., all those that operate to express emotion.—**forms:** appearances.584. **his conceit:** his conception of the part.—**For Hecuba:** Priam's wife [that is, for a fiction. Shakespeare, however, may be introducing a sly compliment to literature's emotional effect. EDS.]. 587. **the motive:** the incentive. 590. **Make mad...free:** by his description of the crime he would drive those spectators mad who had any such sin on their conscience, and would horrify even the innocent. 591. **Confound the ignorant:** confuse even those who have no knowledge of the crime being played on stage. [EDS.]—**amaze:** stun. 594. **A dull...muddy-mettled rascal:** a stupid and poor-spirited wretch. *Mettle* (the same word as *metal*) is often used for one's "material" or "quality," and so for one's "spirit" or "temper."—**peak:** go moping about. To *peak* is, literally, to "pine away." 595. **Like John-a-dreams:** like one in a dream. —**unpregnant of my cause:** with no real sense of mission for the cause to which I should be devoted. 597. **property...life:** all that he possessed: crown, queen, his very life. 598. **defeat:** destruction. 598-615. **Am I a coward?** Hamlet rages against himself for stupid inactivity. He has done nothing to avenge his father and seems incapable of doing anything; he wonders if he is a coward. At the end of the soliloquy, he finds a way out of his dilemma: he will get better evidence that the vision's word. "The play's the thing!" It will force the King to confession, and then Hamlet can act when once he "knows his course." 601-2. **gives me...lungs?** "You lie in your throat" was a greater insult than simply "You lie," because it implied that the lie was deliberate and not a casual lip-falsehood. "As deep as to the lungs" is, then, a lie "in the superlative degree." 603. **'Swounds:** by God's wounds. [The oath, said by Hamlet when alone, shows that he is capable of rough language. EDS.] 604. **pigeon-livered...gall:** The supposed gentleness of the dove was explained in the old physiology on the theory that it had no gall and hence no bitterness or capacity for resentment. 606. **kites:** birds of prey. [EDS.]

With this slave's offal. Bloody, bawdy villain.
Remorseless, treacherous, lecherous, kindless villain.
O, vengeance!
Why, what an ass am I. This is most brave,   610
That I, the son of a dear father murthered,
Prompted to my revenge by heaven and hell,
Must (like a whore) unpack my heart with words
And fall a-cursing like a very drab,
A scullion.   615
Fie upon't! foh! About, my brain. Hum, I have heard
That guilty creatures, sitting at a play,
Have by the very cunning of the scene
Been struck so to the soul that presently
They have proclaimed their malefactions;   620
For murther, though it have no tongue, will speak
With most miraculous organ. I'll have these players
Play something like the murther of my father
Before mine uncle. I'll observe his looks;
I'll tent him to the quick. If he but blench,   625
I know my course. The spirit that I have seen
May be a devil; and the devil hath power
T' assume a pleasing shape; yea, and perhaps
Out of my weakness and my melancholy,
As he is very potent with such spirits,   630
Abuses me to damn me. I'll have grounds
More relative than this. The play's the thing
Wherein I'll catch the conscience of the King   *Exit.*

[margin handwritten: satan may have sent a spirit in the looks of father]

[handwritten: which King]

[handwritten: can he trust the ghost?]

608. **Remorseless:** pitiless. Comparing the King to Pyrrhus: see line 513.—**kindless:** unnatural. 610. **brave:** noble; [sarcastic. EDS.]. 612. **by heaven and hell:** Heaven prompts him to revenge because his uncle deserves punishment; hell, because he is actuated by anger and hatred. 613. **unpack:** relieve. 615. **scullion:** a kitchen wench [i.e., a low person. EDS.]. 616. **About:** Go to work. 618. **cunning of the scene:** the skill with which the play was acted. 619. **presently:** on the spot. 621-2. **For murther...organ:** The doctrine that "murder will out," [that is, will be revealed. EDS.]. 625. **tent:** probe.—**blench:** flinch. 630. **As he is:** as well may be the case, for he is.—**such spirits:** such a temperament [as mine. It was thought that those with a melancholic *humor* had too much black bile and therefore were vulnerable to evil spirits. EDS.] 631. **Abuses:** deceives (by appearing in the likeness of my father and falsely accusing my uncle of murder).—**to damn me:** by persuading me to kill an innocent man. [Hamlet does not recognize another possibility; that though the murder is a fact the spirit is tempting him to commit a sin, since regicide was considered wrong under virtually all conditions. This problem is complicated by the fact that it is difficult to bring a legally elected king to justice. EDS.] 632. **More relative:** referring back more surely from the evidence to the fact, hence, more positive, cogent, and conclusive than the spirit's word.

ACT III

SCENE I. [*Elsinore. A room in the Castle.*]

Enter King, Queen, Polonius, Ophelia, Rosencrantz, Guildenstern, and Lords.

KING	And can you by no drift of circumstance
	Get from him why he puts on this confusion,
	Grating so harshly all his days of quiet
	With turbulent and dangerous lunacy?
ROSENCRANTZ	He does confess he feels himself distracted, 5
	But from what cause he will by no means speak.
GUILDENSTERN	Nor do we find him forward to be sounded,
	But with a <u>crafty madness</u> keeps aloof
	When we would bring him on to some confession
	Of his true state.
QUEEN	Did he receive you well? 10
ROSENCRANTZ	Most like a gentleman.
GUILDENSTERN	But with much forcing of his disposition.
ROSENCRANTZ	Niggard of question, but of our demands
	Most free in his reply.
QUEEN	Did you assay him
	To any pastime? 15
ROSENCRANTZ	Madam, it so fell out that certain players
	We o'erraught on the way. Of these we told him,
	And there did seem in him a kind of joy
	To hear if it. They are here about the court,
	And, as I think, they have already order 20
	This night to play before him.
POLONIUS	'Tis most true;
	And he beseeched me to entreat your Majesties
	To hear and see the matter.

ACT III. SCENE I.
1. **by no drift of circumstance:** by maneuvering the conversation. [EDS.] 2. **puts on this confusion:** acts in this crazy way. 3. **grating:** disturbing. [EDS.] 8. **crafty:** contrived or skillful. [EDS.] 12. **disposition:** mood. Guildenstern noticed Hamlet's efforts to be cordial. 13-14. **Niggard...reply:** [He was stingy with conversation but answered our questions readily. EDS.] *Free* does not imply that the answers were satisfactory. 13. **question:** talk.—**demands:** questions. 14-15. **assay...pastime:** try to attract him to any amusement, in order to relieve his mind. 17. **o'erraught:** overtook and passed. 23. **the matter:** the performance.

KING   With all my heart, and it doth much content me
                     To hear him so inclined.   25
                     Good gentlemen, give him a further edge
                     And drive his purpose on to these delights.

ROSENCRANTZ   We shall, my lord.
                                         Exeunt Rosencrantz and Guildenstern.

KING   Sweet Gertrude, leave us too; †‡
                     For we have closely sent for Hamlet hither,
                     That he, as 'twere by accident, may here   30
                     Affront Ophelia.
                     Her father and myself (lawful espials)
                     Will so bestow ourselves that, seeing unseen,
                     We may of their encounter frankly judge
                     And gather by him, as he is behaved,   35
                     If't be th' affliction of his love, or no,
                     That thus he suffers for.

QUEEN   I shall obey you;
                     And for your part*, Ophelia, I do wish
                     That your good beauties be the happy cause
                     Of Hamlet's wildness. So shall I hope your virtues   40
                     Will bring him to his wonted way again,
                     To both your honors.

OPHELIA   Madam, I wish it may.
                                                         [*Exit Queen.*]

POLONIUS   Ophelia, walk you here. — Gracious, so please you,
                     We will bestow ourselves. —[*To Ophelia*] Read on this book,
                     That show of such an exercise may color   45
                     Your loneliness. — We are oft to blame in this,

---

24. **content me:** please me. [The King and Queen have avoided contact with Hamlet, it appears, and a public entertainment provides an opportunity to be with him in public. Hamlet has his first opportunity to talk to his mother alone in 3.4. He has his first opportunity to be with the King alone in 3.3. EDS.] 29-37. The King confides in the Queen his plans to spy on Hamlet and Ophelia. [She is his partner also when he sets Rosencrantz and Guildenstern to spy on Hamlet, 2.2.19-26. [EDS.] 29. **closely:** privately. 31. **Affront:** meet face to face. 32. **lawful:** rightful. [EDS.]—**espials:** spies. 33. **bestow ourselves:** station ourselves. 34. **encounter:** meeting.—**frankly:** freely. 35. **as he is behaved:** as he behaves. 40-2. **So shall I hope...honors:** This could suggest to Ophelia and her father that the marriage which Polonius had thought impossible might be agreeable to the Queen. 43. **Gracious:** my gracious lord. 44. **bestow ourselves:** take our places behind the arras.—**book:** A prayer book (see line 89) or some book of devotion. 45-6. **color your loneliness:** supply an excuse for being alone. [EDS.]

---

†   Wirth's Gertrude objects to the idea of spying with shakes of her head. The actual spying takes
      place in a new scene; she is not present and thus never agrees.

‡   28-37. Almereyda's Polonius wires a weeping Ophelia for high-tech spying on the two lovers.

*   Almereyda's Gertrude does not sound sincere, and Ophelia does not respond to her.

'Tis too much proved, that with devotion's visage
And pious action we do sugar o'er
The devil himself.

KING   [*aside*] O, 'tis too true. *learn that ghost is telling truth*
How smart a lash that speech doth give my conscience.   50
The harlot's cheek, beautified with plast'ring art,
Is not more ugly to the thing that helps it
Than is my deed to my most painted word.
O heavy burthen.

POLONIUS   I hear him coming. Let's withdraw, my lord.   55

Exeunt [King and Polonius].

Enter Hamlet.

HAMLET   To be, or not to be — that is the question:**   *to be = to suffer*
Whether 'tis nobler in the mind to suffer   *i.e. still; let things happen*
The slings and arrows of outrageous fortune
Or to take arms against a sea of troubles,   *not to be = take arms against*
And by opposing end them. To die—to sleep—   60
No more; and by a sleep to say we end
The heartache, and the thousand natural shocks
That flesh is heir to. 'Tis a consummation
Devoutly to be wished. To die — to sleep.
To sleep — perchance to dream: ay, there's the rub.   65

46-9. **We...himself:** Polonius's comment about hypocrisy applies to himself, of course, as well as to people in general. 47. **proved:** found true by experience. 49–54. **'tis...burthen:** [Here, for the first time, the audience learns that the Ghost told the truth about the King. EDS.] This remark of the King's is an aside and is therefore sincere; the King, like Macbeth, has sinned hideously and his conscience, like Macbeth's, torments him. Herein he differs from such hardened villains as Iago in *Othello* and Edmund in *King Lear*. [After the prayer scene (3.3), the King no longer expresses pangs of conscience. EDS.] 52. **to:** in comparison with. The haggard cheek under the paint is ugly in contrast with the paint that beautifies it. 56–88. In this famous soliloquy Hamlet is often thought to be dallying with suicide. Others disagree. [If Hamlet is aware that he is being overheard, then his speech is no longer a soliloquy and his sincerity may then be questioned. EDS.] 57. **in the mind:** This modifies *nobler*, not *suffer*: "Does it show a nobler quality of mind to submit or to resist?" 59-60. **to take arms...end them:** When troubles come like an onrushing sea, suicide is like the act of a warrior who runs to meet the waves, sword in hand, thus opposing them until they close over his head and his troubles are ended. [From another perspective, Hamlet's choice is simply between "suffering" (enduring) life's troubles or "taking arms" (fighting) against them; that is, the choice does not imply ending one's life but merely ending what makes life troublesome. EDS.] 61. **No more:** With a pause after *sleep* he means that to die is simply to sleep. Said another way, with no pause between *sleep* and *no* (as in the Second Quarto and First Folio), he suggests that in dying he would not be subject to bad dreams because death ends all. Later (65-9), he considers the opposite possibility, that death does not end bad dreams. [EDS.] 63. **a consummation:** a result. [EDS.] 65. **the rub:** the difficulty. A metaphor from bowling. A *rub* is any obstruction which hinders or deflects the course of the bowl.

**   Q1 *Hamlet,* followed in part by Olivier, Zeffirelli and others, position the "to-be-or-not-to-be" speech *after* the nunnery scene 88-157. Scott places it in the previous scene. Zeffirelli places it just after the King says, "madness in great ones must not unwatched go" (3.1.196).

[handwritten margin notes: no one knows whats after death – how do we know its not worse than living – unknown ↓ might as well stay + live]

For in that sleep of death what dreams may come
When we have shuffled off this mortal coil,
Must give us pause. There's the respect
That makes calamity of so long life.
For who would bear the whips and scorns of time,   70
Th' oppressor's wrong, the proud man's contumely,
The pangs of despised love, the law's delay,
The insolence of office, and the spurns
That patient merit of th' unworthy takes,
When he himself might his quietus make   75
With a bare bodkin? Who would these fardels bear,
To grunt and sweat under a weary life,
But that the dread of something after death —

[handwritten margin notes: father returned but in different form]

The undiscovered country, from whose bourn
No traveler returns — puzzles the will,   80
And makes us rather bear those ills we have
Than fly to others that we know not of?
Thus conscience does make cowards of us all,   *– all afraid of the unknown – cowards for staying*

[handwritten margin notes: conscience ↓ resolution/thought ↑ action]

And thus the native hue of resolution
Is sicklied o'er with the pale cast of thought,   85
And enterprises of great pith and moment
With this regard their currents turn awry
And lose the name of action. — Soft you now.
The fair Ophelia. — Nymph, in thy orisons
Be all my sins rememb'red.†

[handwritten: power in the thinking not action]

67. **shuffled...coil:** disentangled ourselves from the tumult of human affairs. *Coil* carries not only the sense of "turmoil" but probably also suggests "something that entangles us," something "coiled about us" (like a rope). 68. **respect:** consideration. 69. **calamity of so long life:** so lasting. If it were not for bad dreams after death, Hamlet argues, no one would endure misfortune long. 70. **time:** the times. 72. **The pangs...love:** The pain of unrequited love. —**despised:** rejected, unvalued; accented on first syllable. [EDS.] 75. **his quietus make:** settle his account. *Quietus est* is an old formula for "his account has been settled." [A person could settle his account by killing himself. EDS.] 76. **a bare bodkin:** 1. hairpin; 2. small dagger, typically used by a woman. [EDS.]—**these fardels:** these burdens. 77. **grunt:** groan. 79. **undiscovered:** unexplored—therefore, mysterious.—**bourn:** boundary. 80. **No traveler returns:** Critics have worried over this, since, they remark, the Ghost had returned. But Hamlet is thinking of living human beings, not of ghosts; [moreover, the Ghost cannot return at will; dawn recalls him to purgatory. EDS.] —**puzzles:** confuses, so that it cannot act. 83. **conscience:** sense of morality. [EDS.] 84. **And thus:** Hamlet extends his observations to the whole subject of *irresolution* as caused by *fear of the consequences* of any act.—**native hue of resolution:** The natural complexion of resolution is ruddy. 85. **cast:** shade (of color).—**thought:** despondency. 86. **pith:** importance.—**moment:** importance. [EDS.] 87. **With this regard:** on this account. 88. **Soft you now:** Hush. [This suggests that Hamlet has been speaking aloud. EDS.] 89. **Nymph:** A courtly way of addressing a lady, not uncommon in the old language of compliment.

† In Zeffirelli's film, during the exchange between Hamlet and Ophelia, a conspicuous shadow cast upon a wall implies the spying presence of Polonius and the King, whereas in Branagh's *Hamlet*, they are secreted behind a wall of mirrored doors.

OPHELIA	Good my lord,	90
	How does your honor for this many a day?	
HAMLET	I humbly thank you; well, well, well.	
OPHELIA	My lord, I have remembrances of yours	
	That I have longed long to re-deliver.	
	I pray you, now receive them.	
HAMLET	No, not I.	95
	I never gave you aught.	
OPHELIA	My honored lord, you know right well you did,	
	And with them words of so sweet breath composed	
	As made the things more rich. Their perfume lost,	
	Take these again; for to the noble mind	100
	Rich gifts wax poor when givers prove unkind.	
	There, my lord.	
HAMLET	Ha, ha. Are you honest?	
OPHELIA	My lord? _chaste_	
HAMLET	Are you fair?	105
OPHELIA	What means your lordship?	
HAMLET	That if you be honest and fair, your honesty should	
	admit no discourse to your beauty.	
OPHELIA	Could beauty, my lord, have better commerce than	
	with honesty?	110
HAMLET	Ay, truly; for the power of beauty will sooner transform	
	honesty from what it is to a bawd than the force of	
	honesty can translate beauty into his likeness. This was	
	sometime a paradox, but now the time gives it proof. I did love	
	you once.	116
OPHELIA	Indeed, my lord, you made me believe so.	

---

91. **many a day:** She does not mean since she's last seen him, since he came to her closet only a day or so before; she means since they have communicated as lovers, about two months before. On the other hand, Shakespeare often treats time very malleably, counting on his listening audiences not to recall specific time markers. With this line and her mention of "givers" who "prove unkind" (101), Ophelia seems to consider herself the injured person, not the one who, as she told her father (2.1.108-9), had prevented Hamlet from meeting her. It may be this falsehood, if it is false, that makes Hamlet suspicious of her. [EDS.] 95-6. Hamlet denies having given her anything; we have to believe her, however, because we have heard his poem (2.2.116-19). [EDS.] 103. **honest:** chaste. [From 103-57 the lines are prose, befitting the coarse content. EDS.] 109. **commerce:** association. 113-14. **translate:** transform. 114. **his:** its. 115. **sometime:** once.—**now...proof:** Hamlet may be thinking of his mother's sexuality, which well might make him feel that there is no purity left in the world.

HAMLET   You should not have believed me; for virtue cannot
                so inoculate our old stock but we shall relish of it. I loved
                you not.   120

OPHELIA   I was the more deceived.

to him this is equated w/ sexual dishonesty

HAMLET *tied to*   Get thee to a nunnery. Why wouldst thou be a
his guilt w/   breeder of sinners? I am myself indifferent honest, but yet I
his mother   could accuse me of such things that it were better my mother
he is tainted   haft not borne me. I am very proud, revengeful, ambitious;
bc of her +   with more offences at my beck than I have thoughts to put
other way   them in, imagination to give them shape, or time to act them in.
around   What should such fellows as I do, crawling between earth and
                heaven? We are arrant knaves all; believe none of us. Go
                thy ways to a nunnery. Where's your father?†   134

OPHELIA   At home, my lord.‡   *her existence doesn't exist w/o him*
                                      ↳ difference btwn mother/father

HAMLET *moment*   Let the doors be shut upon him, that he may play the
he knows that   fool nowhere but in's own house. Farewell.
even she is now
truthe to manipulate
OPHELIA   O, help him, you sweet heavens.   138

HAMLET   If thou dost marry, I'll give thee this plague for thy
                dowry: be thou as chaste as ice, as pure as snow, thou shalt
                not escape calumny. Get thee to a nunnery. Go, farewell. Or
                if thou wilt needs marry, marry a fool; for wise men know
                well enough what monsters you make of them. To a nunnery,
                go; and quickly too. Farewell.   146

OPHELIA   O heavenly powers, restore him.

118-19. **virtue cannot so inoculate our old stock:** virtue cannot, by grafting on the basic essence, so change the original sin (inherited from Adam) that we shall not still have some flavor of it. The image is that of a crabtree in which a bud or a shoot of a better sort has been set as a graft. 121. **I was the more deceived:** As she had told her father, she had believed his vows of love. [EDS.] 122. **nunnery:** 1. convent 2. possibly, house of prostitution. [EDS.] 123. **indifferent honest:** tolerably virtuous. 125. **ambitious:** Whether or not Hamlet suspects that Ophelia is a decoy, or that there are listeners, he is prudent enough to encourage the notion that thwarted ambition is the cause of his madness, as Rosencrantz and Guildenstern, perhaps coached by the King, had guessed (2.2.258). Soon, however, Hamlet assigns another cause, women's wanton sexuality (152). 133. **We:** we men. 133-4. **Go thy ways:** Go along; literally, on your way. 134. **Where's your father?** A sudden non-sequitur and a difficult question for Ophelia. [EDS.] 145. **monsters:** Alluding to the favorite Elizabethan jest of the horns supposed to grow upon a man's head, if his wife is unfaithful.

---

†   Scott's passionate Ophelia kisses Hamlet, and he responds with even greater passion until, standing next to the cabinet where the spies are hiding, he asks her "Where's your father?"

‡   Ophelia may be docile as in Kozintsev, or she may not say the line at all as in Almereyda. She may say it bitterly or reluctantly.

"Where's your father?" (3.1.134). Almereyda's Hamlet (Ethan Hawke) discovers that Ophelia (Julia Stiles) has been wired for sound to permit the King and Polonius to overhear their conversation at a distance.

HAMLET

I have heard of your paintings too, well enough. God *reflection of*
hath given you one face, and you make yourselves another. *1.2*
You jig, you amble, and you lisp; you nickname God's *inside vs outside*
creatures and make your wantonness your ignorance. Go to,
it: women in — I'll no more on't. it hath made me mad. I say, we will have no
general moe marriages. Those that are married already —all but one
— shall live; the rest shall keep as they are. To a nunnery, go.

Exit.

OPHELIA

O, what a noble mind is here o'er-thrown.* *foreshadowing*
The courtier's, scholar's, soldier's, eye, tongue, sword,
Th' expectancy and rose of the fair state, 160
The glass of fashion and the mould of form,
Th' observed of all observers — quite, quite down.

---

148. **your paintings:** i.e., those applications of make-up by you ladies, [a typical use of *your* in a general rather than specific sense, as in 5.1.187, "*your water*" [EDS.]. 150. **jig…amble:** Two kinds of affected gait. 150-1: **you nickname…ignorance:** You give new and affected names to ordinary things and then pretend that this affectation of yours is due to ignorance, that you really do not know what these common objects are called. *Wantonness* often means "affectation" [as well as promiscuity. EDS.]. 156. **no moe marriages:** no more marriages, [a declaration that he will not marry her. EDS.]. 156. **all but one:** The audience can surmise that Hamlet means the King. 158–162. This passage suggests that Ophelia has not known Hamlet to be of a melancholy temperament. [Verse resumes and continues to the scene's end. EDS.] 159. **The courtier's…sword:** the courtier's eye, the scholar's tongue, the soldier's sword. 160. **Th' expectancy…state:** the hope and the adornment of our country, which is made fair by him. 161. **glass:** mirror.—**the mould of form:** model for others to follow. [EDS.] 162. **of:** by.

---

* While Scott's Ophelia tearfully speaks; the camera catches, through a window, Hamlet raging outdoors.

And I, of ladies most deject and wretched,
That sucked the honey of his music vows,
Now see that noble and most sovereign reason,   165
Like sweet bells jangled, out of tune and harsh;
That unmatched form and feature of blown youth
Blasted with ecstasy. O, woe is me   *madness*
T' have seen what I have seen, see what I see.

Enter King and Polonius.

KING   Love? his affections do not that way tend;   170
                Nor what he spake, though it lacked form a little,
                Was not like madness. There's something in his soul
                O'er which his melancholy sits on brood;
                And I do doubt the hatch and the disclose
                Will be some danger; which for to prevent,   175
                I have in quick determination
                Thus set it down: he shall with speed to England
                For the demand of our neglected tribute.
                Haply the seas, and countries different,
                With variable objects, shall expel   180
                This something-settled matter in his heart,
                Whereon his brains still beating puts him thus
                From fashion of himself. What think you on't?

POLONIUS   It shall do well. But yet do I believe
                The origin and commencement of his grief   185
                Sprung from neglected love. — How now, Ophelia?
                You need not tell us what Lord Hamlet said.
                We heard it all. — My lord, do as you please;

---

163. **deject:** cast down. 164. **music vows:** sweet-sounding promises. [EDS.] 165. **most sovereign:** Since the reason should govern all the faculties. 166. **jangled:** out of tune. [EDS.] 167. **blown:** full-blown, in full blossom. This is indicative of Hamlet's age. His youth has come to full flower; he has arrived at early manhood. 168. **ecstasy:** madness. 170. **affections:** feelings, inclinations. 172. **madness:** The King may refuse to believe that Hamlet's words suggest madness—though others interpret them so—because he wants to act against Hamlet. Or he may have heard the soliloquy, evidently said aloud (see 88). As in the source, madness might protect Hamlet from danger. [EDS.] 174. **doubt:** suspect. [EDS.] 175. **prevent:** forestall. 176. **I...determination:** Before putting Polonius's theory to the test, he had already decided to get Hamlet out of the country. [EDS.] 177. **to England:** Since the King has no soliloquy here, the audience cannot gather his purpose, which, if it includes murder, he might keep from Polonius. [EDS.] 180. **variable objects:** the variety of sights incidental to travel. 181. **something-settled matter:** somewhat incessant subject of thought. 182-3. **Whereon...himself:** the constant beating of his brains on which subject (whatever it is) makes him act unnaturally. 184. **It shall do well:** It will be certain to help. The King's prescription of foreign travel is, in fact, a standard one for illness, and Polonius sees nothing objectionable in it. [However, the plan contradicts the Queen's wish to keep Hamlet at Elsinore. See her comment in 3.4.200-1: "Alack, I had forgot. 'Tis so concluded on." This was not something she desired. EDS.] 186. **neglected:** that met with no response.

But if you hold it fit, after the play
Let his queen mother all alone entreat him   190
To show his grief. Let her be round with him;
And I'll be placed, so please you, in the ear
Of all their conference. If she find him not,
To England send him; or confine him where
Your wisdom best shall think.

KING   It shall be so.   195
              Madness in great ones must not unwatched go.

                                                Exeunt.

SCENE II. [*Elsinore. A hall in the Castle.*]

Enter Hamlet and three of the Players.

HAMLET   Speak the speech, I pray you, as I pronounced it to†
              you, trippingly on the tongue. But if you mouth it, as many
              of our players do, I had as live the town crier spoke my lines.
              Nor do not saw the air too much with your hand, thus, but
              use all gently; for in the very torrent, tempest, and (as I may   5
              say) whirlwind of your passion, you must acquire and beget
              a temperance that may give it smoothness. O, it offends me
              to the soul to hear a robustious periwig-pated fellow tear a
              passion to tatters, to very rags, to split the ears of the groundlings,
              who (for the most part) are capable of nothing but
              inexplicable dumb shows and noise. I would have such a fellow

---

191. **round:** outspoken, [blunt. EDS.]. 193. **find him not:** do not discover his secret trouble. 194.
confine... think: This cold-blooded agreement to Hamlet's incarceration may mark the beginning of
Ophelia's madness. [EDS.]
SCENE II.
1. Some people understand Hamlet's advice to the players to embody Shakespeare's own views on the
art of acting. Moderation and common sense are key. 2. **trippingly:** easily, i.e., without exaggerated
emphasis and therefore like the language of real life.—**mouth it:** To *mouth* a word is to hold it long in the
mouth before allowing it to pass the lips; it is not a natural way of speaking. 3. **live:** rather; pronounced
leave. [EDS.]. 3. **the town crier:** Since the town crier wishes to be heard distinctly at some distance,
he must mouth his words, and the result is a kind of loud singsong. 7. **temperance:** moderation. 8.
robustious: boisterous.—**periwig-pated:** [A *periwig* is a wig; a *pate* is the top of the skull. EDS.] Actors
wore wigs, but these were not the fashion in society. 9. **the groundlings:** spectators who stood in the
yard, which was the cheapest place in the theater; [paying a penny to stand in the yard. EDS.]. 13.
capable of: able to appreciate.—**inexplicable dumb shows:** Action without words; [pantomime. EDS.].
The Dumb Show was an important element in early plays, but was losing favor when Shakespeare wrote.
[The play-within has a dumb show to mime the play's action. See 3.2.146 ff. EDS.]

---

†   Scott's Hamlet, make-up on his face, is lecturing the actor playing Lucianus.

whipped for o'erdoing Termagant. It out-herods Herod. Pray
you avoid it.   16

PLAYER   I warrant your honor.

HAMLET   Be not too tame neither; but let your own discretion
be your tutor. Suit the action to the word, the word to the
action; with this special observance, that you o'erstep not the
modesty of nature: for anything so overdone is from the purpose
of playing, whose end, both at the first and now, was and is,
to hold, as 'twere, the mirror up to nature; to show virtue
her own feature, scorn her own image, and the very age and
body of the time his form and pressure. Now this overdone,
or come tardy off, though it make the unskilful laugh, cannot
but make the judicious grieve; the censure of the which one
must in your allowance o'erweigh a whole theatre of others.
O, there be players that I have seen play, and heard others
praise, and that highly (not to speak it profanely), that, neither
having the accent of Christians, nor the gait of Christian,
pagan, nor man, have so strutted and bellowed that I have
thought some of Nature's journeymen had made men, and not
made them well, they imitated humanity so abominably.

PLAYER   I hope we have reformed that indifferently with us, sir.   41

HAMLET   O, reform it altogether. And let those that play your
clowns speak no more than is set down for them. For there be
of them that will themselves laugh, to set on some quantity

---

15. **Termagant...Herod:** In the Middle Ages all Mohammedans were thought to be idolaters, and the
romances give them *Termagant* as their deity. *Mahound* is *Mohammed,* but the origin of *Termagant* is
unknown. Since the Saracens were regarded as a ferocious race, their gods were described as violent
in word and deed. The god or fiend Termagant seems to have been a character in certain old English
plays (now lost), and his part was undoubtedly acted with plenty of sound and fury. Herod was a
well-known character in the medieval Biblical dramas, and his part was that of a raging tyrant. 21.
modesty: moderation. 22. **at the first:** i.e., when the art of acting was first invented. 23. **to hold...
nature:** a reference to the widely-held view that drama reflects life and in doing so reveals the virtues
and vices of the time. [EDS.] 24. **feature:** form. 24-5. **the very age and body of the time:** the times
exactly as they are. 25. **his:** its.—**pressure:** [likeness. EDS.]; literally, impression, as in wax. 31. **come
tardy off:** inadequate. [EDS.]—**the unskilful:** the injudicious or undiscriminating among the audience.
32. **the censure of the which one:** the opinion of a single one of the judicious. 33. **in your allowance:**
in your estimation. [EDS.] —**o'erweigh...others:** Be more significant than the praise of the injudicious.
[EDS.] 35. **not to speak it profanely:** Hamlet apologizes for his apparent flippancy in comparing the
creation of roles by actors with the Creator's. 35-7. **neither...men:** Actors' depictions of various kinds
of men sometimes imitate nature so poorly that it is as if a beginner were at work. [EDS.] 36. **strutted
and bellowed:** These bad actors' unrealistic acting. 37. **journeymen:** common workmen, not artisans.
[EDS.] 39. **abominably:** Spelled *abhominably* in the Folios and Quartos. The word was thought to be
derived from *ab homine* and carried the sense of "in a way contrary to what is natural in man." 41.
indifferently: pretty well. 43. **clowns:** rustic fellows and buffoons, such as the gravedigger in 5.1.
—**speak no more...for them:** The Elizabethan clowns used to improvise freely, and sometimes even
to engage in conversation with the audience. 43-4. **there be of them:** there are some of them. 44.
—**quantity:** small quantity.

of barren spectators to laugh too, though in the mean time
some necessary question of the play be then to be considered.
That's villanous and shows a most pitiful ambition in the fool
that uses it. Go make you ready.   50

Exeunt Players.

Enter Polonius, Rosencrantz, and Guildenstern.

How now, my lord? Will the King hear this piece of work?

POLONIUS   And the Queen too, and that presently.

HAMLET   Bid the players make haste. (*Exit Polonius.*)
                Will you two help to hasten them?

BOTH   We will, my lord.   *Exeunt they two.*

HAMLET   What, ho, Horatio.

Enter Horatio.

HORATIO   Here, sweet lord, at your service.

HAMLET   Horatio, thou art e'en as just a man
                As e'er my conversation coped withal.   60

HORATIO   O, my dear lord.

HAMLET   Nay, do not think I flatter;
                For what advancement may I hope from thee,
                That no revenue hast but thy good spirits
                To feed and clothe thee? Why should the poor be flattered?
                No, let the candied tongue lick absurd pomp,   65
                And crook the pregnant hinges of the knee
                Where thrift may follow fawning. Dost thou hear?
                Since my dear soul was mistress of her choice
                And could of men distinguish, her election
                Hath sealed thee for herself. For thou hast been 70
                As one, in suff'ring all, that suffers nothing;
                A man that Fortune's buffets and rewards
                Hast ta'en with equal thanks; and blest are those

---

45. **barren:** stupid. 47. **villainous:** vulgar.—**fool:** actor who plays the clown's part (with an obvious pun
on the foolishness of the actor himself). 50. **uses:** practices. —**make you ready:** put on your costumes.
52. **presently:** at once. 53-4. [Hamlet politely gets rid of Polonius, Rosencrantz and Guildenstern
to talk privately with Horatio. EDS.] 58. **sweet:** dear. 59. **just:** "well-balanced." 60. **conversation:**
association.—**coped withal:** dealt with. The whole clause means "as ever I have associated with." 63.
revénue: Accented on the second syllable. 65. **candied:** sweetened for flattery. [EDS.] —**absurd pomp:**
personification: ridiculously pretentious person. [EDS.] 66. **pregnant hinges:** supple joints; always ready
to kneel, seeking favors. 67. **thrift:** prosperity. 68. **was...choice:** had the power of discriminating.
69-70. **her election...herself:** Because Hamlet admires Horatio's character, he has chosen him as his
special friend. 71. **in suff'ring...nothing:** Horatio is stoical. 72-3. **Fortune's...thanks:** Horatio remain
calm whatever Fortune brings him, bad or good.

Whose blood and judgment are so well commingled
That they are not a pipe for Fortune's finger   75
To sound what stop she please. Give me that man
That is not passion's slave, and I will wear him
In my heart's core, ay, in my heart of heart,
As I do thee. Something too much of this.
There is a play to-night before the King   80
One scene of it comes near the circumstance,
Which I have told thee, of my father's death.
I prithee, when thou seest that act afoot,
Even with the very comment of thy soul
Observe my uncle. If his occulted guilt   85
Do not itself unkennel in one speech,
It is a damned ghost that we have seen,
And my imaginations are as foul
As Vulcan's stithy. Give him heedful note;
For I mine eyes will rivet to his face,   90
And after we will both our judgments join
In censure of his seeming.

HORATIO   Well, my lord.
If he steal aught the whilst this play is playing,
And scape detecting, I will pay the theft.

*Sound a flourish. Enter Trumpets and Kettledrums. Danish march. Enter King, Queen,
Polonius, Ophelia, Rosencrantz, Guildenstern, and other Lords attendant, with the
Guard carrying torches.*

HAMLET   They are coming to the play. I must be idle.   95
                 Get you a place.

KING   How fares our cousin Hamlet?

---

74. **blood and judgment:** passion and intellectual power. [EDS.] 76. **To sound what stop she please:** to
play upon them [as if they were flutes. The stops are the means to make sounds. EDS.] Horatio possesses
both passion and judgment in a well-balanced combination. Thus he neither acts over-hastily, nor delays
when action is needed. 78. **in my heart of heart:** in the very heart of my heart. 79. **Something too
much of this:** Hamlet feels that his frank praise of Horatio has gone so far as to be embarrassing to them
both. 82. **have told thee:** Thus we learn that Hamlet has told Horatio the Ghost's story; [the play often
suggests that there is action between the lines. EDS.] 84. **with...soul:** with your full attention. [EDS.] 85.
occulted: craftily hidden. 86. **in one speech:** the "dozen or sixteen lines" which Hamlet had written for
the express purpose (2.2.566). 87. **a damnèd ghost:** a demon—not my father's spirit. See 2.2.626-31. 88.
my imaginations: i.e., my belief in my uncle's guilt. 89. **stithy:** forge [associated with hell. EDS.] Since
Vulcan is the god of smiths, his forge must be sooty above all others. 92. **In censure of his seeming:**
in passing judgment on his appearance and behavior. [Hamlet does not intend to do anything during
the play; afterwards he will consult with Horatio. EDS.] 93. **If he steal aught:** If he manages to conceal
anything. [EDS.] 94. **pay the theft:** answer for it. [EDS.] 95. **idle:** foolish in my words and actions. Hamlet
does not pretend to be insane when he is alone with Horatio, who is in his confidence. Here he expressly
tells his friend that it is time to act the madman again, since the others are coming. 97. **cousin:** nephew.
[i. e., kinsman; The King does not call Hamlet *son* here (as he had in 1.2.64) EDS.]

HAMLET	Excellent, i' faith; of the chameleon's dish. I eat the air, promise-crammed. You can not feed capons so. 100
KING	I have nothing with this answer, Hamlet. These words are not mine.
HAMLET	No, nor mine now. [*To Polonius*] My lord, you played once i' th' university, you say?
POLONIUS	That did I, my lord, and was accounted a good actor. 106
HAMLET	What did you enact?
POLONIUS	I did enact Julius Caesar; I was killed i' th' Capitol; Brutus killed me.
HAMLET	It was a brute part of him to kill so capital a calf there. Be the players ready?
ROSENCRANTZ	Ay, my lord. They stay upon your patience.
QUEEN	Come hither, my dear Hamlet, sit by me.
HAMLET	No, good mother. Here's metal more attractive.
POLONIUS	[*to the King*] O, ho. do you mark that?
HAMLET	Lady, shall I lie in your lap? [*Sits down at Ophelia's feet.*]
OPHELIA	No, my lord. 120
HAMLET	I mean, my head upon your lap?
OPHELIA	Ay, my lord.
HAMLET	Do you think I meant country matters?
OPHELIA	I think nothing, my lord.

99-100 **the chameleon's dish...capons so:** When I ought to be on the throne myself, can I be satisfied with such promises as you have made me? The chameleon was supposed to live on air. but capons need real food. [Though his first soliloquy did not express any regret about his not having been elected king, Hamlet may have developed the feeling that he should have been elected (see 2.2.258; 3.1.125, 3.4.99-101, 5.2.65). Certainly, by hinting at his ambition, Hamlet is disturbing the King's peace of mind. EDS.] 101-2. **I have...mine:** I have nothing to do with this answer; your reply does not fit my question. Hamlet has twisted the sense of *How fares* (How are you?), as if the King had asked about his diet. 103. **No, nor mine now:** "A man's words, says the proverb, are his own no longer than he keep them unspoken." 104. **i' th' university:** [Polonius has had a university education. EDS.] All the great European universities produced plays on festal occasions. 108. **Capitol:** The assassination of Caesar took place in the Capitol.—**Brutus killed me:** Polonius would not have condescendingly added this bit of superfluous information if he had not been treating Hamlet as a lunatic. [He mistakes lunacy for stupidity. EDS.] 110. **a brute part:** [brutal action. EDS.] A stock pun. Hamlet's use of so coarse and stale a witticism accords with his acting the madman.—**part:** "deed."—**calf:** fool. [EDS.] 114. **stay... patience:** await your leisure. 118. **in your lap:** a crude sexual proposition, which Ophelia rejects. [EDS.] 123. **country matters:** Hamlet asks, "When you said 'no,' did you think I meant something obscene?" He might emphasize the first syllable to create a sexual pun. [EDS.]

| HAMLET | That's a fair thought to lie between maids' legs. | 126 |

| OPHELIA | What is, my lord? |

| HAMLET | Nothing. |

| OPHELIA | You are merry, my lord. |

| HAMLET | Who, I? | 130 |

| OPHELIA | Ay, my lord. |

HAMLET   O God, your only jig-maker. What should a man
do but be merry? For look you how cheerfully my mother looks,
and my father died within 's two hours.   135

OPHELIA   Nay, 'tis twice two months, my lord.

HAMLET   So long? Nay then, let the devil wear black, for I'll
have a suit of sables. O heavens. die two months ago, and not
forgotten yet? Then there's hope a great man's memory may
outlive his life half a year. But, by'r Lady, he must build
churches then; or else shall he suffer not thinking on, with
the hobby-horse, whose epitaph is "For O, for O, the
hobby-horse is forgot."   145

Hautboys play. The dumb show enters.[†]

Enter a King and a Queen very lovingly; the Queen embracing him, and he her. She kneels, and makes show of protestation unto him. He takes her up, and declines his head upon her neck. He lays him down upon a bank of flowers. She, seeing him asleep, leaves him. Anon comes in a fellow, takes off his crown, kisses it, pours poison in the sleeper's ears, and leaves him. The Queen returns, finds the King dead, and makes passionate action. The Poisoner with some three or four Mutes, come in again, seem to condole with her. The dead body is carried away. The Poisoner wooes the Queen with gifts; she seems harsh and unwilling awhile, but in the end accepts his love.

Exeunt.

---

132. **your only jig-maker:** the best of all writers of comic songs. 135. **'s two hours:** this two hours. 136. **twice two months:** About four months have passed since the King's death. 138. **I'll have a suit of sables:** *Sable* often means "black"; but Hamlet says *sables,* splendid and dignified attire (not mourning clothes). 142. **by 'r Lady:** by our Lady (the Virgin Mary). **build...not thinking on:** build churches to honor his memory or submit to being forgotten. 144. **hobby-horse:** The hobby-horse was a very ancient character in May games and Morris dances. In Shakespeare's time, he was frequently omitted, partly because the Puritans regarded him as a remnant of heathen superstition. [He was famous for wanton behavior disguised as frivolity. EDS.] *After* 145. **Stage Direction: dumb show:** A pantomime showing the action that follows. [EDS.]

---

†   Richardson's King is as confused by the over-the-top performance of the dumb show as the first-time viewer is, solving the apparent problem of how the King manages not to react to the dramatization of his crimes. Many productions solve the problem by eliminating the dumb show or the-play-within-the play (165-238; 266-71) or by having the King paying no attention at all to the dumb show.

OPHELIA	What means this, my lord?
HAMLET	Marry, this is miching malhecho; it means mischief.
OPHELIA	Belike this show imports the argument of the play. *guesses* 150 *correctly?*

Enter Prologue.

show of intelligence

HAMLET	We shall know by this fellow. The players cannot keep counsel; they'll tell all.
OPHELIA	Will he tell us what this show meant?
HAMLET	Ay, or any show that you'll show him. Be not you 155 ashamed to show, he'll not shame to tell you what it means.
OPHELIA	You are naught, you are naught. I'll mark the play. *understands him*
PROLOGUE	For us, and for our tragedy, Here stooping to your clemency, 160 We beg your hearing patiently.
HAMLET	Is this a prologue, or the posy of a ring?
OPHELIA	'Tis brief, my lord.
HAMLET	As woman's love.

Enter [two Players as] King and Queen.

PLAYER KING	Full thirty times hath Phoebus' cart gone round‡ 165 Neptune's salt wash and Tellus' orbed ground, And thirty dozen moons with borrowed sheen About the world have times twelve thirties been, Since love our hearts, and Hymen did our hands, Unite comutual in most sacred bands. 170

---

148. **What means this?** Since her question suggests the pantomime is not clear to her, the King might also miss its significance. Or he understands and shows amazing self-control. 149. **miching malhecho:** sneaking crime. *Malhecho* is Spanish for "misdeed." In one interpretation, Hamlet did not know the actors would give away the plot in a dumb show and accuses them of foiling his plan. In another, the mischief is the crime of murder that the King had committed. Since the pantomime is silent, in performance the King can be otherwise occupied. 150. **Belike...play:** Ophelia guesses that the dumb show indicates the plot of the play. 152. **cannot keep counsel:** keep a secret. 154-8. Hamlet makes sexually explicit puns, and Ophelia is savvy enough to understand them. 158. **naught:** naughty. Ophelia reproves Hamlet for his loose talk. 162. **the posy of a ring:** the short rhyming verse on a ring. *Posy* is a contraction of *poesy* or poetry. [*Ring* sometimes has a sexual meaning, and Hamlet's other off color remarks may imply such a meaning here. EDS.] 165. **Phoebus' cart:** the chariot of the sun. 166. **Neptune's salt wash:** the surging waves of the sea.—**Tellus' orbed ground:** this globe; the earth. —**borrowed:** i.e., from the sun.

---

‡   Though primed for laugher, Zeffirelli's King appears decidedly guilty while watching the play; then stunned, as he abruptly stands and, before calling for lights, points with recognition to the player poisoning the player King. BBC's King remains cool throughout and shames Hamlet for his outrageous behavior.

PLAYER QUEEN   So many journeys may the sun and moon
Make us again count o'er ere love be done.
But woe is me. you are so sick of late,
So far from cheer and from your former state,
That I distrust you. Yet, though I distrust,   175
Discomfort you, my lord, it nothing must;
For women's fear and love holds quantity,
In neither aught, or in extremity.
Now what my love is, proof hath made you know;
And as my love is sized, my fear is so.   180
Where love is great, the littlest doubts are fear;
Where little fears grow great, great love grows there.

PLAYER KING   Faith, I must leave thee, love, and shortly too;
My operant powers their functions leave to do.
And thou shalt live in this fair world behind,   185
Honored, beloved, and haply one as kind
For husband shalt thou —

PLAYER QUEEN   O, confound the rest.
Such love must needs be treason in my breast.
In second husband let me be accurst.
None wed the second but who kill's the first.   190

HAMLET   [*aside*] Wormwood, wormwood.

PLAYER QUEEN   The instances that second marriage move
Are base respects of thrift, but none of love.
A second time I kill my husband dead
When second husband kisses me in bed.   195

PLAYER KING   I do believe you think what now you speak;
But what we do determine oft we break.
Purpose is but the slave to memory,
Of violent birth, but poor validity;

---

175. **I distrust you:** I am anxious about you. After this line the Second Quarto inserts "For women feare too much, euen as they loue," and begins 176 with "And." 177. **holds quantity:** maintain proportion. 179. **proof:** experience. 184. **My operant powers:** my vital forces—**leave to do:** cease to act. 187. **O, confound the rest:** O, may God destroy that which you were about to say; may it never come to pass! 189. **In...accurst:** If I take a second husband, may he prove a curse to me. 190. **None...first:** Let no woman wed a second husband unless she has murdered her first husband. [In Saxo's version, the Queen and the Court know that her second husband murdered her first; his justfication being the old King's supposed plan to murder his Queen. EDS.] 191 **Wormwood:** a bitter-tasting medicinal plant, its juice sometimes used to poison worms. Because the Player's words allude to the Old King's poisoning, they evoke Hamlet's words. [EDS.] 192. **instances:** causes.—**move:** prompt. 193. **respects of thrift:** considerations of worldly welfare. 194. **A second...dead:** I kill my dead husband a second time, as it were, by this act of unfaithfulness. 198. **Purpose...memory:** We cannot hold fast to our purposes when we have forgotten what prompted them. 199. **validity:** strength.

Which now, like fruit unripe, sticks on the tree,   200
But fall unshaken when they mellow be.
Most necessary 'tis that we forget
To pay ourselves what to ourselves is debt.
What to ourselves in passion we propose,
The passion ending, doth the purpose lose.   205
The violence of either grief or joy
Their own enactures with themselves destroy.
Where joy most revels, grief doth most lament;
Grief joys, joy grieves, on slender accident.
This world is not for aye, nor 'tis not strange   210
That even our loves should with our fortunes change;
For 'tis a question left us yet to prove,
Whether love lead fortune, or else fortune love.
The great man down, you mark his favorite flies,
The poor advanced makes friends of enemies;   215
And hitherto doth love on fortune tend,
For who not needs shall never lack a friend,
And who in want a hollow friend doth try,
Directly seasons him his enemy.
But, orderly to end where I begun,   220
Our wills and fates do so contrary run
That our devices still are overthrown;
Our thoughts are ours, their ends none of our own.
So think thou wilt no second husband wed;
But die thy thoughts when thy first lord is dead.   225

PLAYER QUEEN   Nor earth to me give food, nor heaven light,
Sport and repose lock from me day and night,
To desperation turn my trust and hope,
An anchor's cheer in prison be my scope,
Each opposite that blanks the face of joy   230
Meet what I would have well, and it destroy,

is Hamlets action but in words? [handwritten marginal note]

200-1. **like fruit...be:** A purpose holds until the moment for action, as fruit hangs on the tree so long as it is unripe; but one's purposes fail of their own accord when the moment for action arrives. 203-5. **To pay ourselves...lose:** A purpose is an obligation laid upon us by ourselves; and we readily excuse ourselves for neglecting it, for one is an indulgent creditor to oneself. 206-7. **The violence...destroy:** When either grief or joy is violent, it exhausts itself, and thus resolutions formed under its impulse come to naught. 207. **Their own enactures:** their purposed acts. 208. **Where...lament:** excessively emotional people feel extremes of both joy and sorrow. [EDS.] 209. **on slender accident:** as a result of any trifling occurrence. 216. **hitherto:** so far, in human history. 218-19. **who in want...enemy:** An insincere friend may prove himself an enemy when tested. [EDS.] 221. **contráry:** accented on the second syllable. 222. **devices:** purposes.—**still:** constantly. 228–9. Omitted in the Folio. 229. **An anchor's cheer:** an anchorite's (religious hermit's) diet.—**my scope:** the limit of my enjoyment of life. 230. **blanks the face of joy:** either "turns it pale" (the proper hue of joy being rosy-red) or "turns it to a blank," "deprives it of all expression."

	Both here and hence pursue me lasting strife,	
	If, once a widow, ever I be wife.	
HAMLET	If she should break it now.	
PLAYER KING	'Tis deeply sworn. Sweet, leave me here awhile.	235
	My spirits grow dull, and fain I would beguile	
	The tedious day with sleep.	
PLAYER QUEEN	Sleep rock thy brain,	

[He] sleeps.

And never come mischance between us twain.

Exit.

HAMLET	Madam, how like you this play?	
QUEEN	The lady doth protest too much, methinks.	240
HAMLET	O, but she'll keep her word.	
KING	Have you heard the argument? Is there no offence in't?	
HAMLET	No, no. They do but jest, poison in jest; no offence i' th' world.	245
KING	What do you call the play?	
HAMLET	"The Mousetrap." Marry, how? Tropically. This play is the image of a murther done in Vienna. Gonzago is the duke's name; his wife, Baptista. You shall see anon. 'Tis a knavish piece of work; but what o' that? Your Majesty, and we that have free souls, it touches us not. Let the galled jade winch; our withers are unwrung.	

Enter Lucianus.

	This is one Lucianus, nephew to the King	
OPHELIA	You are as good as a chorus, my lord.	255

---

232. **here and hence:** in this world and the next. 236. **My spirits grow dull:** I am tired. [EDS.] 240. **The lady doth protest too much:** The player queen insists too vehemently (and thus perhaps suspiciously). [EDS.] 242. **the argument:** an outline of the plot. When a play was presented at court, it was customary to submit such an outline in order to avoid incidents that might be offensive to the State or Church. 242. **no offence:** nothing offensive. 244. Hamlet's reply, with the reference to poison, is meant to give another turn to the screw. Hamlet picks up the King's words and twists the sense: "There's no crime in the play—nothing but playful poisoning."—**jest:** pretend. [EDS.] 247. **"The Mousetrap":** the trap in which he'll "catch the conscience of the King." [Or since the King has called Gertrude his mouse (3.4.183) perhaps it will catch her also. EDS.]—**Tropically:** metaphorically. 248. **the image:** the exact representation. 252. **free:** innocent. 252-3. **galled jade winch:** To *gall* is to "rub off the skin so as to make a sore spot"; *jade* is a common term for an old, mean horse. [In other words, let the one who's rubbed sore be the one to wince. EDS.] 253. **withers:** the ridge between a horse's shoulders.—**unwrung:** not chafed, and therefore not sensitive. Our consciences are clear. 255. **a chorus:** a character who explains to the audience.

HAMLET	I could interpret between you and your love, if I could see the puppets dallying.
OPHELIA	You are keen, my lord, you are keen.
HAMLET	It would cost you a groaning to take off my edge.

260

OPHELIA	Still better, and worse.
HAMLET	So you must take your husbands. —Begin, murtherer. Pox, leave thy damnable faces, and begin. Come, the croaking raven doth bellow for revenge.

265

LUCIANUS	Thoughts black, hands apt, drugs fit, and time agreeing; Confederate season, else no creature seeing; Thou mixture rank, of midnight weeds collected, With Hecate's ban thrice blasted, thrice infected, Thy natural magic and dire property On wholesome life usurp immediately.

270

Pours the poison in his ears.

HAMLET	He poisons him i' th' garden for's estate. His name's Gonzago. The story is extant, and written in very choice Italian. You shall see anon how the murtherer gets the love of Gonzago's wife.

275

OPHELIA	The King rises.
HAMLET	What, frighted with false fire?

256-7. **I could...dallying:** If I could look on at a scene of dalliance between your lover and you, I could tell what it meant. By the *puppets* Hamlet means Ophelia and her imagined lover. Puppet shows regularly had an interpreter, who sometimes sat on the stage. [EDS.] 258. **keen:** Ophelia responds to the sting of his remark. [EDS.] 260. **It...edge:** With the word *edge* playing on the word *keen*, Hamlet tells her that it would cost her dearly, perhaps in childbirth, to satisfy his desire. [EDS.] 261. **better, and worse:** keener as to wit, but more offensive as to meaning. [Ophelia notices Hamlet's crudeness and responds wittily. EDS.] 262. **So:** i.e., for better, for worse.—**you:** you women.—**must take:** An allusion to the Anglican marriage service (1559), in which the bride and groom promise to "take" each other "for better" or "for worse." Also, "must take" may be a pun on "mis-take": wives who are unfaithful *mistake* their lovers for their husbands. (See *Winter's Tale* 2.1.81). [EDS.] 263. **Pox:** Plague on it! 264-5. **the croaking...revenge:** Hamlet quotes from an old revenge play, *The True Tragedy of Richard III*, 1594: "The screeking Rauen sits croking for reuenge." [The raven is traditionally a bird of ill-omen. EDS.] 267. **Confederate...seeing:** the time being in league with me (since this is a favorable moment), and nobody except my confederate, the time, seeing what I am about. 268. **midnight weeds:** Poisonous and magic herbs were thought to derive additional power from being collected at some special time, as, for example, at midnight. 269. **With Hecate's ban:** by the curse (the evil spell) of Hecate, the goddess of witchcraft and black magic. 272-5. **He poisons...wife:** Does Hamlet say this aloud or is he whispering to Ophelia? [EDS.] 276. **rises:** The King's reaction must be determined in performance. He may show his guilt or not. The next scene shows that the play has stung him into remorse. 277. **false fire:** the harmless discharge of a gun loaded with powder only (without a ball). [It's not clear why Hamlet should say this if he thinks that the play has reached its mark: the king's conscience. This difficult line is not in the Second Quarto but is found in both the Folio and First Quarto. One commentator suggests that perhaps the lines that Hamlet had inserted in the play (2.2.566) were yet to come and were even more stinging than those already performed. EDS.]

Queen	How fares my lord?
Polonius	Give o'er the play.
King	Give me some light.† Away.	280
All	Lights, lights, lights.

Exeunt all but Hamlet and Horatio.

Hamlet   Why, let the strucken deer go weep,
                  The hart ungalled play;
                  For some must watch, while some must sleep:
                  Thus runs the world away.   285
        Would not this, sir, and a forest of feathers — if the rest of my
        fortunes turn Turk with me — with two Provincial roses on
        my razed shoes, get me a fellowship in a cry of players, sir?

Horatio   Half a share.   290

Hamlet   A whole one I.
                  For thou dost know, O Damon dear,
                  This realm dismantled was
                  Of Jove himself; and now reigns here
                  A very, very — pajock.   295

Horatio   You might have rhymed.

Hamlet   O good Horatio, I'll take the ghost's word for a
        thousand pound. Didst perceive?

Horatio   Very well, my lord.

Hamlet   Upon the talk of the poisoning?   300

Horatio   I did very well note him.

Hamlet   Aha. Come, some music. Come, the recorders.

---

280. **some light:** The King calls for the torchbearers to conduct him to his chamber. 282. **strucken:** wounded. [EDS.] 283. **ungalled:** uninjured. [EDS.] 286. **this:** this way in which I've spoken these verses; [or, the way I have handled this theatrical entertainment. EDS.]. —**feathers:** actors wore feathers in their hats. 287. **fortunes turn Turk:** the image means "if my fortunes turn against me"; Turks, who are Muslims, are considered by Christians to be heathens. [EDS.]—**Provincial roses:** huge rosettes. 288. **razed:** ornamented by crosscuts in a pattern.—**a cry:** a pack, used ordinarily of hounds, but here jokingly of actors. 290. **Half a share:** In Shakespeare's time each regular member of a company of players had his proportion of the receipts instead of a salary. Some had a full share, less important members half a share. 295. **pajock:** peacock. The peacock had an evil reputation for cruelty and lust in the natural history of Shakespeare's day; [and was also symbolic of Pride. EDS.]. 296. **rhymed:** i.e., by saying *ass* instead of *pajock.* 302. **recorders:** wooden flute-like instruments.

---

†   Olivier's Hamlet triumphantly wields a torch as a weapon, thrusting it into the King's face; the BBC's King is the one calmly holding the torch as he peers into Hamlet's face.

For if the King like not the comedy,
Why then, belike he likes it not, perdy.   305
Come, some music.

Enter Rosencrantz and Guildenstern.

GUILDENSTERN	Good my lord, vouchsafe me a word with you.
HAMLET	Sir, a whole history.
GUILDENSTERN	The King, sir —

310

HAMLET	Ay, sir, what of him?
GUILDENSTERN	Is in his retirement, marvelous distempered.
HAMLET	With drink, sir?
GUILDENSTERN	No, my lord; rather with choler.

315

HAMLET   Your wisdom should show itself more richer to signify
this to the doctor; for for me to put him to his purgation
would perhaps plunge him into far more choler.   319

GUILDENSTERN   Good my lord, put your discourse into some frame,
and start not so wildly from my affair.

HAMLET   I am tame, sir; pronounce.

GUILDENSTERN   The Queen, your mother, in most great affliction of
spirit hath sent me to you.

HAMLET   You are welcome.   325

GUILDENSTERN   Nay, good my lord, this courtesy is not of the right
breed. If it shall please you to make me a wholesome answer,
I will do your mother's commandment; if not, your pardon
and my return shall be the end of my business.   330

HAMLET   Sir, I cannot.

GUILDENSTERN   What, my lord?

HAMLET   Make you a wholesome answer; my wit's diseased.
But, sir, such answer as I can make, you shall command; or   335

---

305. **belike:** probably.—**perdy:** An old-fashioned oath (*par dieu*) [by God. EDS.], used colloquially for "assuredly." *Perdy* and *comedy* made a good rhyme in Elizabethan pronunciation. 312. **distempered:** out of sorts. 314. **drink:** [Hamlet tauntingly guesses the king is drunk. EDS.] Hamlet later calls him "the bloat King" (3.4.182), again alluding to drunkenness. 315. **choler:** bile; [anger. EDS.]. In the speech that follows, Hamlet puns on the word, pretending to take Guildenstern to mean indigestion (which is caused by an excess of stomach acid or bile, a synonym for choler). 316. **should:** would surely. —**for… purgation:** One continuous pun: *Purgation* means (1) [using laxatives to ease stomach problems. EDS.] and (2) purification of the soul by confession and penance. 320. **frame:** coherent form. Hamlet's speech sounds to Guildenstern like madness. 327. **wholesome:** rational. 334-7. **But, sir…say:** Hamlet pretends to make a strong effort to fix his wandering wits upon the subject.

rather, as you say, my mother. Therefore no more, but to the
matter. My mother, you say —

ROSENCRANTZ   Then thus she says: your behavior hath struck her
into amazement and admiration.

HAMLET   O wonderful son, that can so stonish a mother. But is
there no sequel at the heels of this mother's admiration? Impart.

ROSENCRANTZ   She desires to speak with you in her closet ere you go to bed. 344

HAMLET   We shall obey, were she ten times our mother. Have
you any further trade with us?

ROSENCRANTZ   My lord, you once did love me.

HAMLET   And do still, by these pickers and stealers.   349

ROSENCRANTZ   Good my lord, what is your cause of distemper? You
do surely bar the door upon your own liberty, if you deny your
griefs to your friend.

HAMLET   Sir, I lack advancement.   354

ROSENCRANTZ   How can that be, when you have the voice of the King
himself for your succession in Denmark?

HAMLET   Ay, sir, but "while the grass grows" — the proverb is
something musty.   359

Enter the Players with recorders.

O, the recorders! Let me see one. To withdraw with you —
why do you go about to recover the wind of me, as if you
would drive me into a toil?

GUILDENSTERN   O my lord, if my duty be too bold, my love is too unmannerly.

---

336. **to the matter:** Let us return to the subject 339. **amazement and admiration:** confusion and
wonder. 344. **closet:** private sitting room (see 2.1.77). 346. **trade:** business.—**us:** Hamlet's intentional
use of the royal *we* is perhaps intended to remind Rosencrantz of the idea that his madness sprang
from thwarted ambition, and Rosencrantz accordingly makes one more attempt to induce Hamlet to
reveal the cause of his insanity. 349. **by these pickers and stealers:** by these ten fingers; by this hand.
The phrase comes from the catechism of the Church of England, where one is told to keep one's hands
from "picking [pick-pocketing, EDS.] and stealing." 350. **distemper:** disorder of mind. 351. **liberty:**
Rosencrantz hints that Hamlet may be put under restraint (as a lunatic) if he stubbornly refuses to tell
what ails him. 354, **I lack advancement:** Hamlet recurs to the cause Rosencrantz and Guildenstern
have discussed with him (2. 2. 249 ff.). 355. **the voice of the King:** The King proclaimed Hamlet his
successor in 1.2.109. 358. **while the grass grows:** The saying is, "While the grass is growing, the horse
starves." Hamlet implies that to wait for "advancement" that is so far off is very unsatisfying. 359.
something: somewhat. —**musty:** out of fashion. [EDS.] 360. **To withdraw:** to step aside so as to be
out of the hearing of the others. 361. **go about:** try.—**to recover...of me:** As in hunting, getting to the
windward of the prey so as to surprise it. [EDS.] 362. **into a toil:** into a trap. [EDS.] 363. **if my duty...
unmannerly:** If, in my devotion to your interests, I am too bold in questioning you, it is my love that
causes this breach of good manners.

HAMLET	I do not well understand that. Will you play upon this pipe?	366
GUILDENSTERN	My lord, I cannot.	
HAMLET	I pray you.	
GUILDENSTERN	Believe me, I cannot.	
HAMLET	I do beseech you.	370
GUILDENSTERN	I know no touch of it, my lord.	
HAMLET	It is as easy as lying. Govern these ventages with your fingers and thumbs, give it breath with your mouth, and it will discourse most eloquent music. Look you, these are the stops.	376
GUILDENSTERN	But these cannot I command to any utt'rance of harmony. I have not the skill.	
HAMLET	Why, look you now, how unworthy a thing you make of me. You would play upon me; you would seem to know my stops; you would pluck out the heart of my mystery; you would sound me from my lowest note to the top of my compass; and there is much music, excellent voice, in this little organ, yet cannot you make it speak. 'Sblood, do you think I am easier to be played on than a pipe? Call me what instrument you will, though you can fret me, you cannot play upon me.	

Enter Polonius.

	God bless you, sir.	390
POLONIUS	My lord, the Queen would speak with you, and presently.	
HAMLET	Do you see yonder cloud that's almost in shape of a camel?	
POLONIUS	By th' mass, and 'tis like a camel indeed.	395
HAMLET	Methinks it is like a weasel.	
POLONIUS	It is backed like a weasel.	
HAMLET	Or like a whale.	
POLONIUS	Very like a whale.	399

372. **as easy as lying:** A proverbial phrase [meaning that Guildenstern should be able to play the pipe as easily as he has lied. EDS.]. —**ventages:** wind-holes. 386. **organ:** any musical instrument. 388. **fret:** small bars of wire or wood on a stringed instrument to guide the fingering. Hamlet puns on the sense of "worry," "agitate." 391. **presently:** without delay. 393–9. **Do you see...whale:** Polonius humors the supposed madman.

HAMLET	Then will I come to my mother by-and-by. — They fool me to the top of my bent. — I will come by-and-by.
POLONIUS	I will say so. *I can't take this anymore* Exit.
HAMLET	"By-and-by" is easily said. — Leave me, friends. 405

[*Exeunt all but Hamlet.*]

'Tis now the very witching time of night,
When churchyards yawn, and hell itself breathes out
Contagion to this world. Now could I drink hot blood
And do such bitter business as the day
Would quake to look on. Soft. now to my mother.   410
O heart, lose not thy nature; let not ever
The soul of Nero enter this firm bosom.
Let me be cruel, not unnatural;
I will speak daggers to her, but use none.
My tongue and soul in this be hypocrites —   415
How in my words somever she be shent,
To give them seals never, my soul, consent.   *Exit.*

SCENE III. [*A room in the Castle.*]

Enter King, Rosencrantz, and Guildenstern.

KING	I like him not, nor stands it safe with us† To let his madness range. Therefore prepare you; I your commission will forthwith dispatch,

---

400. **by-and-by:** immediately. 401. **bent:** An idiom from archery; [the bow has its bent when it is drawn as far as it can be. EDS.]. 408. **Contagion:** Two ideas combine in this poetic figure. In the night, evil spirits and malign influences were supposed to have more power than by day; and at the same time the night air was regarded as charged with actual infection.—**Now could...blood:** Hamlet imagines himself here as capable of any atrocity in the way of revenge. 410. **Soft:** wait. [EDS.] 411. **Nature:** natural feelings of a son for his mother. [EDS.] 412. **Nero:** Roman Emperor who murdered his mother [Agrippina. EDS.]. 415. **tongue and soul...be hypocrites:** His soul is to pretend a savage purpose which it does not feel, and his words are to express it. 416. **How...somever:** howsoever much.—**shent:** violently criticized. 417. **To give them seals:** To confirm or fulfill them by action.

SCENE III.

1. **I like him not:** I do not like his behavior.—**with us:** The royal *we*—"with me as King." 2. **range:** wander. [EDS.] 3. **your commission:** Rosencrantz and Guildenstern are to convey a letter to the King of England. —**will forthwith dispatch:** cause to be drawn up right away. [Since the King says that he will have a letter prepared, it seems that it has not yet been written and thus that its content might now be influenced by the events at "The Mousetrap" or that he may have planned murder all along. We learn later that the commission orders England to put Hamlet to death (4.3.60–7). How much Rosencrantz

---

†   Without the King's knowledge, Almereyda's Hamlet takes the place of the King's chauffeur; Rosencrantz and Guildenstern talk to the King via car phone and thus confirm Hamlet's suspicions of them.

	And he to England shall along with you.
	The terms of our estate may not endure	5
	Hazard so near us as doth hourly grow
	Out of his lunacies.

GUILDENSTERN   We will ourselves provide.
                Most holy and religious fear it is
                To keep those many many bodies safe
                That live and feed upon your Majesty.   10

ROSENCRANTZ   The single and peculiar life is bound
                With all the strength and armor of the mind
                To keep itself from noyance; but much more
                That spirit upon whose weal depends and rests
                The lives of many. The cesse of majesty   15
                Dies not alone, but like a gulf doth draw
                What's near it with it. It is a massy wheel,
                Fixed on the summit of the highest mount,
                To whose huge spokes ten thousand lesser things
                Are mortised and adjoined; which when it falls,   20
                Each small annexment, petty consequence,
                Attends the boist'rous ruin. Never alone
                Did the king sigh, but with a general groan.

KING   Arm you, I pray you, to this speedy voyage;
                For we will fetters put upon this fear,   25
                Which now goes too free-footed.

BOTH   We will haste us.

                                              Exeunt Gentlemen.

                        Enter Polonius.

POLONIUS   My lord, he's going to his mother's closet.
                Behind the arras I'll convey myself
                To hear the process. I'll warrant she'll tax him home;
                And, as you said, and wisely was it said,   30

---

and Guildenstern know is never clear; Hamlet, however, appears to blame them (5.2.57), and earlier he had suspected foul play (3.4.202-5; 4.3.50). Shakespeare doesn't bother to resolve the problem of how, if the commission had not yet been drawn up, Hamlet knows, when he speaks to his mother in the next scene, that "There's letters sealed" (3.4.202). This sort of inconsistency apparently did not worry Shakespeare; it's hardly something audiences notice. EDS.] 5. **The terms of our estate:** "my kingly office." 11. **peculiar:** private. [Rosencrantz embroiders on the theme introduced by Guildenstern in the previous lines. EDS.] 13. **noyance:** harm. 15. **cesse:** cessation. 16. **a gulf:** a whirlpool. 17-23. **a massy wheel...groan:** The comparison to the wheel of Fortune that brings down everything attached to it, when it falls, is hardly one that will please the King: he does not respond at all to Rosencrantz's elaborate and failed effort at flattery. [EDS.] 22. **ruin:** downfall. 24. **Arm you:** prepare yourselves. 28. **convey myself:** slip quietly, without being seen. 29. **the process:** their conversation.—**tax him home:** take him to task soundly.

'Tis meet that some more audience than a mother,
Since nature makes them partial, should o'er-hear
The speech, of vantage. Fare you well, my liege.
I'll call upon you ere you go to bed
And tell you what I know.

KING   Thanks, dear my lord.   35

                                        Exit [Polonius].

O, my offence is rank, it smells to heaven;
It hath the primal eldest curse upon't,
A brother's murther. Pray can I not,
Though inclination be as sharp as will.
My stronger guilt defeats my strong intent,   40
And, like a man to double business bound,
I stand in pause where I shall first begin,
And both neglect. What if this cursèd hand
Were thicker than itself with brother's blood,
Is there not rain enough in the sweet heavens   45
To wash it white as snow? Whereto serves mercy
But to confront the visage of offence?
And what's in prayer but this twofold force,
To be forestalled ere we come to fall,
Or pardoned being down? Then I'll look up;   50
My fault is past. But, O, what form of prayer
Can serve my turn? "Forgive me my foul murther"?
That cannot be; since I am still possessed
Of those effects for which I did the murther —
My crown, mine own ambition, and my queen.   55
May one be pardoned and retain th' offence?
In the corrupted currents of this world
Offence's gilded hand may shove by justice,

---

33. **of vantage:** from a favorable position. 37. **the primal eldest curse:** See *Genesis* 4.10–12, [Cain's murder of his brother Abel. EDS.] 39. **Though inclination...will:** though I not only *wish* to pray, but feel a strong *impulse* toward prayer. 41. **double business bound:** in duty bound to two conflicting goals. 43. **neglect:** leave undone. 47. **Whereto...offence?** For what purpose does God's mercy *exist*, if not to confront a man's guilt when that appears as accuser before the Great Judge, and thus to procure his pardon? 48. **this twofold force:** He means the two points that follow in the next two lines. [EDS.] 49. **To...fall:** To be prevented before we commit the crime: "Lead us not into temptation." [EDS.] 50. **Or...down:** Or to "Forgive us our trespasses" 54. **effects:** gains. [In order to obtain forgiveness, one must make restitution: the King cannot do this because he refuses to give up what he gained from his crime. EDS.] 55. **mine own ambition:** the satisfaction of my lust for power.—**my queen:** Note that "my queen" is the climax (compare 1.5.75). The murder was a "crime of passion." 56. **th' offence:** that which has been gained by the crime. 57. **the corrupted currents:** the evil courses; [in this world below heaven. EDS.]. 58. **Offence's gilded hand:** the guilty hand, if lined with gold, [a pun on gild and guilty. EDS.].

And oft 'tis seen the wicked prize itself
Buys out the law; but 'tis not 'so above.   60
There is no shuffling; there the action lies
In his true nature, and we ourselves compelled,
Even to the teeth and forehead of our faults,
To give in evidence. What then? What rests?
Try what repentance can. What can it not?   65
Yet what can it when one cannot, repent?
O wretched state! O bosom black as death!
O liméd soul, that, struggling to be free,
Art more engaged! Help, angels. Make assay.
Bow, stubborn knees; and heart with strings of steel,   70
Be soft as sinews of the new-born babe.
All may be well.†   *He kneels.*

                        Enter Hamlet.

HAMLET   Now might I do it pat, now he is praying;‡
                And now I'll do't, and so he goes to heaven,
                And so am I revenged.* That would be scanned.   75
                A villain kills my father; and for that,
                I, his sole son, do this same villain send
                To heaven.
                Why, this is hire and salary, not revenge.

59-60. **the wicked prize...law:** a part of the illicit winnings may be used to bribe the judge. 60. **'tis not so above:** It's not that way in Heaven. 61. **There:** *There* stressed: in Heaven. [EDS.] 61-2. **there the action...nature:** *There* (in God's court) the lawsuit must be absolutely in accord with the facts. 61. **lies:** a legal term. [EDS.] An action at law is said to *lie* when it may legally be brought. 62-4. **we...evidence:** We must meet our sins face to face, for they are present in court to accuse us; and thus we are forced to testify against ourselves. 64. **What rests?** What remains for me to do? 65. **Try...not?** Repentance can accomplish anything. [EDS.] 66. **Yet...repent?** But what if one cannot repent? The ability to repent is considered to be a gift of grace. [EDS.] 68. **liméd soul:** The figure is that of a bird caught upon a twig smeared with the sticky substance called birdlime. The harder it struggles, the more it is besmeared and ensnared ("engaged"). Thus the King's soul, in its efforts to find some escape from guilt, merely succeeds in convincing itself that no escape is possible, since he can neither pray nor repent. 69. **Make assay:** "Though prayer seems impossible, yet make the attempt." 73. **pat:** readily.—**praying:** and therefore off his guard. 75. **That would be scanned:** That should be looked at closely; that is, Hamlet should examine it closely. [EDS.] 79. **this is hire and salary:** As if I had hired him to murder my father and were now paying him his wages.

---

†   Almereyda's Hamlet, listening to the King's anguish, cannot kill him. Zeffirelli sets this scene in
    a chapel, with the King kneeling before the communion altar.

‡   Flashcuts in Branagh's film show Hamlet, who has entered in the priest's booth adjacent to the
    penitent's, pierce the King through the ear with a blade. This image is in Hamlet's mind only as
    we see the King a moment later still alive, praying. Olivier's Hamlet is restrained from killing the
    King by a statue of a mild Jesus above the kneeling King.

*   Scott's Hamlet is about to strike when the Ghost's arm enters the frame and pushes down Hamlet's
    raised sword.

He took my father grossly, full of bread,   80
With all his crimes broad blown, as flush as May;
And how his audit stands, who knows save heaven?
But in our circumstance and course of thought,
'Tis heavy with him; and am I then revenged,
To take him in the purging of his soul,   85
When he is fit and seasoned for his passage? No.
Up, sword, and know thou a more horrid hent.
When he is drunk asleep; or in his rage;
Or in th' incestuous† pleasure of his bed;   90
At gaming, swearing, or about some act
That has no relish of salvation in't —
Then trip him, that his heels may kick at heaven,
And that his soul may be as damned and black
As hell, whereto it goes. My mother stays.   95
This physic but prolongs thy sickly days.   *Exit.*

KING   [*rises*] My words fly up, my thoughts remain below.
                  Words without thoughts never to heaven go.   *Exit.*

SCENE IV. [*The Queen's closet.*]

Enter Queen‡ and Polonius.

POLONIUS   He will come straight. Look you lay home to him.
                  Tell him his pranks have been too broad to bear with,
                  And that your Grace hath screened and stood between
                  Much heat and him. I'll silence me even here.

---

80. **grossly:** not purified by repentance, confession, and absolution.—**full of bread:** full of worldly pleasures (as opposed to prayer and fasting). 81. **crimes:** sins.—**broad blown:** in full bloom. Compare 1.5.76: "Cut off even in the blossoms of my sin."—**flush:** full of life and vigor. 82. **audit:** final account (in the book of judgment). 83. **in our...thought:** judging as well as possible and letting our thoughts take their natural course, we must conclude, etc. "Our course of thought" is contrasted with God's complete knowledge; and what makes the difference is that we are merely mortals. 85. **in the purging of his soul:** cleansing of his sins. [EDS.] 86. **seasoned:** thoroughly prepared.—**his passage:** from this world to the next. 88. **Up, sword...hent:** Back, sword, into thy sheath, and be seized at a more horrid moment, when his death will involve his damnation. 92. **relish:** taste. 93-5. **that his heels...hell:** so that he may fall headlong to hell. 96. **physic:** remedy: refers to the King's protecting himself through prayer or to Hamlet's sparing him by postponing revenge or perhaps to both. [EDS.]
SCENE IV.
1. **straight:** immediately.—**lay home to him:** rebuke him; Polonius repeats to the Queen what he has just said to the King (3.3.29). [EDS.] 2. **pranks:** misbehavior. [EDS.]— **broad:** unrestrained. [EDS.] 4. **heat:** anger (on the King's part).—**silence me:** stop talking and hide myself.

---

†   Flash cuts in Branagh's film show the King drinking, tossing Gertrude on her bed, as in earlier scenes.

‡   Scott's Queen is dressed as she was for the play, bejeweled with revealing décolletage.

	Pray you be round with him.	5
HAMLET	(*within*) Mother, mother, mother.	
QUEEN	I'll warrant you; fear me not. Withdraw; I hear him coming. [*Polonius hides behind the arras.*]	

Enter Hamlet.

HAMLET	Now, mother, what's the matter?	
QUEEN	Hamlet, thou hast thy father much offended.	
HAMLET	Mother, you have my father much offended.	10
QUEEN	Come, come, you answer with an idle tongue.	
HAMLET	Go, go, you question with a wicked tongue.	
QUEEN	Why, how now, Hamlet?	
HAMLET	What's the matter now?	
QUEEN	Have you forgot me?	
HAMLET	No, by the rood, not so. You are the Queen, your husband's brother's wife, And (would it were not so) you are my mother.	15
QUEEN	Nay, then I'll set those to you that can speak.	
HAMLET	Come, come, and sit you down. You shall not budge. You go not till I set you up a glass Where you may see the inmost part of you.*	20
QUEEN	What wilt thou do? Thou wilt not murther me? Help, help, ho.	
POLONIUS	[*behind*] What, ho. help, help, help.	
HAMLET	[*draws*] How now? a rat? Dead for a ducat, dead. [*Makes a pass through the arras and kills Polonius.*]	
POLONIUS	[*behind*] O, I am slain.**	

---

5. **round:** outspoken. 7. **fear me not:** Do not be afraid that I shall spare him. 7-20. Note the *stichomythia,* the alternation of speeches, line by line, [dialogue delivered as a sort of verbal ping-pong. EDS.]. 11. **idle:** foolish. 14. **Have you forgot me?** Have you forgotten who I am [and the honor you owe me as your mother and your queen? EDS.].—**by the rood:** by the cross. [EDS.] 17. **those:** She implies a threat. 19. **a glass:** a mirror. 21. **What wilt thou do?** Some menace in Hamlet's action alarms the Queen. 23. **a rat?** Hamlet, being in the Queen's private space where he would expect to be alone with her in complete privacy, calls the person behind the arras "a rat." [EDS.]—**for a ducat:** I'll bet a ducat [gold coin. EDS.].

---

*   Zeffirelli's Hamlet speaks angrily to his mother, his drawn sword held toward her, its tip touching her chest, thus forcing her upon the bed.

**   Branagh's Polonius is visible, having fallen outside the arras, with plenty of blood flowing.

QUEEN	O me, what hast thou done?	
HAMLET	Nay, I know not. Is it the King?	25
QUEEN	O, what a rash and bloody deed is this.	
HAMLET	A bloody deed — almost as bad, good mother, As kill a king, and marry with his brother.	
QUEEN	As kill a king?	
HAMLET	Ay, lady, it was my word.	30

[*Lifts up the arras and sees Polonius.*]

Thou wretched, rash, intruding fool, farewell.
I took thee for thy better.† Take thy fortune.
Thou find'st to be too busy is some danger.
Leave wringing of your hands.‡ Peace. sit you down
And let me wring your heart; for so I shall   35
If it be made of penetrable stuff;
If damnéd custom have not brazed it so
That it is proof and bulwark against sense.

QUEEN	What have I done that thou dar'st wag thy tongue In noise so rude against me?	
HAMLET	Such an act	40

That blurs the grace and blush of modesty;
Calls virtue hypocrite; takes off the rose
From the fair forehead of an innocent love,
And sets a blister there; makes marriage vows
As false as dicers' oaths. O, such a deed   45
As from the body of contraction plucks
The very soul, and sweet religion makes
A rhapsody of words. Heaven's face doth glow;
Yea, this solidity and compound mass,

---

25. **Is it the King?** What does Hamlet believe? [EDS.] 28. **As kill…brother:** A plain accusation that the Queen was an accomplice in the murder of her husband. Her response apparently convinces Hamlet of her innocence because he does not mention it again. 33. **too busy:** too meddlesome. 37. **custom:** habitual wrongdoing. [EDS.] See lines 161-5. 38. **proof:** armor.—**sense:** feeling. 40. **Such an act:** Hamlet upbraids his mother for her sexuality [and for choosing a lesser man than his father as a second husband. See lines 53-81. EDS.]. 41. **grace:** beauty. 42. **the rose:** symbol of beauty and perfection. [EDS.] 44. **a blister:** adulterous women and prostitutes were branded on the forehead. [EDS.] 46. **contraction:** the obligation of the marriage contract. 47. **religion:** the marriage vow. 48. **A rhapsody of words:** mere senseless verbiage. 49. **this solidity:** the earth. [EDS.] — **compound mass:** Our globe is a harmonious compound of the four elements: [air, earth, fire, water. EDS.].

---

†   Zeffirelli's Hamlet and his mother kneel together over Polonius body; as they do so, Hamlet's shows a moment of genuine regret and frustration over having killed the wrong man.

‡   Branagh's Gertrude wrings Polonius's hand. Scott's Hamlet leads her to a chair and sits on the floor below her.

	With tristful visage, as against the doom,	50
	Is thought-sick at the act.	
QUEEN	Ay me, what act,	
	That roars so loud and thunders in the index?	
HAMLET	Look here upon this picture, and on this,*	
	The counterfeit presentment of two brothers.	
	See what a grace was seated on this brow;	55
	Hyperion's curls; the front of Jove himself;	
	An eye like Mars, to threaten and command;	
	A station like the herald Mercury	
	New lighted on a heaven-kissing hill:	
	A combination and a form indeed	60
	Where every god did seem to set his seal	
	To give the world assurance of a man.	
	This was your husband. Look you now what follows.	
	Here is your husband, like a mildewed ear	
	Blasting his wholesome brother. Have you eyes?	65
	Could you on this fair mountain leave to feed,	
	And batten on this moor? Ha, have you eyes?	
	You cannot call it love; for at your age love vs lust	
	The heyday in the blood is tame, it's humble,**	
	And waits upon the judgment; and what judgment	70
	Would step from this to this? Sense sure you have,	
	Else could you not have motion; but sure that sense	
	Is apoplexed; for madness would not err,	
	Nor sense to ecstasy was ne'er so thralled	
	But it reserved some quantity of choice	75

50. **tristful:** sad.— **as against the doom:** as if at the approach of the Day of Judgment. 51. **thought-sick:** sick at heart. 52. **the index:** The *index* of a book was the "table of contents." 53. **this picture:** *Station* ("attitude in standing") in line 58 suggests that this portrait was full-length, and if so, the portrait of her new husband was doubtless of the same sort. 54. **counterfeit presentment:** representation in portraiture. 56. **Hyperion:** sun god. [EDS.] See 1.2.140.—**front:** forehead.—**Jove:** See 3.2.294. 58. **station:** posture in standing. 62. **a man:** Compare 1.2.187-8. 65. **Blasting:** infecting. Compare 1.3.39. [EDS.]—**his:** its. 66. **leave:** cease. 67. **batten:** gorge yourself. 68. **at your age:** Hamlet's belief that his mother is too old to feel passionate love is an indication of his youth. 69. **The heyday in the blood:** the liveliness of youthful passion; "the compulsive ardor" (line 86).—**tame:** under control. 70. **waits upon:** defers to. 71. **Sense sure you have:** ability to react to sensations. [EDS.] 72-6. **that sense... difference:** Never before were you unable to distinguish between two such different choices. [EDS.] 73. **apoplexed:** paralyzed. [EDS.] 74. **ecstasy:** madness. 75. **quantity:** small amount.—**choice:** the power of discrimination.

*   Scott's Hamlet has brought with him the snapshot of his father; the photo of Claudius is in her locket.

**   Like many Hamlets, Branagh's throws Gertrude on her bed, but after the Ghost admonishes him, he sits her down on a settee (line 140).

To serve in such a difference. What devil was't
That thus hath cozened you at hoodman-blind?
Eyes without feeling, feeling without sight,
Ears without hands or eyes, smelling sans all,
Or but a sickly part of one true sense   80
Could not so mope.
O shame, where is thy blush? Rebellious hell,
If thou canst mutine in a matron's bones,
To flaming youth let virtue be as wax
And melt in her own fire. Proclaim no shame   85
When the compulsive ardor gives the charge,
Since frost itself as actively doth burn,
And reason panders will.

QUEEN   O Hamlet, speak no more.
Thou turn'st mine eyes into my very soul,
And there I see such black and grainéd spots   90
As will not leave their tinct.

HAMLET   Nay, but to live
In the rank sweat of an enseaméd bed,
Stewed in corruption, honeying and making love
Over the nasty sty.

movie: almost assults her—oedipus

QUEEN   O, speak to me no more.
These words like daggers enter in mine ears.   95
No more, sweet Hamlet.

HAMLET   A murtherer and a villain.
A slave that is not twentieth part the tithe
Of your precedent lord; a vice of kings;†

---

76. **To serve:** enough sense to choose. 77. **cozened:** tricked.—**hoodman-blind:** blindman's buff. The Queen, Hamlet implies, had made her choice with as little discrimination as that shown by the *hoodman* (or blinded person) in blindman's buff, who seizes upon anybody within reach and cannot tell one from another. 78–81. Omitted in the Folios.—**sans:** without.—**so mope:** be so dull and lazy. 82-3. **Rebellious hell:** Hamlet speaks of the baser elements in our nature as rising in mutiny against our nobler selves. 83-4. **If thou...as wax:** If a mature woman can so fall, untried youth should be excused. [EDS.] 86. **gives the charge:** makes the attack [on virtue. EDS.]. 88. **reason panders will:** reason, which should control desire, becomes basely subservient to it, [acting as a "pimp" for sexual desire. EDS.]. 90. **grainéd:** [steeped in color-fast red dye; *scarlet* is associated with sexual sin. EDS.]; *grain* was a kind of scarlet dye.—**leave their tinct:** give up their color. 92. **enseaméd:** soaked in grease; [bed linens soiled by lust. EDS.]. 93. **Stewed:** implying "stews," or brothels. [EDS.] 94 **sty:** pig pen; also a brothel. [EDS.] 97. **the tithe:** the tenth part. 98. **a vice of kings:** a rascally buffoon among kings. The *vice* in the medieval morality plays was a comic character [who was also a trickster. EDS.].

---

†   Scott's Gertrude hears something; the camera cuts to Polonius, bloody, standing; he falls revealing the ghost behind him; Hamlet falls backward, terrified.

	A cutpurse of the empire and the rule,	
	That from a shelf the precious diadem stole	100
	And put it in his pocket.	
QUEEN	No more.	

Enter the Ghost [in his nightgown].

HAMLET	A king of shreds and patches.‡ —	
	Save me and hover o'er me with your wings,	
	You heavenly guards. What would your gracious figure?	
QUEEN	Alas, he's mad.	105
HAMLET	Do you not come your tardy son to chide,	
	That, lapsed in time and passion, lets go by	
	Th' important acting of your dread command?	
	O, say.	
GHOST.	Do not forget. This visitation	110
	Is but to whet thy almost blunted purpose.	
	But look, amazement on thy mother sits.	
	O, step between her and her fighting soul.	
	Conceit in weakest bodies strongest works.	
	Speak to her, Hamlet.	

---

99. **cutpurse:** Literally, "one who steals money by cutting a hole in the purse" (worn at the belt); thus, "a pickpocket" in general; here, "a sneaking thief." Claudius has been legally elected king; as Hamlet says to Horatio, Claudius had "popped in between th' election and my hopes" (5.2. 65), [evidently with Polonius's help (1.2.47-9). EDS.]. 101. **Enter the Ghost:** Ghosts had the power of appearing and speaking to one person while remaining invisible and inaudible to all others present.—**in his nightgown:** These words are in the First Quarto only. [Hamlet's description in 135 suggests any kind of attire, including the same armor he had on in act one.] 102. **A king of shreds and patches:** Often taken as alluding to the motley attire of a fool or jester; but apparently Hamlet means merely that Claudius's royalty is a threadbare, patched-up thing. He has compared him to a clown, then to a pickpocket and sneak-thief, now to a ragged vagabond. Compare the First Quarto: "a king of clowts, of very shreds." 107. **lapsed in time and passion:** [lost opportunity and desire. EDS.] Literally, *lapsed* means "having slipped or failed." 108. **important:** momentous. 110. **Do not forget:** compare 1.5.91. —**This visitation:** Since the Ghost arrives in the midst of Hamlet harangue against his mother, it seems it comes to protect her from his attack; notably, it had not come to encourage Hamlet as he weighed whether to kill the King at prayer. [EDS.] 111. **blunted purpose:** Since the Ghost had asked Hamlet to "Let not the royal bed of Denmark be A couch for luxury and damned incest" (1.5.82-3), perhaps it thinks that Hamlet is taking longer than necessary to accomplish that goal. The other aspect of Hamlet's purpose is to revenge the murder in some way that the Ghost had not specified. [EDS.] 112. **amazement:** confusion. 114. **Conceit:** imagination (which forms, in the Queen's mind, a vivid image of her guilt).

---

‡   Zeffirelli's Hamlet and his mother kiss frantically, if not passionately, an action which seems to summon the Ghost's final appearance. Branagh's Ghost appears between Hamlet and Gertrude. He has changed: sweet music and a beneficent look on his face, a robe instead of armor, all suggest that the purgatorial fires have had a good effect. "Do not forget" in this film could mean "Do not forget your prayers for me." No Ghost mentions his murderer specifically here, but Branagh implies that the Ghost has forgotten the murderer.

| HAMLET | How is it with you, lady? | 115 |

QUEEN   Alas, how is't with you,
That you do bend your eye on vacancy,
And with th' incorporal air do hold discourse?
Forth at your eyes your spirits wildly peep;
And, as the sleeping soldiers in th' alarm,   120
Your bedded hairs, like life in excrements,
Start up and stand an end. O gentle son,
Upon the heat and flame of thy distemper
Sprinkle cool patience. Whereon do you look?

HAMLET   On him, on him! Look you how pale he glares.   125
His form and cause conjoined, preaching to stones,
Would make them capable. — Do not look upon me,
Lest with this piteous action you convert
My stern effects. Then what I have to do
Will want true color — tears perchance for blood.   130

QUEEN   To whom do you speak this?

HAMLET   Do you see nothing there?

QUEEN   Nothing at all; yet all that is I see.

HAMLET   Nor did you nothing hear?

QUEEN   No, nothing but ourselves.

HAMLET   Why, look you there. Look how it steals away.
My father, in his habit as he lived.   135
Look where he goes even now out at the portal.

Exit Ghost.

QUEEN   This is the very coinage of your brain.
This bodiless creation ecstasy
Is very cunning in.

HAMLET   Ecstasy?
My pulse as yours doth temperately keep time   140
And makes as healthful music. It is not madness
That I have uttered. Bring me to the test,
And I the matter will reword; which madness

---

118. **incorporal:** bodiless. 119. **spirits:** In moments of excitement the *spirits* or "vital forces" were thought to come, as it were, to the surface, and to cause various symptoms of agitation, such as a wild glare in the eyes. 120. **th' alarm:** the call to arms. 121. **bedded:** smooth, flat. [EDS.] See 1.5.18. —**excrements:** The hair and nails, being not a part of the body but rather something growing out of it, were often so called. 122. **an end:** on end. [EDS.] 123. **distemper:** distraction. 124. **patience:** self-control. 127. **capable:** capable of feeling and emotion. 128. **convert:** change utterly. 129. **effects:** deeds. 130. **color:** emotion. [EDS.] 135. **in his habit as he lived:** dressed as he was when alive. 138. **ecstasy:** madness.—**cunning:** skilful.

Would gambol from. Mother, for love of grace,
Lay not that flattering unction to your soul,   145
That not your trespass but my madness speaks.
It will but skin and film the ulcerous place,
Whiles rank corruption, mining all within,
Infects unseen. Confess yourself to heaven;
Repent what's past; avoid what is to come;   150
And do not spread the compost on the weeds
To make them ranker. Forgive me this my virtue;
For in the fatness of these pursy times
Virtue itself of vice must pardon beg —
Yea, curb and woo for leave to do him good.   155

QUEEN   O Hamlet, thou hast cleft my heart in twain.

HAMLET   O, throw away the worser part of it,
And live the purer with the other half.
Good night — but go not to my uncle's bed.
Assume a virtue, if you have it not.   160
That monster, custom, who all sense doth eat
Of habits evil, is angel yet in this,
That to the use of actions fair and good
He likewise gives a frock or livery,
That aptly is put on. Refrain tonight,   165
And that shall lend a kind of easiness
To the next abstinence; the next more easy;
For use almost can change the stamp of nature,

---

144. **gambol from:** "wander away from in a fantastic way."—**for love of grace:** for God's sake. 145. **flattering unction:** soothing ointment. Hamlet urges his mother to take his reproofs and exhortations seriously and not as the ravings of a maniac. 148. **mining:** undermining. [EDS.] 147. **skin:** provide a covering. [EDS.] 152–5. **Forgive me...good:** "I must ask you to forgive my action in thus upbraiding you, though it is a good action (a virtue) on my part; for, in these corrupt times, the virtuous cannot chide the vicious without asking pardon for the liberty, indeed, they must bend the knee (*curb*) and beg for leave to benefit them by such needed reproof." Hamlet feels some compunction at his own harsh language, but he justifies it in the very act of apologizing. 153. **fatness...times:** Hamlet compares these corrupt times to a body that is unhealthily corpulent. 156. **cleft...twain:** Hamlet's immediate reply is an order or a suggestion that she throw away the bad part of her heart. [EDS.] 160. **Assume...not:** "Force yourself to act virtuously, even if you are not virtuously inclined." 161–5. **That monster...put on:** Custom, who is a monster because he takes away our feeling of the badness of our evil habits, is yet an angel in this point, namely, that Custom likewise makes good actions easy. *Monster* and *angel* stand in antithesis. The Folios omit the passage. The Second Quarto reads *deuill* for *evil*. Many editors retain *devil*; but *evil* is necessary to mark the antithesis between bad habits and good, and *monster* makes a satisfactory antithesis to *angel*. 164. **frock or livery:** With a slight pun on *habits*, [which refers also to clothing. EDS.]. 165. **That aptly is put on:** that is easy to wear. Because he is speaking of the good effects of habit, the figure is not meant to suggest fraud or the concealment of evil intent under a cloak of virtue. 166. **shall:** will certainly. 167–70. **the next...potency:** Omitted in the Folios. 168. **use:** habit. —**can...nature:** For, as the proverb runs, "habit is a second nature."

	And either [master] the devil, or throw him out	
	With wondrous potency. Once more, good night;	170
	And when you are desirous to be blest,	
	I'll blessing beg of you. —For this same lord,	
	I do repent; but heaven hath pleased it so,	
	To punish me with this, and this with me,	
	That I must be their scourge and minister.	175
	I will bestow him, and will answer well	
	The death I gave him. So again, good night.	
	I must be cruel, only to be kind;	
	Thus bad begins, and worse remains behind.	
	One word more, good lady.	
QUEEN	What shall I do?	180
HAMLET	Not this, by no means, that I bid you do:	
	Let the bloat King tempt you again to bed;	
	Pinch wanton on your cheek; call you his mouse;	
	And let him, for a pair of reechy kisses,	
	Or paddling in your neck with his damned fingers,	185
	Make you to ravel all this matter out,	
	That I essentially am not in madness,†	
	But mad in craft. 'Twere good you let him know;	
	For who that's but a queen, fair, sober, wise,	
	Would from a paddock, from a bat, a gib,	190
	Such dear concernings hide? Who would do so?	

---

169. **either master:** The devil (evil) in a person's character may be kept under control by good habits, or it may even be eradicated thereby. 171-2. **And when...you:** And when you show some sign of wishing for the blessing of heaven, I will be once more your dutiful son and ask your blessing at parting, as I used to do. 171. **you:** Emphatic. 172. **For:** as for. 174. **To punish me with this:** Hamlet sees that the King will perceive that he killed Polonius by mistake for him, and will take measures accordingly. See line 211; 4.1.13–15. [Also, Hamlet, as a moral person, might feel painful remorse for this accident. EDS.] **—and this:** and this dead man. 175. **their scourge and minister:** heaven's plague (punishing) and heaven's agent; minister of divine retribution. *Their* refers to heaven (line 173). The use of a plural pronoun to refer to the singular noun *heaven* is common. 176. **bestow him:** stow him away; dispose of him. **—will answer well:** Hamlet is ready to pay a penalty for this crime. [EDS.] 178. **cruel...kind:** Hamlet says that his harsh treatment of his mother is meant to cure her of her sinful choices. [EDS.] 179. **Thus...behind:** Thus, in this interview, I have made a bad beginning (by killing Polonius when I meant to kill the King); but there is worse to come: that is, either the King will kill me or I shall kill the King. The Queen does not understand this vague threat. *Thus* is the Folio reading. The Quartos have *This* [perhaps referring to the dead body of Polonius. EDS.]. 181. **not this:** Hamlet announces that what he is about to say is meant sarcastically and is the opposite of what he wants her to do. [EDS.] 182. **bloat:** swollen with drinking. 183. **mouse:** A common pet name. 184. **reechy:** smelly. 186. **ravel...out:** [tell all. EDS.] 187. **essentially:** in fact. 188. **in craft:** pretending madness. [EDS.] 190. **paddock:** toad.—**gib:** tomcat. The word is a contraction of *Gilbert,* commonly a cat's name. These animals were regarded as unclean or dangerous [and were supposed to be chosen by witches as pets or "familiars." EDS.]. 191. **Such dear concernings:** matters of such importance.

---

†   Though Scott's Hamlet has moments of lucidity, he is more unhinged than most others.

"I must to England" (3.4.199). In Zeffirelli's film, Hamlet and his mother forge a bond at this point.

	No, in despite of sense and secrecy,	
	Unpeg the basket on the house's top,	
	Let the birds fly, and like the famous ape,	
	To try conclusions, in the basket creep	195
	And break your own neck down.	
QUEEN	Be thou assured, if words be made of breath,	
	And breath of life, I have no life to breathe	
	What thou hast said to me.	
HAMLET	I must to England; you know that?‡	
QUEEN	Alack,	200
	I had forgot. 'Tis so concluded on.	

193–6. **Unpeg...down:** Refers to a fable, in which an ape finds a basket full of birds on the housetop, and opens it. When the birds fly away, the ape gets into the basket and jumps out in an attempt to fly, but falls from the roof and breaks his neck. 195. **To try conclusions:** to experiment. 196. **down:** by the fall. 197-9. **Be thou assured...to me:** Gertrude says here that she will not reveal what she has heard. [EDS.] 200. **I must to England:** The King does not announce this voyage to Hamlet until 4.3.48, and then Hamlet pretends to take it as a novelty. The present passage shows that he had already learned of the project. [The King had thought of a trip for Hamlet as early as 3.1.176-83. See also note 3.3.3. EDS.] 200. **Alack:** an expression of sorrow at the coming separation. The Queen doesn't suspect the King's evil purpose.

‡   Zeffirelli breaks up Hamlet's exchange with his mother and moves its conclusion forward to 4.3, after the King's aside: "Do it England" (67). The scene is set out of doors, as Hamlet prepares to leave for England, with Rosencrantz and Guildenstern. A close shot of Hamlet embracing and kissing his mother is followed by a closeup of the Queen's face, her eyes filled with tears, her expression suggesting that a new bond has been forged between her and her son.

HAMLET   There's letters sealed; and my two schoolfellows,
                Whom I will trust as I will adders fanged,
                They bear the mandate; they must sweep my way
                And marshal me to knavery. Let it work;   205
                For 'tis the sport to have the enginer
                Hoist with his own petar; and 't shall go hard
                But I will delve one yard below their mines
                And blow them at the moon. O, 'tis most sweet
                When in one line two crafts directly meet.   210
                This man shall set me packing.
                I'll lug the guts into the neighbor room. —
                Mother, good night. — Indeed, this counselor
                Is now most still, most secret, and most grave,
                Who was in life a foolish prating knave.   215
                Come, sir, to draw toward an end with you.
                Good night, mother.
                        [*Exit the Queen Then*] *exit Hamlet, tugging in Polonius.*

ACT IV

SCENE I. [*Elsinore. A room in the Castle.*]

Enter King [and Queen, with Rosencrantz and Guildenstern].

KING   There's matter in these sighs. These profound heaves
                You must translate; 'tis fit we understand them.
                Where is your son?

QUEEN   Bestow this place on us a little while.

202-10. **There's letters…directly meet:** The Folio omits lines 202–10. 203. **adders fanged:** poisonous snakes. 205. **marshall:** lead the way. [EDS.]—**knavery:** some crime against myself. The precise nature of the plan Hamlet does not discover until they are at sea, when he opens the sealed commission (5.2.25). 207. **Hoist:** blown up.—**petar:** petard, a kind of bomb used for blowing gates open. 210. **When… meet:** Another figure from warfare: Hamlet imagines two opposing plotters (the King and himself) digging a mine and a countermine and suddenly coming face to face in their excavations. 211. **packing:** With a pun: (1) carrying a load on my back; (2) leaving the country in haste (on account of Polonius's death). 214. **most grave:** Another pun. [Polonius is finally serious, and he is ready for the grave. EDS.] Compare *Romeo and Juliet*, 3.1.90-1, where Mercutio, mortally wounded, says to Romeo, "Ask for me tomorrow, and you shall find me a grave man." 216. **to draw…with you:** to come to the end of my business with you. From this point in the source story the Queen assists Hamlet in his plans of revenge, [and the First Quarto expresses that assistance in a scene between her and Horatio not found in the Second Quarto or the Folio. EDS.].

ACT IV. SCENE I.
1. **matter:** meaning.—**prófound:** deep. 3. **your son:** [*her* son, no longer *his*. EDS.] 4. **Bestow this place on us:** leave us. [Since they don't enter in the Folio, her request is in the Quarto only. EDS.]

[*Exeunt Rosencrantz and Guildenstern.*]
Ah, mine own lord, what have I seen tonight.

KING   What, Gertrude? How does Hamlet?

QUEEN   Mad as the sea and wind when both contend
                Which is the mightier. In his lawless fit,
                Behind the arras hearing something stir,
                Whips out his rapier, cries "A rat, a rat."   10
                And in this brainish apprehension kills
                The unseen good old man.

KING   O heavy deed.
                It had been so with us, had we been there.
                His liberty is full of threats to all —
                To you yourself, to us, to every one.   15
                Alas, how shall this bloody deed be answered?
                It will be laid to us, whose providence
                Should have kept short, restrained, and out of haunt
                This mad young man. But so much was our love
                We would not understand what was most fit,   20
                But, like the owner of a foul disease,
                To keep it from divulging, let it feed
                Even on the pith of life. Where is he gone?

QUEEN   To draw apart the body he hath killed;
                O'er whom his very madness, like some ore   25
                Among a mineral of metals base,
                Shows itself pure. He weeps for what is done.†

KING   O Gertrude, come away.
                The sun no sooner shall the mountains touch
                But we will ship him hence; and this vile deed   30
                We must with all our majesty and skill

---

7. **Mad:** The Queen does as she has promised Hamlet; she does not give him away. Or she truly believes Hamlet is mad. [EDS.] 11. **brainish apprehension:** insane notion. 12. **good old man:** The regard of the King and Queen for Polonius is evident throughout the play; [he is the one who helped them to their thrones. EDS.]. 13. **It had been so with us:** The King immediately perceives that Hamlet [whether sane or not. EDS.] had intended to kill him when he thrust his sword through the tapestry; and henceforth he has no doubt that Hamlet is his mortal enemy.—**us:** me. The "royal *we.*" 14. **His liberty:** unrestrained freedom. [EDS.] 16. **answered:** explained: Polonius is an important public figure. 17. **to us:** "to me, the King." So also *our* in line 19.—**providence:** foresight. 18. **short:** on a short leash.—**out of haunt:** away from others. 20. **We would not:** Affection blinded me. [EDS.] 22. **divulging:** coming to light. 25. **ore:** precious metal (especially gold). 26. **mineral:** mine or metallic vein. 27. **He weeps:** Gertrude may be lying to protect Hamlet. [EDS.] 31. **We must…excuse:** I must defend with all my royal authority and excuse with all my skill.

---

†   Branagh's Gertrude lies in saying this.

Both countenance and excuse. Ho, Guildenstern!
Enter Rosencrantz and Guildenstern.
Friends both, go join you with some further aid.
Hamlet in madness hath Polonius slain,
And from his mother's closet hath he dragged him.   35
Go seek him out; speak fair, and bring the body
Into the chapel. I pray you haste in this.
                        Exeunt [Rosencrantz and Guildenstern].
Come, Gertrude,‡ we'll call up our wisest friends
And let them know both what we mean to do
And what's untimely done. [So haply slander —]   40
Whose whisper o'er the world's diameter,
As level as the cannon to his blank,
Transports his poisoned shot — may miss our name
And hit the woundless air. — O, come away.
My soul is full of discord and dismay.   45
                        Exeunt.*

SCENE II. [Elsinore. A passage in the Castle.]

                    Enter Hamlet.

HAMLET   Safely stowed.**
GENT.   (within) Hamlet. Lord Hamlet.

HAMLET   But soft. What noise? Who calls on Hamlet? O, here they come.

                Enter Rosencrantz and Guildenstern.

ROSENCRANTZ   What have you done, my lord, with the dead body?   5

---

33. **with some further aid:** Once Rosencrantz and Guildenstern catch up with him in 4.3, Hamlet is under surveillance and has no opportunity to attack the King. 40. **And what's untimely done:** Both Second Quarto and Folio omit the rest of this line and the Folio omits lines 41–4 (through *air*). 41. **o'er...diameter:** across the breadth of the world. 42. **As level:** with as sure an aim.—**his blank:** its mark. The *blank* is literally the white circle or spot at the center of the target. 44. **woundless:** invulnerable. 45. **My soul...dismay:** An expression of the turmoil in the King's mind. The death of Polonius is a serious matter, likely to shake his throne; [the rhyming couplet at the end reinforces the idea. EDS.]. After 45. **Exeunt:** The manner of their exit will suggest their present relationship. [EDS.]
SCENE II.
1. **Safely stowed:** [Safely hidden. EDS.] Hamlet has not yet recovered from the excited mood in which we saw him at the end of Act III, hence the flippancy of his language.

---

‡   Branagh's King holds Gertrude tight; she responds to him. Olivier's queen rejects him.
*   Branagh inserts a new scene: soldiers search for Hamlet, rushing in on a sleeping Ophelia, looking under her sheets as she screams in panic for Hamlet.
** Scott's Hamlet tucks the body into the cabinet where Polonius had spied on him and Ophelia.

HAMLET	Compounded it with dust, whereto 'tis kin.
ROSENCRANTZ	Tell us where 'tis, that we may take it thence And bear it to the chapel.
HAMLET	Do not believe it.
ROSENCRANTZ	Believe what? 10
HAMLET	That I can keep your counsel, and not mine own. Besides, to be demanded of a sponge, what replication should be made by the son of a king?
ROSENCRANTZ	Take you me for a sponge, my lord? 15
HAMLET	Ay, sir; that soaks up the King's countenance, his rewards, his authorities. But such officers do the King best service in the end. He keeps them, like an ape, in the corner of his jaw; first mouthed, to be last swallowed. When he needs what you have gleaned, it is but 20 squeezing you and, sponge, you shall be dry again.
ROSENCRANTZ	I understand you not, my lord.
HAMLET	I am glad of it. A knavish speech sleeps in a foolish ear.
ROSENCRANTZ	My lord, you must tell us where the body 25 is and go with us to the King.
HAMLET	The body is with the King, but the King is not with the body. The King is a thing —
GUILDENSTERN	A thing, my lord?
HAMLET	Of nothing. Bring me to him. Hide fox, and all after!† 30

Exeunt.

---

6. **whereto 'tis kin:** See *Genesis* 3.19: ["thou art dust and to dust shalt thou return." EDS.]. 11. **keep your counsel:** keep your secrets. Hamlet suggests that he knows well enough (but will not tell) what they and the King have in mind regarding him. See 3.4.202–10. 12. **demanded of:** interrogated by.— **replication:** formal answer. 15. **Take you me for a sponge?** one who sucks up the wealth and advantage around him. [EDS.] 16. **countenance:** favor. 18. **like an ape:** as an ape keeps things which he intends to devour. The text follows the Folio. The Second Quarto reads "like an apple"; [as an ape eats an apple. EDS.]. 24. **A knavish speech...ear:** "*My* knavish speech sleeps in (is not understood by) your foolish ear." 28, 29. **The body...body:** Perhaps a reference to the King's "two bodies," one being mortal and the other divine. [EDS.] 30. **Of nothing:** Compare *Psalm* 144. 4: "Man is like a thing of naught: his time passeth away like a shadow." The phrase had become an idiom to express the utmost contemp.—**Hide fox, and all after:** Omitted in the Quartos. Doubtless the formula of a child's game similar to hide-and-seek. One person (the fox) hides, and the other players are to find him if they can. As he speaks, Folio Hamlet runs off as if he were the fox ("Catch me if you can!"), and is followed by Rosencrantz and Guildenstern.

†   Branagh's Ophelia comes face to face with Hamlet in the midst of this line; he turns from her as he says the rest of the line. She continues shouting for him as he runs to momentary safety in his study.

SCENE III. [*Elsinore. A room in the Castle.*]

Enter King.

KING

I have sent to seek him and to find the body.
How dangerous is it that this man goes loose.
Yet must not we put the strong law on him.
He's loved of the distracted multitude,
Who like not in their judgment, but their eyes;   5
And where 'tis so, th' offender's scourge is weighed,
But never the offence. To bear all smooth and even,
This sudden sending him away must seem
Deliberate pause. Diseases desperate grown
By desperate appliance are relieved,   10
Or not at all.‡

Enter Rosencrantz.

How now? What hath befall'n?

ROSENCRANTZ

Where the dead body is bestowed, my lord,
We cannot get from him.

KING

But where is he?

ROSENCRANTZ

Without, my lord; guarded, to know your pleasure.

KING

Bring him before us.   15

ROSENCRANTZ

Ho, Guildenstern. Bring in my lord.

Enter Hamlet and Guildenstern [with Attendants].

KING

Now, Hamlet, where's Polonius?

HAMLET

At supper.

KING

At supper? Where?   19

SCENE III.
1. The Folio has the stage direction "*Enter King*"; the Second Quarto, "*Enter King, and two or three.*" [The King here may be speaking to "his wisest friends, mentioned earlier (4.1.31-2, 38-40). Compare his words when alone at the end of the scene. EDS.] 4. **of:** by.—**distracted:** turbulent. Note the wildness of the mob described in 4.5.99–108.—**multitude:** Hamlet's popularity is one reason the King has to be cautious in putting him out of the way; another reason is the Queen's love for her son. 5. **in:** in accordance with. 7. **bear:** manage. 8. **sudden:** The sending away may seem sudden to the courtiers but the King has planned it since eavesdropping on Hamlet (3.1.177). 9. **Deliberate pause:** the outcome of careful thought. 9-11. **Diseases...at all:** Proverbial: "To desperate diseases must desperate Medicines be applyde." 12. **bestowed:** hidden. 14. **guarded:** under guard. [EDS.]

---

‡   Branagh's King says these lines to himself. In other versions he is speaking to the "wisest friends" he had mentioned in 4.1.38. When counselors are present in the scene, he behaves kindly towards Hamlet, but alone with his flatterers, he can show his cruelty—as does Branagh's King.

HAMLET	Not where he eats, but where he is eaten.
	A certain convocation of politic worms are e'en at him.
	Your worm is your only emperor for diet. We fat
	all creatures else to fat us, and we fat ourselves for maggots.
	Your fat king and your lean beggar is but variable service —
	two dishes, but to one table. That's the end. 25
KING	Alas, alas.
HAMLET	A man may fish with the worm that hath eat of
	a king, and eat of the fish that hath fed of that worm.
KING	What dost thou mean by this?
HAMLET	Nothing but to show you how a king may go a 30
	progress through the guts of a beggar.
KING	Where is Polonius?
HAMLET	In heaven. Send thither to see. If your messenger
	find him not there, seek him I' th' other place yourself.
	But indeed, if you find him not within this month, 35
	you shall nose him as you go up the stairs into the lobby.
KING	Go seek him there. [*To Attendants.*]
HAMLET	He will stay till you come.*
	[*Exeunt Attendants.*]
KING	Hamlet, this deed, for thine especial safety, —
	Which we do tender as we dearly grieve 40
	For that which thou hast done, — must send thee hence
	With fiery quickness. Therefore prepare thy self.
	The bark is ready and the wind at help,
	Th' associates tend, and everything is bent
	For England.

21. **politic:** skilled in statecraft.—**e'en:** just now; at this moment. 22-5. **Your worm...table:** Compare Montaigne's *Essays,* 2. 2 (Florio's translation, 1603): "The heart and life of a mighty and triumphant Emperour, is but the break-fast of a seely-little Worme." 22. **Your:** The general *your* as in 5.1.187. 24. **variable service:** two ways of serving the same kind of food. 26-9. *King.* **Alas...that worm:** Omitted in the Folios. 27-8. **A man...that worm:** Hamlet expresses a similar idea in 5.1.224-6. [EDS.] 31. **progress:** a journey of state undertaken by a monarch from one part of his realm to another. Queen Elizabeth and James I made such progresses. [Greenblatt detects much in this passage, including: (1) a lightly-veiled death threat against King Claudius; (2) a parody of the transubstantiation debate (the changing of bread and wine into the real presence of Christ's body and blood); (3) an allusion to the Diet of Worms (1521), wherein Luther's teachings were refuted by the papal nuncio, Cardinal Alexander, and Luther was banned from his homeland (*Purgatory* 241). EDS.] 35. **indeed:** In the emphatic sense: "in fact," "to speak plainly." 36. **shall nose him:** smell him. 39-41. **Hamlet...hence:** The King says he is equally concerned about Hamlet's safety and about the murder; taking both into consideration, he must send Hamlet away. [EDS.] 43. **at help:** favorable. 44. **Th' associates:** Rosencrantz and Guildenstern.—**tend:** await your convenience.—**bent:** ready. A figure from archery.

* Scott's Hamlet says this line with a smile and then sees a somber Ophelia facing him.

HAMLET	For England?	
KING	Ay, Hamlet.	
HAMLET	Good.	45
KING	So is it, if thou knew'st our purposes.	
HAMLET	I see a cherub that sees them.	
	But come, for England. Farewell, dear mother.	
KING	Thy loving father, Hamlet.	
HAMLET	My mother. Father and mother is man and wife;	50
	man and wife is one flesh; and so, my mother.	
	Come, for England.	*Exit.*
KING	Follow him at foot; tempt him with speed aboard.	
	Delay it not; I'll have him hence tonight.	
	Away. for everything is sealed and done	55
	That else leans on th' affair. Pray you make haste.	

                      [Exeunt Rosencrantz and Guildenstern.]

         And, England, if my love thou hold'st at aught, —
         As my great power thereof may give thee sense,
         Since yet thy cicatrice looks raw and red
         After the Danish sword, and thy free awe   60
         Pays homage to us, — thou mayst not coldly set
         Our sovereign process, which imports at full,
         By letters congruing to that effect,
         The present death of Hamlet. Do it, England;
         For like the hectic in my blood he rages,   65
         And thou must cure me. Till I know 'tis done,
         Howe'er my haps, my joys were ne'er begun.

---

47. **I see a cherub:** Hamlet expresses obliquely the suspicion he has about the King's purpose [EDS.] 48. **dear mother:** The Queen is not present. The King corrects Hamlet as if he is speaking to a madman. 51. **one flesh:** Biblical allusion, see for example, Genesis 2.24 and Mark 10.8. 53. **at foot:** closely. [EDS.]—**tempt him:** coax him. 56. **leans on the affair:** appertains to the business. 57. **England:** King of England.—**at aught:** at any value. 58. **As...sense:** as my great power may well give thee a feeling of the value of my favor. 59. **cicatrice:** scar. [EDS.] 60-1. **thy free...us:** though technically free, yet you stand in awe of me and pay homage accordingly. 61. **coldly set:** regard indifferently. 62. **process:** instructions. 63. **letters:** This sealed mandate to the English king is distinct from the "commission" given to Rosencrantz and Guildenstern. Its contents are a secret. Their commission gives them custody of the mandate and of Hamlet and directs them to deliver it and him. They are apparently ignorant of its contents [though they may reason to suspect what the King plans. EDS.]—**congruing to:** in complete agreement with. The Folio reads *coniuring,* i.e., calling upon him solemnly.—**effect:** result. 64. **present:** immediate. Thus, for the first time, we learn specifically of the King's plan. 65. **the hectic:** a continuous fever. 67. **Howe'er my haps:** whatever my past or future fortune.

SCENE IV. [*Near Elsinore.*]†

Enter Fortinbras with his Army over the stage.

FORTINBRAS	Go, Captain, from me greet the Danish King
	Tell him that by his license Fortinbras
	Craves the conveyance of a promised march
	Over his kingdom. You know the rendezvous.
	If that his Majesty would aught with us, 5
	We shall express our duty in his eye;
	And let him know so.
CAPTAIN	I will do't, my lord.
FORTINBRAS	Go softly on.

Exeunt [all but the Captain].

Enter Hamlet, Rosencrantz, [Guildenstern,] and others.

HAMLET	Good sir, whose powers are these?
CAPTAIN	They are of Norway, sir. 10
HAMLET	How purposed, sir, I pray you?
CAPTAIN	Against some part of Poland.
HAMLET	Who commands them, sir?
CAPTAIN	The nephew to old Norway, Fortinbras.
HAMLET	Goes it against the main of Poland, sir, 15
	Or for some frontier?
CAPTAIN	Truly to speak, and with no addition,
	We go to gain a little patch of ground
	That hath in it no profit but the name.
	To pay five ducats, five, I would not farm it; 20
	Nor will it yield to Norway or the Pole
	A ranker rate, should it be sold in fee.
HAMLET	Why, then the Polack never will defend it.

SCENE IV

3. **conveyance:** free passage over Danish soil. [EDS.] 6. **in his eye:** in his royal presence. 8. **softly:** slowly. 9–66. The omission of these lines in the Folio shortens the play very slightly. Critics have advanced various arguments for its omission. Most actors of Hamlet prefer to keep it. [It is here in his last soliloquy, moreover, that Hamlet commends Fortinbras as worthy of emulation, and this explains, perhaps, Hamlet's vote for Fortinbras's succession to the Danish throne (5.2.367). EDS.] 9. **powers:** troops. 15. **the main:** the whole country. 19. **the name:** Emphatic: "the mere *name* of conquest." 20. **To pay...farm it:** I would not take it on lease at a rental of five ducats a year. 22. **A ranker rate:** a higher rate. If the plot were sold, it would not yield an annual income of more than five ducats.

---

†   In Scott's version this is a nighttime scene, as promised in the King's line 4.3.54.

CAPTAIN	Yes, it is already garrisoned.
HAMLET	Two thousand souls and twenty thousand ducats 25
	Will not debate the question of this straw.
	This is th' imposthume of much wealth and peace,
	That inward breaks, and shows no cause without
	Why the man dies. — I humbly thank you, sir.
CAPTAIN	God b' wi' you, sir. [Exit.]
ROSENCRANTZ	Will't please you go, my lord? 30
HAMLET	I'll be with you straight. Go a little before.

[Exeunt all but Hamlet.]

How all occasions do inform against me‡
And spur my dull revenge. What is a man,
If his chief good and market of his time
Be but to sleep and feed? A beast, no more.   35   *what separates*
Sure he that made us with such large discourse,   *man from beast:*
Looking before and after, gave us not   *reason (+aprehension)*
That capability and godlike <u>reason</u>
To <u>fust</u> in us unused. Now, whether it be
Bestial oblivion, or some craven scruple   40
Of thinking too precisely on th' event, —
critique of reason: A thought which, quartered, hath but one part wisdom
thinking too much   And ever three parts coward, — I do not know
prevents action   Why yet I live to say "This thing's to do,"
Sith I have cause, and will, and strength, and means   45
To do't. Examples gross as earth exhort me.
Witness this army of such mass and charge,
Led by a delicate and tender prince,
Whose spirit, with divine ambition puffed,
Makes mouths at the invisible event,   50

---

26. **debate:** settle by combat. 27. **imposthume:** internal abscess or ulcer. Hamlet means that such wars are the result of the corruption which comes from too much peace and luxury. [Idle hands looking for something to do choose to go to war for no reason except the fame. EDS.] 32. **inform against me:** denounce me. 34. **market of his time:** what he gets in payment for his time. 36. **discourse:** faculty of reasoning. 37. **Looking before and after:** ability to reason logically [and to recollect facts and anticipate events. EDS.] 38. **Godlike:** [reason gives us kinship to God. EDS.] and distinguishes us from beasts. 39. **fust:** grow musty from disuse. 40. **Bestial oblivion:** the dullness of animals. 41. **thinking...event:** considering too carefully what the outcome may be. 43-6. **I do not...do't:** It seems that Hamlet at this moment, under virtual arrest, does not have the means to do what he wants to do. 45. **Sith:** since. 46. **gross:** large, hence "easily seen." 47. **charge:** expense. 50. **Makes mouths at:** holds in contempt.—**event:** outcome.

---

‡   Branagh makes of Hamlet's last soliloquy a rousing pledge to do great things, backed by swelling music, with an ever receding camera seeming to embrace a whole wintry world. The film has an intermission here. Most productions make the speech contemplative or quietly purposeful.

Exposing what is mortal and unsure
To all that fortune, death, and danger dare,
Even for an eggshell. Rightly to be great
Is not to stir without great argument,
But greatly to find quarrel in a straw   55
When honor's at the stake. How stand I then,
That have a father killed, a mother stained,
Excitements of my reason and my blood,
And let all sleep, while to my shame I see
The imminent death of twenty thousand men   60
That for a fantasy and trick of fame
Go to their graves like beds, fight for a plot
Whereon the numbers cannot try the cause,
Which is not tomb enough and continent
To hide the slain? O, from this time forth,   65
My thoughts be bloody, or be nothing worth.

thoughts not actions   *Exit.*

SCENE V. [*Elsinore. A room in the Castle.*]

Enter Horatio, Queen*, and a Gentleman.

QUEEN   I will not speak with her.
GENTLEMAN   She is importunate, indeed distract. Her mood will needs be
            pitied.

QUEEN   What would she have?
GENTLEMAN   She speaks much of her father; says she hears
            There's tricks i' th' world, and hems, and beats her heart;   5
            Spurns enviously at straws; speaks things in doubt,
            That carry but half sense. Her speech is nothing,

---

53–6. **Rightly...stake:** True nobility of soul is to restrain one's self unless there is great cause, but nobly to recognize even a trifle as such a cause, when honor is at issue. Hamlet plays on multiple meanings of the word "great." *Greatly* in line 55 means "nobly," "as a great soul should." 61. **a fantasy:** a whim.—**trick of fame:** a matter affecting one's reputation in the slightest degree. 63. **Whereon... cause:** not big enough to hold the men needed to settle the case by combat. 64. **continent:** receptacle. 66. **My thoughts...bloody:** This is the last time Hamlet expresses this intention; when he speaks next of his cause to Horatio, his words are much milder.

SCENE V
1–20. The text follows the Second Quarto except in line 16 ("Let her come in"), which the Quarto gives to Horatio. The Folio gives it to the Queen, to whom it also assigns "'Twere good...minds." The Gentleman is not in the Folio, which gives his lines to Horatio. 5. **tricks:** deceits. 6. **Spurns enviously at straws:** takes offence at trifles.

*   Scott's Queen sits brooding.

	Yet the unshaped use of it doth move	
	The hearers to collection; they aim at it,	
	And botch the words up fit to their own thoughts;	10
	Which, as her winks and nods and gestures yield them,	
	Indeed would make one think there might be thought,	
	Though nothing sure, yet much unhappily.	

HORATIO   'Twere good she were spoken with; for she may strew
            Dangerous conjectures in ill-breeding minds.   15

QUEEN   Let her come in.

                                        [*Exit Gentleman.*]

            [*Aside*] To my sick soul (as sin's true nature is)
            Each toy seems prologue to some great amiss.
            So full of artless jealousy is guilt
            It spills itself in fearing to be spilt.   20

                    Enter Ophelia distracted.[†]

OPHELIA   Where is the beauteous Majesty of Denmark?

QUEEN   How now, Ophelia?[‡]

OPHELIA   (*sings*)

                How should I your true-love know
                    From another one?
                By his cockle hat and staff   25
                    And his sandal shoon.

8-9. **the unshapéd...collection:** Those who hear her disconnected speech naturally try to make sense of it. —**aim:** guess. 10. **botch...thoughts:** patch the words up to fit what they already think about Polonius's death. [EDS.] 11. **Which:** The antecedent is *words* in the previous line. —**as...them:** These words, uttered as they are with nods and winks, *do* appear to give some ground for suspicion. 15. **ill-breeding:** prone to evil thoughts. 18. **toy:** trifle.—**amiss:** misfortune. 19. **artless jealousy:** unreasonable or unwise suspicion. 20. **spills:** destroys. The guilty person's wariness often causes that person to act suspiciously enough to raise suspicion in others. Thus the Queen's avoidance of Ophelia might have caused that very suspicion which she wished to avoid. [She may wish to avoid Ophelia simply because she cannot bear her suffering. EDS.] —*Enter Ophelia distracted:* So in the Folio. The Second Quarto has simply "*Enter Ophelia*" (after line 16). The First Quarto reads "*Enter Ofelia playing on a Lute, and her haire downe singing.*" 23 ff. The fragments that Ophelia sings appear to be bits that would be familiar to the Elizabethan audience. —**your true-love:** your affianced lover. 25. **cockle hat and staff:** The signs of a pilgrim [someone traveling to a holy place. EDS.]. A cockle shell stuck in the hat was originally a sign that the wearer had been on a pilgrimage to the shrine of St. James at Compostela, in Spanish Galicia. See *Romeo and Juliet* 1.5.96 ff. That lovers are pilgrims and their lady-loves are saints was a common metaphor.

---

†   In Branagh's film, the brutality towards Ophelia begun in 4.2 continues, reflecting the norms of nineteenth–century treatment of the insane. At her entrance, she is straitjacketed. Later, though she had docilely stood waiting to re-enter her padded cell, she is brutally hosed down there.

‡   Scott's Ophelia wears her father's bloody vest and his jacket. The Queen weeps with her. Because Ophelia has been so strong, her madness is most pitiable.

QUEEN   Alas, sweet lady, what imports this song?

OPHELIA   Say you? Nay, pray you mark.

(*Sings*)
> He is dead and gone, lady,
> > He is dead and gone;
> At his head a grass-green turf,
> > At his heels a stone.   30

O, ho!

QUEEN   Nay, but Ophelia —

OPHELIA   Pray you mark.

(*sings*)
> White his shroud as the mountain snow—   35

Enter King.

QUEEN   Alas, look here, my lord.

OPHELIA   (*sings*)
> Larded all with sweet flowers;
> > Which bewept to the grave did not go
> With true-love showers.

KING   How do you, pretty lady?   40

OPHELIA   Well, God dild you. They say the owl was a baker's daughter. Lord, we know what we are, but know not what we may be. God be at your table.

KING   Conceit upon her father.   45

OPHELIA   Pray let's have no words of this; but when they ask you what it means, say you this:

(*Sings*)
> Tomorrow is Saint Valentine's day,*
> All in the morning betime,
> And I a maid at your window,   50

---

26. **imports:** means. [EDS.] 27. **Say you?** Is that what you wish me to tell you? 37. **Larded:** bedecked. 38. **did not go:** All the Quartos and Folios have "not." We are to regard it as Ophelia's insertion in the verse. She suddenly remembers that the words of the song do not quite agree with the facts of her father's burial, which was hasty and without the usual ceremonies. See lines 83–4, 213–15. 41. **God dild you:** God yield (i.e., repay) you. **—the owl:** In folklore, a baker's daughter was turned into an owl when she selfishly denied bread to Jesus. [EDS.] 44. **God be at your table:** In her madness Ophelia uses a form of blessing that might be spoken by one who enters and finds a company at dinner. 45. **Conceit:** imagination, "Her mind is running on her father." 48. **Tomorrow...day:** This song alludes to the custom of the first girl seen by a man on the morning of this day being considered his Valentine or true-love. 49. **betime:** early.

---

*   Ophelia's bawdy song is often accompanied by crude gestures of coitus. The BBC's Ophelia confuses the King with her seductive gestures to him. During Ophelia's song, Branagh intercuts images of Hamlet and Ophelia in bed (the third time her thoughts have turned to their lovemaking) and thus links her song with their affair. Hamlet, like the lover in the song, has abandoned her.

To be your Valentine.

Then up he rose and donned his clothes
    And dupped the chamber door,
Let in the maid, that out a maid *taken virginity*
    Never departed more.   55

KING   Pretty Ophelia.

OPHELIA   Indeed, la, without an oath, I'll make an end on't.
[*Sings*]   By Gis and by Saint Charity,
    Alack, and fie for shame.
Young men will do't if they come to't.   60
    By Cock, they are to blame.

Quoth she, "Before you tumbled me,
    You promised me to wed."

He answers:

"So would I 'a' done, by yonder sun,   65
    An thou hadst not come to my bed."

KING   How long hath she been thus?

OPHELIA   I hope all will be well. We must be patient; but
    father? I cannot choose but weep to think
they would lay him i' th' cold ground. My
brother shall know of it; and so I thank you
for your good counsel. Come, my coach.
Good night, ladies. Good night, sweet
ladies. Good night, good night.   *Exit.*

KING   Follow her close; give her good watch, I pray you.   75
                  [*Exit Horatio.*]

blames her O, this is the poison of deep grief; it springs
madness on fathers death All from her father's death. O Gertrude, Gertrude,†

---

53. **dupped:** opened. 58. **By Gis:** a common contraction of "by Jesus." 61. **Cock:** A vulgar substitute for *God* in oaths [also a bawdy reference to "penis." EDS.] 69. **cannot choose but weep:** cannot help weeping. 76-7. **this is the poison...death:** The King sums up the meaning of Ophelia's madness in the same way the Gentleman had introduced it. Laertes agrees with the King's diagnosis (lines 156 ff.). Disappointed love and Hamlet's madness had made Ophelia "deject and wretched" (3.1.163), but it is the mysterious tragedy of her father's death that has driven her mad. [She may not know that Hamlet had killed him; if she does, that knowledge would exacerbate the effect. The sexuality of her song has suggested to some that she is not as innocent as her brother and father wanted to keep her; but her words could also have been induced by their suspicions of Hamlet's intentions. EDS.] 77. **Gertrude, Gertrude:** The King appeals to her for sympathy in his troubles. [EDS.] 77–96. The King seems to feels genuine sorrow for Polonius and Ophelia; and, besides, their fate has involved him in such difficulties that he seems to be hemmed in by troubles which are ever drawing nearer.

---

†   Starting the scene at this line before returning to its beginning, Branagh reviews images from 4.3 to provide a link between his two acts. Scott's Gertrude is cool to the King, but he does not seem to notice.

When sorrows come, they come not single spies,
But in battalions. First, her father slain;
Next, your son gone, and he most violent author   80
Of his own just remove; the people muddied,
Thick and unwholesome in their thoughts and whispers
For good Polonius' death, and we have done but greenly
In hugger-mugger to inter him; poor Ophelia
Divided from herself and her fair judgment,   85
Without the which we are pictures or mere beasts;
Last, and as much containing as all these,
Her brother is in secret come from France;
Feeds on his wonder, keeps himself in clouds,
And wants not buzzers to infect his ear   90
With pestilent speeches of his father's death,
Wherein necessity, of matter beggared,
Will nothing stick our person to arraign
In ear and ear. O my dear Gertrude, this,
Like to a murd'ring piece, in many places   95
Gives me superfluous death.

                                         A noise within.

QUEEN   Alack, what noise is this?

KING   Where are my Switzers? Let them guard the door.

                    Enter a Messenger.

            What is the matter?

MESSENGER Save yourself, my lord:
The ocean, overpeering of his list,
Eats not the flats with more impetuous haste   100
Than young Laertes, in a riotous head,

78-9. **When...battalions:** Proverbial. [A single soldier (spy) might scope out an enemy's position, but in this case a whole battalion of enemy soldiers (figuratively) assails the King. EDS.] 81. **muddied:** The muddy bottom of the people's minds has been stirred up by angry suspicions, and their thoughts are roiled and turbid. 83. **we:** I—not, you and I.—**done but greenly:** acted with childish folly. 84. **In hugger-mugger:** in haste and secrecy. Polonius had been buried without the ceremonies that befit his rank. See lines 213–15. 89. **Feeds...clouds:** Instead of trying to discover the facts about his father's death, Laertes does nothing but wonder about it, making such wonder his only food for thought. Thus he keeps himself in a state of willful uncertainty and confusion. 90. **wants not buzzers:** lacks not scandalmongers who buzz or whisper in his ear. 92-4. **necessity, of matter beggared:** The necessity of making up a good story without materials drives these scandalmongers to accuse the King. 93. **Will nothing stick:** wont hesitate to personally accuse.—**our person:** me the King, as responsible for the death of Polonius, as his actual murderer. Compare lines 127, 149–152. 94. **In ear and ear:** in one ear and then the other; these "buzzers" surround him. 95. **a murd'ring piece:** a kind of mortar [cannon. EDS.] loaded with a variety of missiles and intended to scatter its shot; also called a *murderer*. 97. **my Switzers:** In Shakespeare's time the Swiss furnished bodyguards to many foreign princes. The Pope still has such a guard in the Vatican. 99–101. **overpeering of his list:** when it towers above its boundary or limit (high-water mark). —**the flats:** the low country near the sea. —**head:** armed band.

O'erbears your officers. The rabble call him lord;
And, as the world were now but to begin,
Antiquity forgot, custom not known,
The ratifiers and props of every word,   105
They cry "Choose we. Laertes shall be King"
Caps, hands, and tongues applaud it to the
clouds, "Laertes shall be King Laertes King"

A noise within.

QUEEN   How cheerfully on the false trail they cry.
            O, this is counter, you false Danish dogs.

KING   The doors are broke.

                Enter Laertes with others.

LAERTES   Where is this king? — Sirs, stand you all without.

ALL   No, let's come in.

LAERTES   I pray you give me leave.

ALL   We will, we will.

LAERTES   I thank you. Keep the door.   *[Exeunt his Followers]*
            O thou vile king,   115
            Give me my father.

QUEEN   Calmly, good Laertes.†

LAERTES   That drop of blood that's calm proclaims me bastard;   foil
            Cries cuckold to my father; brands the harlot ↳Hamlet
            Even here between the chaste unsmirched brows
            Of my true mother.

KING   What is the cause, Laertes,   120
            That thy rebellion looks so giantlike?

103–6. **And…Choose we:** "Let *us* choose!" *Ratifiers and props* refers to *they*, the rabble. 109 ff. In this terrifying situation the Queen appears as a fearless and high-spirited woman, while Claudius meets the furious mob with dignity and courage. 110. **counter:** A hound "hunts counter" (*contre, contra*) when he follows the scent backward—away from the animal pursued. 113. **give me leave:** leave and let me go in alone. 114. **We will:** The fact that Laertes has the mob under control makes him all the more terrifying and emphasizes the King's fortitude. 115 ff. Henceforth Laertes appears as the typical [myopically driven. EDS.] avenger. He serves as a complete foil to Hamlet in this regard. He assumes that the King is somehow guilty of Polonius's death and acts accordingly, without weighing the evidence. Then, informed that Hamlet was the slayer, he joins in the King's plot without scruple and violates his own code of honor. Witness his confession in 5.2.324 ff.

---

†   Gertrude in almost every performance shows her mettle in confronting Laertes. Branagh's
     Gertrude listens carefully as her husband turns Laertes's wrath against Hamlet. Her recognition
     of his betrayal ultimately separates them for the first time.

Let him go, Gertrude. Do not fear our person.
There's such divinity doth hedge a king
That treason can but peep to what it would,
Acts little of his will. Tell me, Laertes,   125
Why thou art thus incensed. Let him go, Gertrude.
Speak, man.

LAERTES   Where is my father?

KING   Dead.

QUEEN   But not by him. —defends Claudius —dependence

KING   Let him demand his fill.

LAERTES   How came he dead? I'll not be juggled with: 130
To hell, allegiance. Vows, to the blackest devil.
Conscience and grace, to the profoundest pit.
I dare damnation. To this point I stand,
That both the worlds I give to negligence,
Let come what comes; only I'll be revenged   135
Most throughly for my father.

KING   Who shall stay you?

LAERTES   My will, not all the world.
And for my means, I'll husband them so well
They shall go far with little.

KING   Good Laertes,
If you desire to know the certainty   140
Of your dear father's death, is't writ in your revenge
That swoopstake you will draw both friend and foe,
Winner and loser?

LAERTES   None but his enemies.

KING   Will you know them then?

LAERTES   To his good friends thus wide I'll ope my arms   145
And, like the kind life-rend'ring pelican,
Repast them with my blood.

---

122. **Let him go, Gertrude:** The Queen has caught hold of Laertes to prevent his attacking the King. [The King repeats his request to the Queen in line 126; she hasn't obeyed him. EDS.] 123. **divinity doth hedge a king:** God protects kings, a nervy statement by a man who murdered a king. [EDS.] 124-5. **peep to:** observe from a distance, approaching no closer than the protecting hedge or barrier which "divine right" builds about the monarch. 132. **grace:** regard for God's laws. 134. **both the worlds:** He cares not what may happen to him, either in this world or the next, if only he can avenge his father's death. Contrast Hamlet's scruple in 2.2.626 ff. 136. **throughly:** thoroughly. 137. **My will...world:** Nothing shall stop me, not even the whole world. 142-3. **That swoopstake...loser:** that you are determined to include in your revenge both friend and foe, as if, in gaming, you were to sweep from the board all the money in sight, whether it belonged to the winner or to the loser. 146. **pelican:** Some people believed that the mother pelican drew blood from her own breast to feed her young.

KING	Why, now you speak
	Like a good child and a true gentleman.
	That I am guiltless of your father's death,
	And am most sensibly in grief for it, 150
	It shall as level to your judgment pierce
	As day does to your eye.

A noise within: "Let her come in."

LAERTES   How now? What noise is that?

Enter Ophelia.[†]

O heat, dry up my brains! Tears seven times salt
Burn out the sense and virtue of mine eye.   155
By heaven, thy madness shall be paid by weight
Till our scale turn the beam. O rose of May.
Dear maid, kind sister, sweet Ophelia.
O heavens. is't possible a young maid's wits
Should be as mortal as an old man's life?   160
Nature is fine in love, and where 'tis fine,
It sends some precious instance of itself
After the thing it loves.

OPHELIA   (*sings*)

  They bore him barefaced on the bier
    (Hey non nony, nony, hey nony)
  And in his grave rained many a tear.
      Fare you well, my dove.

LAERTES   Hadst thou thy wits, and didst persuade revenge,
It could not move thus,   169

OPHELIA   You must sing "A-down a-down, and you
call him a-down-a." O, how the wheel becomes
it. It is the false steward, that stole his master's
daughter.

---

151. **as level:** with as sure an aim.—**pierce:** i.e., through all doubts and obscurities, as the sun pierces the clouds and mists. 153. ***Enter Ophelia:*** This is the first time Laertes has seen Ophelia since she went mad. Her entrance at this crisis revives and intensifies his rage against the unknown murderer, and threatens to undo all that Claudius has accomplished in the way of controlling him. 155. **virtue:** faculty. 161–3. **Nature...loves:** It is natural to give a part of one's self to those whom one loves. EDS.] *Nature* is "human nature." *Instance* combines the two common meanings of "sample" and "proof." Ophelia's nature has sent her "wits" after her father (into the grave), as a precious part of itself in proof of love. 171. **the wheel:** the wheel is the song's refrain, presumably *a-down a-down.* [EDS.] —**becomes it:** suits the ballad and its tune. 172. **It is...steward:** The song tells the story of the false steward.

---

†   Zeffirelli's Ophelia seats herself on the King's throne during her mad scene, quietly sorting small bones and straws while delivering her lines; she comes down from the dais to distribute the strange objects. Branagh's flowers are all imaginary.

Zeffirelli's Ophelia (Helena Bonham Carter) has climbed into the King's throne where she sorts twigs and small bones that figure as the herbs and flowers she distributes (4.5.170-83).

LAERTES   This nothing's more than matter.

OPHELIA   There's rosemary, that's for remembrance.
Pray you, love, remember. And there is pansies,
that's for thoughts.

LAERTES   A document in madness. Thoughts and remembrance
fitted.   179

OPHELIA   There's fennel for you, and columbines. There's
rue for you, and here's some for me. We may
call it herb of grace o' Sundays. O, you must
wear your rue with a difference. There's a daisy.
I would give you some violets, but they withered all

174. **This...matter:** This random talk of hers is more significant (of what she has suffered) than sane speech could be. 175 ff. Whether Ophelia brings flowers and herbs on the stage or simply imagines them, nobody can tell. There is no indication in the old stage directions how the distribution (real or imagined) was made. It is arguable, however, that she gives rosemary and pansies to Laertes, fennel and columbines to the King, and rue to the Queen, saving some for herself. The daisy remains in doubt. Perhaps she gave it to the King or the Queen [see 183 below. EDS.]. 175. **that's for remembrance:** The smell of rosemary was thought to strengthen the memory. 176. **thoughts:** *Pansy* comes from the French *pensée* [meaning *thoughts*. EDS.]. 178. **A document in madness:** A piece of instruction given to me in this mad talk. What the instruction is we learn from the next sentence: "Thoughts and remembrance fit together." 180. **fennel:** a symbol of flattery and deceit. 181 **rue:** Since rue is bitter, and since its name coincides with the verb *rue*, the herb became a symbol for sorrow or repentance. Its name *herb of grace* was associated with the idea of repentance for one's sins. 183. **with a difference:** An heraldic term for a variation (usually slight) in a family coat of arms, indicating that the wearer belonged to a younger branch of the family. Ophelia means merely that the Queen's cause of sorrow differs from hers; but the audience may feel that rue should mean "grief" in Ophelia's case, "repentance for sin" in the Queen's.—**a daisy:** symbolizes dissemblance. [EDS.] 184. **violets:** symbolizes faithfulness. [EDS.]

	when my father died. They say he made a good	
	end.	186
[Sings]	For bonny sweet Robin is all my joy.	
LAERTES	Thought and affliction, passion, hell itself,	
	She turns to favor and to prettiness.	
OPHELIA	(*sings*)	

And will he not come again?   190
And will he not come again?
    No, no, he is dead;
    Go to thy deathbed;
He never will come again.

His beard was as white as snow,   195
All flaxen was his poll.
    He is gone, he is gone,
    And we cast away moan.
God 'a' mercy on his soul.

And of all Christian souls, I pray God. God
b' wi' you.   *Exit.*

LAERTES	Do you see this, O God?	201
KING	Laertes, I must commune with your grief,	
	Or you deny me right. Go but apart,	
	Make choice of whom your wisest friends you will,	
	And they shall hear and judge 'twixt you and me.	205
	If by direct or by collateral hand	
	They find us touched, we will our kingdom give,	
	Our crown, our life, and all that we call ours,	
	To you in satisfaction; but if not,	
	Be you content to lend your patience to us,	210
	And we shall jointly labor with your soul	
	To give it due content.	
LAERTES	Let this be so.	
	His means of death, his obscure funeral —	
	No trophy, sword, nor hatchment o'er his bones,	
	No noble rite nor formal ostentation, —	215

---

187. **For...joy:** From an old song, found in *The Two Noble Kinsmen* (4.1.107-8). 188. **Thought:** melancholy thought, sorrow. Compare 3.1.85. —**passion:** passionate grief. 189. **favor:** beauty. 200. **And...souls:** An old formula of prayer.—**of:** on.—**God b' wi' you:** good-bye. 206. **collateral:** indirect. 207. **touched:** i.e., with guilt in the death of Polonius. 214. **trophy:** anything that serves as a memorial of honor.—**hatchment:** a tablet, with coat of arms and mourning emblems, set up on a tomb or a house-front, or over a gate. 215. **formal ostentation:** due and proper ceremony.

Cry to be heard, as 'twere from heaven to earth,
That I must call't in question.

KING   So you shall;
And where th' offence is let the great axe fall.
I pray you go with me.   *Exeunt.*

SCENE VI. [*Elsinore. Another room in the Castle.*]

Enter Horatio with an Attendant.

HORATIO   What are they that would speak with me?[†]

SERVANT   Seafaring men, sir. They say they have letters for
you.

HORATIO   Let them come in.
                              [*Exit Attendant.*]
I do not know from what part of the world
I should be greeted, if not from Lord Hamlet.   5

Enter Sailors.

SAILOR   God bless you, sir.

HORATIO   Let him bless thee too.
SAILOR.   'A shall, sir, an't please him. There's a letter for you,
sir, — it comes from th' ambassador that was bound
for England — if your name be Horatio, as I am let
to know it is.   11

HORATIO   (*reads the letter*) "Horatio, when thou shalt have overlooked
this, give these fellows some means to the King. They
have letters for him. Ere we were two days old at sea, a
pirate of very war-like appointment gave us chase.
Finding our selves too slow of sail, we put on a compelled
valor, and in the grapple I boarded them. On the instant
they got clear of our ship; so I alone be came their prisoner.

---

216. **as...earth:** as if by a direct summons from God. 217. **That:** so that. 218. **the great axe:** the axe of
vengeance.
SCENE VI.
7-8. There is a mild humor in Horatio's remark, for the sailor (who doubtless looks like the pirate that
he is), may well need God's blessing.—**'A:** He.—**an't:** if it. 12-30. The letter: **overlooked:** read over. —
means: access. — **appointment:** equipment.

---

† Branagh prepares for Horatio's abandonment of Ophelia, whom he has been told to watch
carefully. He sees her safely, as he assumes, in her cell being hosed down. After he turns away, in
a closeup, she slyly opens her mouth showing the key she has somehow obtained.

They have dealt with me like thieves of mercy; but they knew
what they did: I am to do a good turn for them. Let the King
have the letters I have sent, and repair thou to me with as much
speed as thou wouldst fly death. I have words to speak in
thine ear will make thee dumb; yet are they much too light for
the bore of the matter. These good fellows will bring thee
where I am. Rosencrantz and Guildenstern hold their course
for England. Of them I have much to tell thee. Farewell.   30
              "He that thou knowest thine, Hamlet."

Come, I will give you way for these your letters, And do't
the speedier that you may direct me to him from whom
you brought them.   *Exeunt.*

SCENE VII. [*Elsinore. Another room in the Castle.*]

Enter King and Laertes.‡

KING   Now must your conscience my acquittance seal,
              And you must put me in your heart for friend,
              Sith you have heard, and with a knowing ear,
              That he which hath your noble father slain
              Pursued my life.

LAERTES   It well appears. But tell me   5
              Why you proceeded not against these feats
              So crimeful and so capital in nature,
              As by your safety, wisdom, all things else,
              You mainly were stirred up.

KING   O, for two special reasons,

— **thieves of mercy:** merciful robbers.—**they knew what they did:** they understood what was in their own interest.—**a good turn:** to repay their kindness to him, perhaps by seeing to it that their letters get to the King. [EDS.]— **repair:** return. [EDS.]—**too light...matter:** A figure from gunnery: "not weighty enough to do the subject justice."—**good fellows:** Humorously ambiguous; for this phrase was often (and still is) equivalent to "crooks." 32. **give you way:** procure you access. For other indications that Horatio stands well with the King and Queen see 4.5.14–16; 5.1.316.

SCENE VII.
1. **acquittance seal**—exonerate me. [EDS.] 2. **put...friend:** acknowledge me as a friend. [EDS.] 3. **sith**—since. [EDS.] 6. **proceeded:** i.e., by bringing Hamlet to trial for murder and treason.—**feats:** deeds. 8. **your safety:** regard for your own safety. 9. **mainly:** strongly. — **reasons:** These two reasons are apparently genuine. The Queen's love for her son and the King's love for the Queen are strong motives in the drama, and the necessity of taking the Danish people into account has just been proved by their insurrection under the lead of Laertes.

‡   Branagh's King and Laertes drink heavily, as they lay their plans, polishing off nearly half a decanter of liquor.

	Which may to you, perhaps, seem much unsinewed,	10
	But yet to me they are strong. The Queen his mother	
	Lives almost by his looks; and for myself, —	
	My virtue or my plague, be it either which, —	
	She's so conjunctive to my life and soul	
	That, as the star moves not but in his sphere,	15
	I could not but by her. The other motive	
	Why to a public count I might not go	
	Is the great love the general gender bear him,	
	Who, dipping all his faults in their affection,	
	Would, like the spring that turneth wood to stone,	20
	Convert his gyves to graces; so that my arrows,	
	Too slightly timbered for so loud a wind,	
	Would have reverted to my bow again,	
	And not where I had aimed them.	
LAERTES	And so have I a noble father lost;	25
	A sister driven into desp'rate terms,	
	Whose worth, if praises may go back again,	
	Stood challenger on mount of all the age	
	For her perfections. But my revenge will come.	
KING	Break not your sleeps for that. You must not think	30
	That we are made of stuff so flat and dull	
	That we can let our beard be shook with danger,	
	And think it pastime. You shortly shall hear more.	
	I loved your father, and we love ourself,	
	And that, I hope, will teach you to imagine —	35

Enter a Messenger with letters.

	How now? What news?	
MESSENGER	Letters, my lord, from Hamlet:	
	This to your Majesty; this to the Queen	
KING	From Hamlet? Who brought them?	
MESSENGER	Sailors, my lord, they say; I saw them not.	

---

13. **be it either which:** whichever of the two (*virtue* or *plague*) you may choose to call it. 14. **conjunctive:** dear. 15. **in his sphere:** i.e., in its hollow crystalline sphere, concentric with the earth (in accordance with the Ptolemaic astronomy). 16. **motive:** reason. 17. **count:** judgment. —**might:** could. 18. **the general gender:** the common people. 20. **the spring...to stone:** Near Stratford there were springs that contained enough lime to petrify wood. 21. **Convert...graces:** change his impediments to honors. 26. **terms:** condition. 27. **if...again:** if I may commend her for what she was before she lost her mind. 28-9. **Stood challenger...perfections:** was exalted above the whole contemporary world, challenging it to bring forward any other woman to equal her in excellence. 30-5. Here the King shows his bitter enmity toward Hamlet [and determination to act against him. EDS.]. 31. **flat and dull:** incapable of resenting an injury. 33. **shall hear more:** i.e., when the news comes from England. 34. **I...we:** The King changes from the personal *I* to the royal *we*.

| | They were given me by Claudio; he received them | 40 |
| | Of him that brought them. | |

KING   Laertes, you shall hear them.
Leave us.

Exit Messenger.

[*Reads*] "High and Mighty, — You shall know I am
set naked on your kingdom. Tomorrow shall I beg
leave to see your kingly eyes; when I shall (first
asking your pardon thereunto) recount the occasion
of my sudden and more strange return.

"Hamlet."

What should this mean? Are all the rest come back?   50
Or is it some abuse, and no such thing?

LAERTES   Know you the hand?

KING   'Tis Hamlet's character. "Naked."
And in a postscript here, he says "alone."
Can you advise me?

LAERTES   I am lost in it, my lord. But let him come!   55
It warms the very sickness in my heart
That I shall live and tell him to his teeth,
"Thus didest thou."

KING   If it be so, Laertes
(As how should it be so? how otherwise?),
Will you be ruled by me?

LAERTES   Ay, my lord,   60
So you will not o'errule me to a peace.

KING   To thine own peace. If he be now returned,
As checking at his voyage, and that he means
No more to undertake it, I will work him
To an exploit now ripe in my device,   65

---

41. **Of:** from. 46. **your kingly eyes:** A formal and courtly phrase (like "High and Mighty") masking or perhaps sarcastically showing Hamlet's scorn and hatred. Compare 1.2.116: "in the cheer and comfort of our eye"; in 4.4.6: Fortinbras says he is willing to "express our duty in his eye"; and similar expressions in which *eye* is used for "the royal presence." 47. **pardon:** permission. 51. **abuse:** deceit.—**no such thing:** not a reality. 52. **character:** handwriting. 54. **Can...advise me?** The King flatteringly elevates Laertes to the position of chief advisor. [EDS.] 59. **how...otherwise?** How can it be true that he has returned? And yet, on the other hand, how can it be otherwise than true? The King finds it hard to believe that Hamlet has come back; yet he cannot explain the letter upon any other supposition. 60. **Will you be ruled by me?** Even in his perplexity, Claudius is already forming another plan to destroy Hamlet. 61. **So:** provided that. 63. **checking at his voyage:** refusing to continue his voyage. A falcon is said to "check" when she forsakes her proper prey for another inferior kind.

Under the which he shall not choose but fall;
And for his death no wind of blame shall breathe,
But even his mother shall uncharge the practice
And call it accident.

LAERTES   My lord, I will be ruled;
The rather, if you could devise it so   70
That I might be the organ.

KING   It falls right.
You have been talked of since your travel much,
And that in Hamlet's hearing, for a quality
Wherein they say you shine. Your sum of parts
Did not together pluck such envy from him   75
As did that one; and that, in my regard,
Of the unworthiest siege.

LAERTES   What part is that, my lord?

KING   A very riband in the cap of youth —
Yet needful too; for youth no less becomes
The light and careless livery that it wears   80
Than settled age his sables and his weeds,
Importing health and graveness. Two months since
Here was a gentleman of Normandy.
I have seen myself, and served against, the French,
And they can well on horseback; but this gallant   85
Had witchcraft in't. He grew unto his seat,
And to such wondrous doing brought his horse
As had he been incorpsed and demi-natured
With the brave beast. So far he topped my thought.
That I, in forgery of shapes and tricks,   90
Come short of what he did.

LAERTES   A Norman was't?

---

66. **shall not choose but fall:** cannot help falling. 68. **uncharge the practice:** not blame our plot. 71. **the organ:** the agent.—**It falls right:** The circumstances fit your wish. 73. **a quality:** an accomplishment. 74. **Your sum of parts:** the sum total of your accomplishments. 77. **siege:** rank; literally, seat. 78. **A very riband...youth:** an ornament of youth. It was the fashion for courtiers to wear a jewel or ribbon on the cap. 79-82. **youth no less becomes...graveness:** In modern English we should invert the phrase: "The light and trivial sports that characterize youth are just as becoming to the young as the serious and dignified pursuits are to their elders." Shakespeare is fond of metaphors from clothes. 81. **weeds:** attire. 82. **Importing health and graveness:** signifying due care for health and a proper regard for dignity. *Health* is contrasted with *light,* and *graveness* with *careless.* Young men dress lightly and carelessly; their elders wear warmer and more stately attire. 85. **can well on horseback:** are skilful riders. Feats of horsemanship were highly esteemed. 88. **As:** as if.—**incorpsed:** made into one body.—**demi-natured:** so united as to form with the animal a Centaur, half man and half horse. 89. **brave:** noble.—**topped my thought:** surpassed anything that I could even think. 90. **in forgery of shapes and tricks:** in imagining feats of horsemanship.—**did:** Emphatic: "actually performed."

KING	A Norman.
LAERTES	Upon my life, Lamound.
KING	The very same.
LAERTES	I know him well. He is the brooch indeed
	And gem of all the nation.

95

KING	He made confession of you;
	And gave you such a masterly report
	For art and exercise in your defense,
	And for your rapier most especially,
	That he cried out 'twould be a sight indeed

100

	If one could match you. The scrimers of their nation
	He swore had neither motion, guard, nor eye,
	If you opposed them. Sir, this report of his
	Did Hamlet so envenom with his envy
	That he could nothing do but wish and beg

105

| | Your sudden coming o'er to play with you. |
| | Now, out of this — |

| LAERTES | What out of this, my lord? |

KING	Laertes, was your father dear to you?
	Or are you like the painting of a sorrow,
	A face without a heart?

| LAERTES | Why ask you this? |

110

KING	Not that I think you did not love your father;
	But that I know love is begun by time,
	And that I see, in passages of proof,
	Time qualifies the spark and fire of it.
	There lives within the very flame of love

115

| | A kind of wick or snuff that will abate it; |
| | And nothing is at a like goodness still; |

---

96. **He made confession of you:** He admitted that he knew you as an accomplished gentleman. 98. **art and exercise:** skill in both theory and practice.—**defense:** fencing. 101. **scrimers:** fencers (French *escrimeurs*). 104. **with his envy:** This claim does not sound like Hamlet's way. 108. **was your father dear to you?** The treacherous revenge which the King is about to propose is so abhorrent to what he knows to be the feelings of a gentleman that he fears some urging may be necessary. The savage exclamation "To cut his throat i' th' church" convinces him that Laertes will have no scruples (line 127). 111–24. These reflections are curiously similar to the moralizing of the Player King in 3.2.196–209, [and they can suggest the play's criticism of Hamlet's inaction, but then one has to consider the source of these truisms about inaction. EDS.]. 112. **that:** because. 113. **passages of proof:** facts of experience. 114. **qualifies:** weakens. 115–24. Omitted in the Folios. 115-16. **There lives...it:** The very intensity of love serves to abate it, as the flame of a lamp makes the snuff (the charred piece of wick) that deadens the flame and reduces the light. [He may be speaking of his love for the Queen, which has diminished in favor of self-preservation. EDS.] 117. **still:** forever.

For goodness, growing to a plurisy,
Dies in his own too-much. That we would do,
We should do when we would; for this "would" changes,   120
And hath abatements and delays as many
As there are tongues, are hands, are accidents;
And then this "should" is like a spendthrift sigh,
That hurts by easing. But to the quick o' th' ulcer.
Hamlet comes back. What would you undertake   125
To show yourself your father's son in deed
More than in words?

LAERTES   To cut his throat i' th' church.

KING   No place indeed should murther sanctuarize;
Revenge should have no bounds. But, good Laertes,
Will you do this? Keep close within your chamber.   130
Hamlet returned shall know you are come home.
We'll put on those shall praise your excellence
And set a double varnish on the fame
The Frenchman gave you; bring you in fine together
And wager on your heads. He, being remiss,   135
Most generous, and free from all contriving,
Will not peruse the foils; so that with ease,
Or with a little shuffling, you may choose
A sword unbated, and, in a pass of practice,
Requite him for your father.

LAERTES   I will do't.   140
And for that purpose I'll anoint my sword.
I bought an unction of a mountebank,
So mortal that, but dip a knife in it,

---

118. **plurisy:** excess; refers especially to an excess of blood in the system. 119. **his own too-much:** its own excess.—**That:** what. 120. **this "would":** our will to act. 123-4. **And then...easing:** It was believed that a sigh of relief draws blood from the heart and thus weakens it, as when one loses the will to do something but admits inwardly that it must be done *eventually* so that one's conscience is relieved, though one's strength of character is weakened. 124. **to the quick o' th' ulcer:** Let me probe the sore to the quick; that is, Let me put the crucial question without further talk. 127. **To cut his throat i' th' church:** Laertes' ferocity, typical of the unscrupulous "revenger," is enhanced by the King's choric response, in the next line: "Revenge should have no bounds." These lines glance at Hamlet's refusal to kill in the prayer scene (3.3), but again the sources of the opinion have to be weighed in. [EDS.] 132. **We'll put on those shall:** We'll instigate persons who shall. 135. **remiss:** unsuspicious by nature. 136. **generous:** noble-minded. The frankness of the King's praise of Hamlet for qualities that are the opposite of those here shown by Laertes, suggests how sure he now feels of his accomplice. 137. **peruse:** scrutinize. 138. **shuffling:** trickery. 139. **unbated:** not blunted. Rapiers for practice were blunted.—**a pass of practice:** a thrust with this treacherous weapon. *Practice* means "plot," "treachery." 141. **I'll anoint my sword.** [*anoint*: poison. EDS.] This is Laertes at his worst. He forgets his own code of honor, in his reckless pursuit of revenge, although he is aware that Hamlet killed Polonius by mistake for the King. The idea, however, of fencing with poisoned swords is not unknown in Elizabethan literature. 142. **unction:** ointment; [poison. EDS.]. —**mountebank:** quack.

Where it draws blood no cataplasm so rare,
Collected from all simples that have virtue   145
Under the moon, can save the thing from death
This is but scratched withal. I'll touch my point
With this contagion, that, if I gall him slightly,
It may be death.

KING   Let's further think of this,
Weigh what convenience both of time and means   150
May fit us to our shape. If this should fail,
And that our drift look through our bad performance,
'Twere better not assayed. Therefore this project
Should have a back or second, that might hold
If this did blast in proof. Soft. Let me see.   155
We'll make a solemn wager on your cunnings —
I ha't.
When in your motion you are hot and dry —
As make your bouts more violent to that end —
And that he calls for drink, I'll have prepared him   160
A chalice for the nonce; whereon but sipping,
If he by chance escape your venomed stuck,
Our purpose may hold there. — But stay, what noise?

                    Enter Queen.

How now, sweet queen?

QUEEN   One woe doth tread upon another's heel,   165
So fast they follow. Your sister's drowned, Laertes.

LAERTES   Drowned. O, where?

QUEEN   There is a willow grows aslant a brook,[†]
That shows his hoar leaves in the glassy stream.

---

144. **cataplasm:** poultice. 145. **Collected from:** composed of.—**simples:** medicinal plants.—**virtue:** medicinal efficacy. 146. **Under the moon:** i.e., anywhere on earth. An idiomatic phrase. 147. **withal:** with it. 148. **gall:** break the skin; draw blood. 151. **fit us to our shape:** adapt us (in our actions) to our plan. 152. **that...performance:** if our intention should show itself because of our failure to carry it out adroitly.—**that:** if that; if. 155. **did blast in proof:** should burst (fail) when put to the test.—**Soft:** Wait a minute; literally, let's go slowly. 156. **solemn:** formal.—**your cunnings:** your skill as fencers. 158. **dry:** thirsty. 159, **As make...end:** make your bouts vigorous so that he'll be hot and thirsty. 160. **that:** when. 161. **for the nonce:** for that express purpose. 162. **stuck:** thrust. It is the vernacular equivalent of *stoccado,* the Italian fencing term. 165-6. **One woe...follow:** She echoes the King in 4.5.78-9. 169. **hoar:** grey, as the leaves of the willow are on the under side.

---

†   Films often illustrate Gertrude's words while or after she speaks. The gravedigger's and the priest's versions in act V, scene 1 differ from Gertrude's, where the drowning seems accidental. Scott omits her narrative completely, also cutting the two gravediggers.

"There is a willow grows aslant a brook" (4.7.168). Zeffirelli's camera shows Ophelia just before drowning, as the Queen recounts the story of her death (168-81).

	There with fantastic garlands did she come	170
	Of crowflowers, nettles, daisies, and long purples,	
	That liberal shepherds give a grosser name,	
	But our cold maids do dead men's fingers call them.	
	There on the pendent boughs her coronet weeds	
	Clamb'ring to hang, an envious sliver broke,	175
	When down her weedy trophies and herself	
	Fell in the weeping brook. Her clothes spread wide	
	And, mermaid-like, awhile they bore her up;	
	Which time she chanted snatches of old tunes,	
	As one incapable of her own distress,	180
	Or like a creature native and indued	
	Unto that element; but long it could not be	
	Till that her garments, heavy with their drink,	
	Pulled the poor wretch from her melodious lay	
	To muddy death.	
LAERTES	Alas, then she is drowned?	185

170. **There...come.** So the Folio. The Second Quarto reads "therewith fantastique garlands did she make Of Crowflowers," etc. 171. **crowflowers.** Two or three different flowers are so called.—**long purples:** orchids. 172. **liberal:** freely low in their talk. 173. **cold:** chaste.—**dead men's fingers:** Early purple orchids, pale in color, with hand-shaped tubers. [EDS.] 174. **coronet:** woven into wreaths for the head. 175. **envious:** malicious. 179. **tunes.** So the Folio and the First Quarto. The Second Quarto reads *laudes,* i.e., "hymns or psalms of praise." 180. **incapable of:** unaware of. 181. **indued:** adapted by nature.

QUEEN	Drowned, drowned.

LAERTES   Too much of water hast thou, poor Ophelia,
And therefore I forbid my tears; but yet
It is our trick; nature her custom holds,
Let shame say what it will. When these are gone,   190
The woman will be out. Adieu, my lord.
I have a speech of fire, that fain would blaze
But that this folly douts it.   *Exit.*

KING   Let's follow, Gertrude.[†]
How much I had to do to calm his rage.
Now fear I this will give it start again;   195
Therefore let's follow.   *Exeunt.*

ACT V

SCENE I. [*Elsinore. A churchyard.*]

Enter two Clowns, [with spades and pickaxes].

CLOWN   Is she to be buried in Christian burial when she[‡]
willfully seeks her own salvation?

OTHER   I tell thee she is; therefore make her grave straight.
The crowner hath sate on her, and finds it Christian
burial.   5

---

187. **Too much...thou:** This speech would have seemed far less artificial to Shakespeare's contemporaries than it might to us, for such punning expressions had come to be natural in Elizabethan style and were by no means inconsistent with deep feeling. 189. **It is our trick:** To shed tears is a natural human trait. 191. **The woman will be out:** All the womanish qualities of my nature will have spent themselves, and I shall be remorseless in my vengeance. The convention that "tears are womanish" is a recurring theme in Shakespeare, e.g. *Romeo and Juliet* 3.3.114. 193. **this folly douts it:** this natural weakness (my weeping) prevents me from speaking. Laertes can no longer control his weeping.—**douts:** [puts out the speech of fire. EDS.] Compare 1.4.37.

ACT V. SCENE I.
Stage direction. **Clowns:** actors who were meant to amuse the audience; these two are playing a sexton and his assistant. 1. **Christian burial:** Christian funeral service, with burial in consecrated ground, denied to suicides. [EDS.] 1-2. **when she...salvation:** when she willfully seeks to go to heaven before her time. 3. **straight:** immediately. 4. **crowner:** coroner.

---

†   Branagh's King extends his hand, and when the Queen refuses him, he turns away stricken with the recognition that he has lost her.

‡   Zeffirelli, like many other directors, has only one grave digger and thus omits these lines. Branagh retains both.

CLOWN	How can that be, unless she drowned herself in her own defense?
OTHER	Why, 'tis found so.
CLOWN	It must be se offendendo; it cannot be else. For here lies the point: if I drown myself wittingly, it argues an act; and an act hath three branches — it is to act, to do, and to perform; argal, she drowned herself wittingly.
OTHER	Nay, but hear you, Goodman Delver.
CLOWN	Give me leave. Here lies the water; good. Here stands the man; good. If the man go to this water and drown himself, it is, will he nill he, he goes — mark you that. But if the water come to him and drown him, he drowns not himself. Argal, he that is not guilty of his own death shortens not his own life.
OTHER	But is this law?
CLOWN	Ay, marry, is't—crowner's quest law,
OTHER	Will you ha' the truth on't? If this had not been a gentlewoman, she should have been buried out o' Christian burial.
CLOWN	Why, there thou say'st. And the more pity that great folk should have count'nance in this world to drown or hang themselves more than their even-Christen. Come, my spade. There is no ancient gentlemen but gard'ners, ditchers, and grave-makers. They hold up Adam's profession.
OTHER	Was he a gentleman?
CLOWN	'A was the first that ever bore arms,

Line numbers in margin: 13, 25, 35

---

6. **in her own defense:** Self-defense being justification for homicide, the Clown ludicrously jokes that it may justify suicide also. 9. **se offendendo:** in self-*offence*.—the Clown's blunder for *se defendendo,* "in self-defense." [Many of Shakespeare's clowns reach above the language of their social class toward the language of their superiors, producing comical malapropisms; but such errors should not prejudice us against their commonsense humanity. EDS.] 13. **argal:** The Clown's corruption of *ergo,* "therefore," a word often used in formal reasoning. 17. **will he nill he:** will he or will he not; willy-nilly; *nil* is a contraction of *ne* (the negative) and *will.* 25. **quest:** inquest. 26. **an't:** of it. 29. **there thou say'st:** You're right in that. 30. **count'nance:** authorization. The Clown speaks of the liberty to commit suicide as one more unfair advantage which the aristocracy have over the common people. [This is of course a joke, but kings did not overrule the clergy about burial in sacred ground for souls of commoners. See line 252. EDS.] 31. **even-Christen:** fellow Christian. 36. **Was he a gentleman?** The Clown is startled to hear Adam styled a gentleman, for he is familiar with the old rhyme: "When Adam delved and Eve span, Where was then the gentleman?" —'**A:** he.

OTHER	Why, he had none.	
CLOWN	What, art a heathen? How dost thou understand the Scripture? The Scripture says Adam digged. Could he dig without arms? I'll put another question to thee. If thou answerest me not to the purpose, confess thyself —	
OTHER	Go to.	45
CLOWN	What is he that builds stronger than either the mason, the shipwright, or the carpenter?	
OTHER	The gallows-maker; for that frame outlives a thousand tenants.	50
CLOWN	I like thy wit well, in good faith The gallows does well. But how does it well? It does well to those that do ill. Now, thou dost ill to say the gallows is built stronger than the church. Argal, the gallows may do well to thee. To't again, come.	56
OTHER	Who builds stronger than a mason, a shipwright, or a carpenter?	
CLOWN	Ay, tell me that, and unyoke.	
OTHER	Marry, now I can tell.	60
CLOWN	To't.	
OTHER	Mass, I cannot tell.	

Enter Hamlet and Horatio afar off.

| CLOWN | Cudgel thy brains no more about it, for your dull ass will not mend his pace with beating; and when you are asked this question next, say "a grave-maker." The houses he makes lasts till doomsday. Go, get thee to Yaughan; fetch me a stoup of liquor. | |

[Exit Second Clown.]

[Clown digs and] sings.

> In youth when I did love, did love,
>   Methought it was very sweet;   70
> To contract—O—the time for—a—my behove,

---

44. **confess thyself—:** If not interrupted, he would complete the sentence: "confess thyself an ass" or "confess thyself and be hanged," a proverb. [Catholics make a confession before death, especially necessary before a hanging. EDS.] 45. **Go to:** Enough of that and get on with your question. [EDS.] 49. **frame:** structure. 51-2. **does well:** provides a good answer. 59. **unyoke:** unyoke your oxen; call it a day. 62. **Mass:** A common oath, ["By the Mass." EDS.]. 63. **Yaughan:** Yohan or Johan. A local alehouse keeper.—**a stoup:** a big cup. 71. **To contract...behove:** to make time pass pleasantly [and seem shorter. EDS.].

O, methought there—a—was nothing—a—meet.

HAMLET	Has this fellow no feeling of his business, that
	he sings at grave-making?

HORATIO   Custom hath made it in him a property of easiness.   76

HAMLET   'Tis e'en so. The hand of little employment hath the
daintier sense.

CLOWN   (*sings*)

> But age with his stealing steps
>> Hath clawed me in his clutch,
> And hath shipped me intil the land.   80
>> As if I had never been such.

[Throws up a skull.]

HAMLET   That skull had a tongue in it, and could sing once.
How the knave jowls it to the ground, as if 'twere
Cain's jawbone, that did the first murther. This
might be the pate of a politician, which this ass
now o'erreaches; one that would circumvent God,
might it not?

HORATIO   It might, my lord.   89

HAMLET   Or of a courtier, which could say "Good morrow,
sweet lord. How dost thou, good lord?"
This might be my Lord Such-a-one, that
praised my Lord Such-a-one's horse when he
meant to beg it — might it not?

HORATIO   Ay, my lord.   95

HAMLET   Why, e'en so. and now my Lady Worm's, chapless,
and knocked about the mazzard with a sexton's spade.
Here's fine revolution, an we had the trick to see't.
Did these bones cost no more the breeding but to
play at loggets with 'em? Mine ache to think on't.   101

CLOWN   (*sings*)

> A pickaxe and a spade, a spade,
> For and a shrouding sheet;

---

76. **hath made...easiness:** has become uncomplicated by deep thought through practice. [EDS.] 77-8. **The hand...sense:** The hand unaccustomed to manual labor is more sensitive. 79. **clawed:** seized. 79-80. **hath...land:** has stopped my voyage and sent me ashore. 80. **intil:** in to. 84. **jowls:** tosses. 87. **o'erreaches:** gets the better of.—**one...God:** one who disregards God's laws and apparently escapes unscathed. 96–100. **chapless:** lacking the lower jaw.—**mazzard:** Like *pate,* an old word for "head."—**trick:** knack.—**loggets:** little logs—a game in which the players throw pieces of hard wood at a stake or wooden wheel. 103. **For and:** This simply means "and."

O, a pit of clay for to be made
For such a guest is meet   105

Throws up [another skull.]

HAMLET   There's another. Why may not that be the skull of
             a lawyer? Where be his quiddits now, his quillets,
             his cases, his tenures, and his tricks? Why does
             he suffer this rude knave now to knock him about
             the sconce with a dirty shovel, and will not tell
             him of his action of battery? Hum. This fellow
             might be in's time a great buyer of land, with his   111
             statutes, his recognizances, his fines, his double
             vouchers, his recoveries. Is this the fine of his fines,
             and the recovery of his recoveries, to have his fine
             pate full of fine dirt? Will his vouchers vouch him
             no more of his purchases, and double ones too, than
             the length and breadth of a pair of indentures? The
             very conveyances of his lands will scarcely lie in this
             box; and must th' inheritor himself have no more,
             ha?

HORATIO   Not a jot more, my lord.   122

HAMLET   Is not parchment made of sheepskins?

HORATIO   Ay, my lord, and of calveskins too.

HAMLET   They are sheep and calves which seek out assurance
             in that. I will speak to this fellow. Whose grave's
             this, sirrah?

CLOWN   Mine, sir.

[*Sings.*]   O, a pit of clay for to be made
                         For such a guest is meet.   130

---

107. **quiddits:** hair-splitting definitions. *Quiddity (quidditas)* is an old scholastic word for something's "whatness" or its essential nature.—**quillets:** quibbles.—**tenures:** holdings of real estate. 109. **sconce:** head. 111–21. **buyer of land:** There are constant references in Elizabethan and older literature to the ambition of persons not belonging to the "landed gentry" to purchase estates and thus make themselves gentlemen. In this case it is a successful lawyer that Hamlet imagines as the purchaser.—**statutes:** bonds indicating that one person owes another a certain amount of money. [EDS.] —**the fine...his recoveries:** the final outcome of his fines and the total acquired by his recoveries. "Fine and recovery" was a legal process for changing an entailed estate (forced to descend in a limited way, for example, to the nearest male heir however distant from the owner) into an estate in fee simple (absolute possession with freedom to bestow it on anyone).—**double vouchers:** A recovery with "double voucher" was so called because two persons had to "vouch" for or ensure the tenant's title—**his fine pate:** his subtly clever head.—**indentures:** agreements or contracts, drawn up in duplicate on a single sheet, then cut apart in a zigzag (indented) line. Their fitting together at this line was proof of genuineness.—**conveyances:** deeds.—**inheritor:** possessor, owner.—**ha?** An interrogative "huh?" 126. **sirrah?** A form of *sir*, used in addressing an inferior or to express anger or contempt; often (to boys) as a playful and affectionate term.

HAMLET	I think it be thine indeed for thou liest in't.
CLOWN	You lie out on't, sir, and therefore 'tis not yours. For my part, I do not lie in't, yet it is mine.
HAMLET	Thou dost lie in't, to be in't and say it is thine. 'Tis for the dead, not for the quick; therefore thou liest.
CLOWN	'Tis a quick lie, sir; 'twill away again from me to you. 140
HAMLET	What man dost thou dig it for?
CLOWN	For no man, sir.
HAMLET	What woman then?
CLOWN	For none neither.
HAMLET	Who is to be buried in't? 145
CLOWN	One that was a woman, sir; but, rest her soul, she's dead.
HAMLET	How absolute the knave is! We must speak by the card, or equivocation will undo us. By the *Lord*, Horatio, this three years I have taken note of it, the age is grown so picked that the toe of the peasant comes so near the heel of the courtier he galls his kibe. — How long hast thou been a grave-maker?
CLOWN	Of all the days i' th' year, I came to't that day that our last king Hamlet overcame Fortinbras. 157
HAMLET	How long is that since?
CLOWN	Cannot you tell that? Every fool can tell that. It was the very day that young Hamlet was born — he that is mad[†], and sent into England. 162

131–40. Hamlet uses the familiar *thee* and *thou* to the Sexton, but the Sexton uses the respectful *you* in reply. The inevitable pun on *lie* is elaborated into a game of repartee [in alternating short lines, or *stichomythia*. EDS.]. The Sexton wins by punning on *quick*, which Hamlet has used in the sense of "living." **146. rest her soul:** God give her soul repose. **148–55. How absolute the knave is:** How the fellow insists upon accuracy in language.—**by the card:** by the compass, observing every point..— **equivocation:** ambiguity.—**picked:** choice, refined.—**that the toe...courtier:** that the peasant has become almost as polished in language and manners as the courtier.—**galls his kibe:** follows him so closely that he rubs and irritates the sore on the courtier's heel. **157. Fortinbras:** Shakespeare keeps before us this character who appears only twice (in 4.4 and 5.2). See also 1.1.80–95; 1.2.17–25.

---

† Scott's Hamlet has changed; he is now quiet and sane.

HAMLET	Ay, marry, why was he sent into England?	
CLOWN	Why, because 'a was mad. 'A shall recover his wits there; or, if 'a do not, 'tis no great matter there.	
HAMLET	Why?	
CLOWN	'Twill not be seen in him there. There the men are as mad as he.	170
HAMLET	How came he mad?	
CLOWN	Very strangely, they say.	
HAMLET	How strangely?	
CLOWN	Faith, e'en with losing his wits.	
HAMLET	Upon what ground?	175
CLOWN	Why, here in Denmark. I have been sexton here, man and boy, thirty years.	
HAMLET	How long will a man lie i' th' earth ere he rot?	179
CLOWN	Faith, if 'a be not rotten before 'a die (as we have many pocky corses now-a-days that will scarce hold the laying in), 'a will last you some eight year or nine year. A tanner will last you nine year.	
HAMLET	Why he more than another?	185
CLOWN	Why, sir, his hide is so tanned with his trade that 'a will keep out water a great while; and your water is a sore decayer of your whoreson dead body. Here's a skull now. This skull hath lien you i' th' earth three-and-twenty years.	
HAMLET	Whose was it?	192
CLOWN	A whoreson mad fellow's it was. Whose do you think it was?	
HAMLET	Nay, I know not.	195
CLOWN	A pestilence on him for a mad rogue! 'A poured a flagon of Rhenish on my head once. This same skull, sir, was Yorick's skull, the King's jester.	

---

170. **as mad as he:** The supposed eccentricity of Englishmen gave rise to the notion on the Continent that they were a nation of madmen. [Of course, since Shakespeare's audience is English, he expects them to enjoy the joke on themselves. EDS.] 177. **thirty years:** This figure and the "three-and-twenty" in line 191 involve a problem as to Hamlet's age. He appears to be younger than thirty in act 1 but matures as the play proceeds. 183. **year:** An old form of the plural.

HAMLET	This?	200
CLOWN	E'en that.	
HAMLET	Let me see. [*Takes the skull.*] Alas, poor Yorick!‡	

I knew him, Horatio. A fellow of infinite jest, of most excellent
fancy. He hath borne me on his back a thousand times. And now
how abhorred in my imagination it is. My gorge rises
at it. Here hung those lips that I have kissed I know not how
oft. Where be your gibes now? your gambols? your songs?
your flashes of merriment that were wont to set the table on
a roar? Not one now, to mock your own grinning? Quite
chapfall'n?
Now get you to my lady's chamber, and tell her, let
her paint an inch thick, to this favor she must come. Make
her laugh at that. Prithee, Horatio, tell me one thing.   216

HORATIO	What's that, my lord?	
HAMLET	Dost thou think Alexander looked o' this fashion i' th' earth?	
HORATIO	E'en so.	220
HAMLET	And smelt so? Pah!	

[Puts down the skull.]

HORATIO	E'en so, my lord.	
HAMLET	To what base uses we may return, Horatio! Why may not imagination trace the noble dust of Alexander till he find it stopping a bunghole?	226
HORATIO	'Twere to consider too curiously, to consider so.	
HAMLET	No, faith, not a jot; but to follow him thither with modesty enough, and likelihood to lead it; as thus: Alexander died, Alexander was buried, Alexander returneth into dust; the dust is earth; of earth we make loam; and why of that loam (whereto he was converted) might they not stop a beer barrel?	235

---

205. **it:** the mere thought of it, i.e., of his bearing me on his back. 213. **chapfall'n:** lacking the lower jaw, chapless (line 97); with a pun on the sense of "down in the mouth." 215. **favor:** appearance of the face. 227. **too curiously:** with unreasonable ingenuity. Horatio is no "yes man," but he is also less imaginative than Hamlet and thus is a foil for his friend. 231. **modesty:** reasonableness.

---

‡   Branagh has a flashback to Yorick playing and joking with Hamlet as a child. The jester's gap-toothed smile matches the jaw of the skull Hamlet holds.

Imperious Caesar, dead and turned to clay,
Might stop a hole to keep the wind away.
O, that that earth which kept the world in awe
Should patch a wall t' expel the winter's flaw!

But soft, but soft. aside! Here comes the King —   240

*Enter [Priests with] a coffin [in funeral procession], King, Queen, Laertes,
with Lords attendant.*

The Queen, the courtiers. Who is this they follow?
And with such maimed rites? This doth betoken
The corse they follow did with desp'rate hand
Fordo it own life. 'Twas of some estate.[†]
Couch we awhile, and mark.   245

[Retires with Horatio.]

LAERTES   What ceremony else?

HAMLET   That is Laertes,
A very noble youth. Mark.

PRIEST   Her obsequies have been as far enlarged
As we have warranty. Her death was doubtful;   250
And, but that great command o'ersways the order,
She should in ground unsanctified have lodged
Till the last trumpet. For charitable prayers,
Shards, flints, and pebbles should be thrown on her.
Yet here she is allowed her virgin crants,   255
Her maiden strewments, and the bringing home
Of bell and burial.

LAERTES   Must there no more be done?

PRIEST   No more be done.
We should profane the service of the dead
To sing a requiem and such rest to her   260

236–40. An impromptu bit of versification by Hamlet. 236.—**Imperious:** imperial.—**soft:** hush. 241.
Who is this? Hamlet has not heard of Ophelia's death or even of her madness. 244. **Fordo:** destroy.—
it: its.—**estate:** rank. 245. **Couch we:** Let us conceal ourselves. 247. **noble:** referring either to Laertes's
character or to his rank. 250–4. **doubtful:** The Queen has provided one view of Ophelia's death as an
accidental drowning, but since no one saw her die, she could have been a suicide. [EDS.]—**great...
order:** The King's command has prevailed against the usual rule of the Church.—**For:** instead of.—
shards: potsherds, broken pottery. 255. **crants:** garland. The word (variously spelled) is singular, not
plural. It comes from the Dutch *crans* or the German *kranz*. Such a garland, at the burial of a young
woman, was carried to the grave and afterwards hung up in the church. 256. **strewments:** flowers for
a maiden's grave. [EDS.]—**the bringing home:** to the grave—her "long home" (*Ecclesiastes* 12. 5), as a
bride was brought (escorted) to her new home by her friends. 260. **a requiem:** So the Second Quarto.
The Folio reads "sage *Requiem*," i.e., "a requiem in due form."

---

†   Scott's Horatio guesses who is to be buried but does not have a chance to speak.

As to peace-parted souls.

LAERTES   Lay her i' th' earth;
And from her fair and unpolluted flesh
May violets spring. I tell thee, churlish priest,
A minist'ring angel shall my sister be
When thou liest howling.

HAMLET   What, the fair Ophelia?   265

QUEEN   Sweets to the sweet; Farewell.
                                        [Scatters flowers.]
I hoped thou shouldst have been my Hamlet's wife;
I thought thy bride-bed to have decked, sweet maid,
And not have strewed thy grave.

LAERTES   O, treble woe
Fall ten times treble on that cursed head   270
Whose wicked deed thy most ingenious sense
Deprived thee of. Hold off the earth awhile,
Till I have caught her once more in mine arms.
                                        Leaps in the grave.
Now pile your dust upon the quick and dead
Till of this flat a mountain you have made   275
T' o'ertop old Pelion or the skyish head
Of blue Olympus.

HAMLET   [comes forward.] What is he whose grief‡
Bears such an emphasis? whose phrase of sorrow
Conjures the wand'ring stars, and makes them stand
Like wonder-wounded hearers? This is I,   280
Hamlet the Dane.

LAERTES   The devil take thy soul.
                [Jumps out of the grave and grapples with him.]

HAMLET   Thou pray'st not well,
I prithee take thy fingers from my throat;
For, though I am not splenitive and rash,

---

264. **howling:** in hell. [EDS.] 271. **thy most ingenious sense:** thy mind, endowed by nature with the finest faculties. 276. **Pelion:** The high mountain upon which the Giants piled Mount Ossa, in their attempt to scale Mount Olympus, which rose to the home of the gods, in the sky. 279. **Conjures:** lays a spell upon.—**the wand'ring stars:** the planets. *Planet* means "wanderer." 280-1. **This...Dane:** Hamlet here asserts himself as rightful King of Denmark. Compare 1.2.44. The First Quarto alone has the stage direction: *Hamlet leapes in after Leartes.* 282–6. Hamlet's restraint is self imposed, in an attempt to be calm, despite the circumstances.—**splenitive and rash:** Synonymous: "excitable and quick-tempered." The spleen was regarded as the seat of any sudden fit of wrath, laughter, or excitement.

---

‡   Scott's Hamlet speaks quietly until Laertes attacks him (line 286).

| | Yet have I in me something dangerous, | 285 |
| | Which let thy wisdom fear. Hold off thy hand. | |

KING   Pluck them asunder.

QUEEN   Hamlet, Hamlet!

ALL   Gentlemen!

HORATIO   Good my lord, be quiet.

[The Attendants part them.]

HAMLET   Why, I will fight with him upon this theme
             Until my eyelids will no longer wag.   290

QUEEN   O my son, what theme?

HAMLET   I loved Ophelia. Forty thousand brothers
             Could not (with all their quantity of love)
             Make up my sum. What wilt thou do for her?

KING   O, he is mad, Laertes.   295

QUEEN   For love of God, forbear him.

HAMLET   'Swounds, show me what thou't do.
             Woo't weep? woo't fight? woo't fast? woo't tear thyself?
             Woo't drink up esill? eat a crocodile?
             I'll do't. Dost thou come here to whine?   300
             To outface me with leaping in her grave?
             Be buried quick with her, and so will I.
             And if thou prate of mountains, let them throw
             Millions of acres on us, till our ground,
             Singeing his pate against the burning zone,   305
             Make Ossa like a wart. Nay, an thou'lt mouth,
             I'll rant as well as thou.

QUEEN   This is mere madness;
             And thus a while the fit will work on him.
             Anon, as patient as the female dove

---

290. **wag:** move up and down, such motion being the last sign of life in a dying man. 291. **what theme?** The Queen regards Hamlet as raving mad. 292. **I loved Ophelia:** Hamlet's clearest avowal of love for her. 293. **their quantity:** their little bit. 296. **forbear him:** Addressed to Laertes: "Let him alone." 297. **'Swounds:** By the wounds of Christ. [EDS.] — **thou't:** thou wilt. 298. **Woo't:** wilt. The form is a contraction of *wolt,* the *l* having become silent like the letter *l* in *would.* It was either rustic or colloquial, and its use here expresses angry contempt. The whole speech is a kind of passionate parody of the style of Laertes in lines 274–7. 299. **drink up esill:** drain huge cups of vinegar. The word *esill* (Old French *aisil*) was associated with the drink of vinegar and gall given to Christ at his crucifixion (*Matthew* 27.34). This, though intended as an anesthetic, was regarded as an additional torment. 302. **quick:** alive. 305. **the burning zone:** that zone or belt of the celestial sphere that is bounded by the Tropics of Cancer and Capricorn. 306. **Ossa:** See n. 276. [EDS.] 307. **mere:** utter. 309. **patient:** calm.

When that her golden couplets are disclosed,   310
His silence will sit drooping.

HAMLET   Hear you, sir.
What is the reason that you use me thus?
I loved you ever. But it is no matter.
Let Hercules himself do what he may,
The cat will mew, and dog will have his day.   315

Exit.

KING   I pray thee, good Horatio, wait upon him.

Exit Horatio.

[*To Laertes.*] Strengthen your patience in our last night's speech.
We'll put the matter to the present push. —
Good Gertrude, set some watch over your son. —
This grave shall have a living monument.   320
An hour of quiet shortly shall we see;
Till then in patience our proceeding be.

Exeunt.

SCENE II. [*Elsinore. A hall in the Castle.*]†

Enter Hamlet and Horatio.

HAMLET   So much for this, sir; now shall you see the other.
You do remember all the circumstance?

HORATIO   Remember it, my lord!

---

310. **couplets:** twins.—**disclosed:** hatched. 312. **What...thus:** Hamlet seems to have forgotten that he has given Laertes sufficient reason to "use (him) thus." See his recollection, 5.2.75-9. 315. **dog... day:** A familiar proverb. [Hercules himself could not restrain Laertes; but my time will come. EDS.] The King may or may not regard Hamlet's words as a veiled threat. 317-18. These two lines may be heard by Laertes only. 317. **patience:** calm endurance under stress.—**in...speech:** by thinking of what we said last night (with regard to your revenge).—**to the present push:** into immediate action. 320-2. At line 319 the Queen starts to follow Hamlet.—**a living monument:** If the Queen hears this, she may take *living* in the sense of "life-like." To Laertes, however, the words mean that Hamlet, shall be sacrificed as an offering to Ophelia's memory.

SCENE II.
1. **this:** [Like many scenes, this one begins *in medias res,* as if the discussion had begun before the scene started. EDS.] Hamlet has just finished telling Horatio certain early incidents of the voyage.—**the other:** the rest of the story. 2. **the circumstance:** the details which I have told you.

---

†   Branagh opens the scene with a shot re-establishing Francisco as sentry on duty, as in the beginning. Throughout the final scene, Branagh periodically interpolates shots of Fortinbras steadily moving toward Elsinore, the camera then cutting to reveal Francisco's growing concern, while those within the palace remain unaware of the mounting threat to Denmark. Scott's Hamlet is formally dressed and calm.

HAMLET	Sir, in my heart there was a kind of fighting
	That would not let me sleep. Methought I lay	5
	Worse than the mutines in the bilboes. Rashly—
	And praised be rashness for it; let us know,
	Our indiscretion sometime serves us well
	When our deep plots do pall; and that should learn us
	There's a divinity that shapes our ends,	10
	Rough-hew them how we will —
HORATIO	That is most certain.
HAMLET	Up from my cabin,
	My sea-gown scarfed about me, in the dark
	Groped I to find out them; had my desire,
	Fingered their packet, and in fine withdrew	15
	To mine own room again; making so bold
	(My fears forgetting manners) to unseal
	Their grand commission; where I found, Horatio
	(O royal knavery), an exact command,
	Larded with many several sorts of reasons,	20
	Importing Denmark's health, and England's too,
	With, hoo! such bugs and goblins in my life —
	That, on the supervise, no leisure bated,
	No, not to stay the grinding of the axe,
	My head should be struck off.
HORATIO	Is't possible?	25
HAMLET	Here's the commission;‡ read it at more leisure.
	But wilt thou hear me how I did proceed?
HORATIO	I beseech you.
HAMLET	Being thus benetted round with villanies,
	Or I could make a prologue to my brains,	30

---

6. **mutines:** mutineers.—**bilboes:** a kind of portable restraint carried on board ship. They consisted of a heavy horizontal bar of iron, to which were attached rings for the ankles.—**Rashly:** obeying a sudden impulse. 7–11. **And...will:** Parenthetical. 7. **let us know:** let us recognize as a fact of experience. 9. **pall:** fail. 10. **our ends:** the outcome of our plans. 11. **Rough-hew...will:** however we may roughly shape them. [EDS.] 15. **Fingered:** laid hold on. 17. **to:** as to. 20. **Larded:** decorated. 21. **Importing:** signifying.— **health:** welfare. 22. **hoo!** An interjection expressing fright.—**such bugs...life:** interspersed with such outbursts as to the danger of leaving a terrible creature like me alive.—**bugs:** imaginary goblins. 23. **on the supervise:** as soon as the document had been read (by the English king).—**no leisure bated:** with no time wasted for delaying the execution. The whole speech suggests bitter humor. 24. **grinding:** sharpening. [EDS.] 29. **benetted:** surrounded. [EDS.] 30. **Or:** ere. Before he could prepare his brains, they had begun to carry out a plan. —**prologue:** begins the play-metaphor continued in the next line.

---

‡   Some Hamlets rip the commission, leaving him without proof of the King's guilt. Lyth's Horatio uses it at the end to try to "report [Hamlet] and [his] cause aright" (line 350), but neither Fortinbras nor the courtiers are interested: power has shifted and that's all that is important.

They had begun the play. I sat me down;
Devised a new commission; wrote it fair.
I once did hold it, as our statists do,
A baseness to write fair, and labored much
How to forget that learning; but, sir, now   35
It did me yeoman's service. Wilt thou know
Th' effect of what I wrote?

HORATIO   Ay, good my lord.

HAMLET   An earnest conjuration from the King,
As England was his faithful tributary,
As love between them like the palm might flourish,   40
As peace should still her wheaten garland wear
And stand a comma 'tween their amities,
And many such-like as's of great charge,
That, on the view and knowing of these contents,
Without debatement further, more or less,   45
He should the bearers put to sudden death,
Not shriving time allowed.

HORATIO   How was this sealed?

HAMLET   Why, even in that was heaven ordinant.
I had my father's signet in my purse,
Which was the model of that Danish seal;   50
Folded the writ up in the form of th' other,
Subscribed it, gave't th' impression, placed it safely,
The changeling never known. Now, the next day
Was our sea-fight; and what to this was sequent
Thou know'st already.   55

HORATIO   So Guildenstern and Rosencrantz go to't.

HAMLET   Why, man, they did make love to this employment.
They are not near my conscience; their defeat

---

31. **begun the play:** Hamlet describes the event as if it is the action within a play. [EDS.] 32. **fair:** in legible script (proper for a clerk or secretary). 33. **statists:** statesmen. 34. **A baseness:** a lower-class accomplishment. 36. **yeoman's service:** substantial service. 37. **effect:** purport. 39–42. Hamlet satirizes the stately style used by the King in the original. 41. **wheaten garland:** since agriculture can flourish only in peacetime. 42. **a comma:** as a brief link. 43. **as's of great charge:** A pun on *ass* and *as*. *Charge* means "burden" (as applied to the *asses*) and "earnest conjuration" (as applied to the *as's*). [The *as's* introduce all the reasons that Hamlet should be killed. EDS.] 45. **debatement:** discussion. 46. **sudden:** instant. 47. **shriving time:** not even time enough for confession and absolution for their sins. [The Ghost had lamented that he had been sent to his death in just this way. Compare 1.5.75-9. But here Hamlet might mean speed, not literally insufficient time for last rites. EDS.] 48. **ordinant:** operative in controlling events; Hamlet recurs to the thought of the "divinity that shapes our ends" (line 10). 50. **model:** copy. 51. **writ:** document. 52. **impression:** i.e., of the seal. 53. **changeling:** a metaphor: he refers to an elf or imp, often hideously ugly and always malicious, substituted by the fairies for a baby stolen from the cradle. 56. **go to't:** go to their deaths. [EDS.] 58. **defeat:** destruction.

	Does by their own insinuation grow.	
	'Tis dangerous when the baser nature comes	60
	Between the pass and fell incensed points	
	Of mighty opposites.	
HORATIO	Why, what a king is this.	
HAMLET	Does it not, thinks't thee, stand me now upon —	
	He that hath killed my king, and whored my mother;	
	Popped in between th' election and my hopes;	65
	Thrown out his angle for my proper life,	
	And with such coz'nage — is't not perfect conscience	
	To quit him with this arm? And is't not to be damned	
	To let this canker of our nature come	
	In further evil?	70
HORATIO	It must be shortly known to him from England	
	What is the issue of the business there.	
HAMLET	It will be short; the interim is mine,	
	And a man's life's no more than to say "one."	
	But I am very sorry, good Horatio,	75
	That to Laertes I forgot myself;	
	For by the image of my cause I see	
	The portraiture of his. I'll court his favors.	
	But sure the bravery of his grief did put me	
	Into a tow'ring passion.	
HORATIO	Peace. Who comes here?	80

Enter young Osric, a courtier.

| OSRIC | Your lordship is right welcome back to Denmark. | |

---

59. **their own insinuation:** their own act in worming themselves into this affair. Though Rosencrantz and Guildenstern may not have known the King's intention, they had put themselves into his service unreservedly. [In Shakespeare's sources, they knew the King's plan. EDS.] 60. **baser:** Hamlet speaks as a prince, conscious of his royalty and convinced of the difference between kings and common men. *Baser* refers to rank and dignity. These lines imply Claudius's position in the drama. He is Hamlet's "mighty opposite," not a contemptible foe. Hamlet speaks differently about the King at various points. See, e.g. 3.4.53-67; 97-8. 61. **pass:** thrust.—**fell:** fierce. 63-70. Hamlet's constitutional disinclination to deeds of blood is still strong. Now he sums up all the reasons why the King deserves death and adds that he ought to be killed to prevent his doing further mischief. 63. **thinks't thee:** seems it to thee. Compare *methinks,* "it seems to me."—**stand me now upon:** is my duty. 65. **Popped:** Compare what Hamlet says of the King's "stealing the diadem from a shelf and putting it in his pocket" (3.4.100-1).—**election:** Denmark's king was elected from among the royal family by the council of noblemen. [EDS.]—**hopes:** hope to be king. [EDS.] 66. **my proper life:** my own life. 68. **To quit him:** to pay him off. 69. **canker:** cancer or ulcer. 70. **In:** into. 68–80. Omitted in the Second Quarto. 74. **A man's life's..."one:"** Life lasts no longer than it takes to say "one." [EDS.] 77–8. **For...his:** Laertes the revenger serves as a foil to Hamlet the revenger. 78. **court:** The Folio has *count.* 79. **bravery:** ostentation. 81 ff. The language and manners of Osric satirize the affectations of young gentlemen at the English court. [The dialogue gives comic relief. EDS.]

HAMLET	I humbly thank you, sir. [*Aside to Horatio*] Dost know this waterfly?
HORATIO	[*aside to Hamlet*] No, my good lord. 85
HAMLET	[*aside to Horatio*] Thy state is the more gracious; for 'tis a vice to know him. He hath much land, and fertile. Let a beast be lord of beasts, and his crib shall stand at the king's mess. 'Tis a chough; but, as I say, spacious in the possession of dirt. 90
OSRIC	Sweet lord, if your lordship were at leisure, I should impart a thing to you from his Majesty.
HAMLET	I will receive it, sir, with all diligence of spirit. Put 95 your bonnet to his right use. 'Tis for the head.
OSRIC	I thank your lordship, it is very hot.
HAMLET	No, believe me, 'tis very cold; the wind is northerly.
OSRIC	It is indifferent cold, my lord, indeed. 100
HAMLET	But yet methinks it is very sultry and hot for my complexion.
OSRIC	Exceedingly, my lord; it is very sultry, as 'twere — I cannot tell how. But, my lord, his Majesty bade me signify to you that he has laid a great wager on your head. Sir, this is the matter —
HAMLET	I beseech you remember. 108
	[*Hamlet motions him to put on his hat.*]
OSRIC	Nay, good my lord; for mine ease, in good faith. Sir, here is newly come to court Laertes; believe me, an absolute gentleman, full of most excellent differences, of very soft society and great showing. Indeed, to speak feelingly of him, he is the card or calendar of gentry; for you shall find in him the continent of what part a gentleman would see. 116

84. **waterfly:** an unsubstantial creature, all wings and iridescence, skimming along the surface of life. 86. **Thy state...gracious:** Thy condition is the more virtuous. 88. **his crib...mess:** A disrespectful way of saying "He will be sure to be admitted to the King's table." 89. **a chough:** a silly, chattering creature. The term *chough* (pronounced *chuff*) was applied to the jackdaw and other noisy crow-like birds of the same family. 91. **I should:** I was to. 96. **bonnet:** cap. The contest in courtesy is won by Osric, who holds his cap in his hand to the last, as we see from line 109. 100-4. **indifferent:** rather. —**complexion:** temperament.—**I cannot tell how:** somehow or other. 109. **for mine ease:** A common phrase when one politely insists on standing hat in hand. 109–150. **Sir, here...unfellowed:** This is cut down to a single sentence in the Folio: "Sir, you are not ignorant of what excellence Laertes is at his weapon." 110–16. **absolute:** perfect.—**differences:** accomplishments.—**soft society:** agreeable manners,—**great showing:** splendid appearance.—**feelingly:** with a due sense of his merits.—**card or calendar of gentry:** model of courtly manners. As one consults a calendar for sure guidance, so every gentleman may learn how to behave by observing Laertes.—**the continent...see:** whatever qualities one gentleman would like to find in another. A *continent* is literally "that which contains."

HAMLET   Sir, his definement suffers no perdition in you;
                though, I know, to divide him inventorially would dozy th'
                arithmetic of memory, and yet but yaw neither in respect of
                his quick sail. But, in the verity of extolment, I take him to
                be a soul of great article, and his infusion of such dearth and
                rareness as, to make true diction of him, his semblable is his
                mirror, and who else would trace him, his umbrage, nothing
                more.   125

OSRIC   Your lordship speaks most infallibly of him.

HAMLET   The concernancy, sir? Why do we wrap the gentleman
                in our more rawer breath?

OSRIC   Sir?   130

HORATIO   [aside to Hamlet] Is't not possible to understand in another
                tongue? You will do't, sir, really.

HAMLET   What imports the nomination of this gentleman?

OSRIC   Of Laertes?   135

HORATIO   [aside] His purse is empty already. All's golden words are spent.

HAMLET   Of him, sir.

OSRIC   I know you are not ignorant —   140

HAMLET   I would you did, sir; yet, in faith, if you did, it would
                not much approve me. Well, sir?

OSRIC   You are not ignorant of what excellence Laertes is —

117-20. **definement:** definition.—**perdition:** loss.—**to divide…sail:** To make an inventory of his fine
qualities would stagger the reckoning power of one's memory, and yet, after all, the inventory would
come far short of his real excellence. The excellence of Laertes is a fast boat that sails steadily on; the
inventory is another boat, which tries to overtake the leader, but *yaws* continually and thus falls far
behind. A boat yaws when she steers badly, so that she does not hold her course but swings her bow
from side to side and thus loses headway.—**dozy:** confuse, stagger.—**neither:** after all.—**in respect of:**
in comparison with. 120–5. **in…extolment:** to give him the praise he truly deserves.—**of great article:**
An *article* is an "item," but the word is here used collectively: "with great qualities"; "with a great amount
of fine traits."—**his infusion:** the nature with which he is endowed.—**of such dearth and rareness:** of
such rare excellence. *Dearth* and *rareness* mean the same thing: "rarity."—**his semblable is his mirror:**
the only person who resembles him is his own image in the looking glass.—**who else would…more:**
Anybody else who wishes to keep pace with him, can do so only as the shadow follows the substance.
[Hamlet's affected speech here parodies Osric's. EDS.] 128-9. **The concernancy, sir?** What is the purport
of all this?—**Why…breath?** Why do we attempt to describe the gentleman in our words, which are too
crude to do him justice?" 131-6. **Is't…tongue?** Does Osric find it impossible to understand his own
lingo when another man speaks it?—**do't:** succeed in nonplussing Osric.—**nomination:** naming.—
All's: all his. 141-2. **yet…approve me:** If you, who are yourself a fool, supposed me not to be ignorant,
that belief would not be much evidence in my favor.

HAMLET	I dare not confess that, lest I should compare with him in excellence; but to know a man well were to know himself.
OSRIC	I mean, sir, for his weapon; but in the imputation laid on him by them, in his meed he's unfellowed. 150
HAMLET	What's his weapon?
OSRIC	Rapier and dagger.
HAMLET	That's two of his weapons — but well.
OSRIC	The King, sir, hath wagered with him six Barbary horses; against the which he has imponed, as I take it, six French rapiers and poniards, with their assigns, as girdle, hangers, and so. Three of the carriages, in faith, are very dear to fancy, very responsive to the hilts, most delicate carriages, and of very liberal conceit. 160
HAMLET	What call you the carriages?
HORATIO	[*aside to Hamlet*] I knew you must be edified by the margent ere you had done.
OSRIC	The carriages, sir, are the hangers.
HAMLET	The phrase would be more germane to the matter if 165 we could carry cannon by our sides. I would it might be hangers till then. But on. Six Barbary horses against six French swords, their assigns, and three liberal-conceited carriages: that's the French bet against the Danish. Why is this all imponed, as you call it? 170
OSRIC	The King, sir, hath laid that, in a dozen passes between yourself and him, he shall not exceed you three hits; he hath

---

145–48. **I dare not...excellence:** I dare not say that I know how excellent Laertes is, for such an assertion would imply equal excellence on my own part, since only the excellent can judge of excellence.—**to know a man...himself:** to know someone else, one must first know oneself. [EDS.] 149. **imputation:** reputation. 150. **them:** i.e., his weapons.—**meed:** excellence. 152. **Rapier and dagger:** In fencing it was common to carry a dagger in the left hand to assist in warding off the blows or thrusts of one's opponent. 153. **two:** Hamlet is merely quibbling over Osric's affected use of *weapon* as a plural.—**but well:** but never mind. 154–60. **Barbary horses:** Proverbially the finest in Shakespeare's day.—**imponed:** wagered.—**assigns:** accessories.—**hangers:** straps attaching the sword to the belt.—**dear to fancy:** tastefully designed.—**responsive to the hilts:** complementing the hilts in design.—**of very liberal conceit:** elegantly conceived designed. 162-3. **edified by the margent:** instructed by a marginal note. This remark is omitted in the Folio. 164–6. **carriages:** Hamlet makes fun of Osric's affected use, which suggests a gun carriage, the wheeled frame that *carries* a cannon. 173-6. **laid:** wagered.—**a dozen passes:** The terms of the wager: a dozen passes, or "bouts," with the King betting that Laertes's total score shall not exceed Hamlet's by three hits. Thus if the score stood 7 for Laertes and 5 for Hamlet, the King would win; so also if it stood 6 to 6, or 6 to 4 with two draws. But if it stood Laertes 8, Hamlet 4, the King would lose, so also if it stood 7 to 4, with one draw. *Twelve for nine,* however, cannot by any twist be brought into accord with these terms.

laid on twelve for nine, and it would come to immediate trial
if your lordship would vouchsafe the answer.

HAMLET   How if I answer no?   177

OSRIC   I mean, my lord, the opposition of your person in trial.

HAMLET   Sir, I will walk here in the hall. If it please his
Majesty, it is the breathing time of day with me. Let the foils
be brought, the gentleman willing, and the King hold his
purpose, I will win for him if I can; if not, I will gain nothing
but my shame and the odd hits,   185

OSRIC   Shall I redeliver you e'en so?

HAMLET   To this effect, sir, after what flourish your nature will.

OSRIC   I commend my duty to your lordship.

HAMLET   Yours, yours. [*Exit Osric.*] He does well to commend
it himself; there are no tongues else for's turn.   192

HORATIO   This lapwing runs away with the shell on his head.

HAMLET   He did comply with his dug before he sucked it. Thus
has he, and many more of the same bevy that I know the drossy
age dotes on, only got the tune of the time and outward habit
of encounter — a kind of yesty collection, which carries them
through and through the most fanned and winnowed opinions;
and do but blow them to their trial — the bubbles are out.   202

Enter a Lord.

LORD   My lord, his Majesty commended him to you by young
Osric, who brings back to him, that you attend him in the hall.
He sends to know if your pleasure hold to play with Laertes,
or that you will take longer time.

HAMLET   I am constant to my purposes; they follow the King's
pleasure. If his fitness speaks, mine is ready; now or   210
whensoever, provided I be so able as now.

—**vouchsafe the answer:** consent to meet Laertes in this match. 180–5. **the breathing time of day with me:** the time of day when I take my exercise. 186. **redeliver you:** carry back your reply. 189–92. **I commend my duty:** I declare myself your humble servant. Hamlet puns on *commend*, which meant also "to praise."—**for's turn:** for his purpose. 193. **This...head:** Horatio implies that Osric is very young. [EDS.] — **lapwing:** proverbially cautious bird [noted for drawing intruders away from its nest. EDS.]. 194. **comply:** use, i.e., ceremonious language during the most intimate and ordinary of acts. 195-6. **the drossy age:** the degenerate present. 196-7. **outward habit of encounter:** the fashionable habits of society, with a pun on *habit* in the sense of "clothing." *Encounter* means "meeting." 200. **yesty collection:** frothy mess. 200-1. **carries...opinions:** These trivial accomplishments make them acceptable even to the choicest and most refined judgment. *Fanned* and *winnowed* [tried and tested. EDS.] are identical in sense. The Second Quarto reads "prophane and trennowed"; the Folio, "fond and winnowed." 203-18. **commended him:** sent his compliments. — **If his fitness speaks:** If his convenience calls for the match.

LORD	The King and Queen and all are coming down.
HAMLET	In happy time.
LORD	The Queen desires you to use some gentle entertainment to Laertes before you fall to play.
HAMLET	She well instructs me. 218

[Exit Lord.]

HORATIO	You will lose this wager, my lord.
HAMLET	I do not think so. Since he went into France I have been in continual practice. I shall win at the odds. But thou wouldst not think how ill all's here about my heart. But it is no matter.
HORATIO	Nay, good my lord —
HAMLET	It is but foolery; but it is such a kind of gaingiving as would perhaps trouble a woman.
HORATIO	If your mind dislike anything, obey it. I will forestall their repair hither and say you are not fit. 229
HAMLET	Not a whit, we defy augury; there's a special providence in the fall of a sparrow. If it be now, 'tis not to come; if it be not to come, it will be now; if it be not now, yet it will come: the readiness is all. Since no man knows aught of what he leaves, what is't to leave betimes? Let be. 235

Enter King, Queen, Laertes, [Osric], and Lords, with other Attendants
with foils and gauntlets. A Table and flagons of wine on it.

KING	Come, Hamlet, come, and take this hand from me.

[The King puts Laertes' hand into Hamlet's.]

HAMLET	Give me your pardon, sir. I have done you wrong; But pardon't, as you are a gentleman. This presence knows, And you must needs have heard, how I am punished 240

— **In happy time:** very opportunely. — **to use…entertainment:** to meet Laertes in a cordial and friendly way. — **fall to play:** begin to fence. 222–8. **how ill…heart:** how uneasy I feel. Hamlet has a presentiment of evil..—**gaingiving:** misgiving.—**obey it:** Horatio, the philosopher, urges Hamlet to obey his instinctive reluctance of mind. 230. **we:** i.e., men like us, who believe in God's providence. 231. **sparrow:** *Matthew* 10.29: "Are not two sparrows sold for a farthing? and one of them shall not fall on the ground without your Father." Compare *Luke* 12.6.—**it:** death. 234. **is all:** is the only important matter. 234-5. **Since…betimes?** [Since, once dead, no one knows what he leaves behind, what difference does it make to leave at once? EDS.] Shakespeare may be thinking of Michel de Montaigne's Essay on "Learning how to Die." The Second Quarto reads "since no man of ought he leaues, knowes what ist to leaue betimes, let be"; the Folio, "since no man ha's ought of what he leaues. What is't to leaue betimes?" The Folio omits "Let be." 235. **Let be:** Let it go. 239. **This presence:** the King and Queen, in whose presence I speak.

With sore distraction. What I have done
That might your nature, honor, and exception
Roughly awake, I here proclaim was madness.
Was't Hamlet wronged Laertes? Never Hamlet.
If Hamlet from himself be ta'en away,   245
And when he's not himself does wrong Laertes,
Then Hamlet does it not, Hamlet denies it.
Who does it, then? His madness. If't be so,
Hamlet is of the faction that is wronged;
His madness is poor Hamlet's enemy.   250
Sir, in this audience,
Let my disclaiming from a purposed evil
Free me so far in your most generous thoughts
That I have shot my arrow o'er the house
And hurt my brother.

two Hamlets

LAERTES   I am satisfied in nature,   255
Whose motive in this case should stir me most
To my revenge. But in my terms of honor
I stand aloof, and will no reconcilement
Till by some elder masters of known honor
I have a voice and precedent of peace   260
To keep my name ungored. But till that time
I do receive your offered love like love,
And will not wrong it.

HAMLET   I embrace it freely,
And will this brother's wager frankly play.
Give us the foils. Come on.

LAERTES   Come, one for me.   265

HAMLET   I'll be your foil, Laertes. In mine ignorance
Your skill shall, like a star i' th' darkest night,
Stick fiery off indeed.

LAERTES   You mock me, sir.

HAMLET   No, by this hand.

---

242. **exception:** disapproval. 249. **faction:** party. 251. **this audience:** this royal audience. 253-4. **so far...That:** so far that you may believe that. 255-61. Though his *natural* inclination is satisfied, yet he will ask the advice of older guardians of reputation and the rules of honor whether his obligations to his *honor* can be contented with Hamlet's apology. 259. **masters:** experts in these questions. 260. **a voice... peace:** a decision that may serve as a precedent for reconciliation. 261. **ungored:** free from disgrace. 264. **frankly:** with a heart free from rancor. 266. **your foil:** A pun. A *foil* is a weapon. It also means "a bit of tinsel placed under a gem to enhance its brilliiancy," and so, "that which sets off something by contrast." 268. **Stick fiery off:** stand out in brilliant contrast.

KING	Give them the foils, young Osric. Cousin Hamlet,	270
	You know the wager?	
HAMLET	Very well, my lord.	
	Your Grace has laid the odds o' th' weaker side.	
KING	I do not fear it, I have seen you both;	
	But since he is bettered, we have therefore odds.	
LAERTES	This is too heavy; let me see another.	
HAMLET	This likes me well. These foils have	
	all a length?	

Prepare to play.

OSRIC	Ay, my good lord.	
KING	Set me the stoups of wine upon that table.	
	If Hamlet give the first or second hit,	
	Or quit in answer of the third exchange,	280
	Let all the battlements their ordnance fire;	
	The King shall drink to Hamlet's better breath,	
	And in the cup an union shall he throw	
	Richer than that which four successive kings	
	In Denmark's crown have worn. Give me the cups;	285
	And let the kettle to the trumpet speak,	
	The trumpet to the cannoneer without,	
	The cannons to the heavens, the heaven to earth,	
	"Now the King drinks to Hamlet." Come, begin.	
	And you the judges, bear a wary eye.	290
HAMLET	Come on, sir.	
LAERTES	Come, my lord.	*They play.*
HAMLET	One.	
LAERTES	No.	
HAMLET	Judgment!	
OSRIC	A hit, a very palpable hit.	
LAERTES	Well, again.	
KING	Stay, give me drink. Hamlet, this pearl is thine;	
	Here's to thy health.	

---

272. **odds:** i. e., in the value of the stake. The King's stake is much greater than that of Laertes. 274. **is bettered:** has improved since he went to France.—**odds:** i.e., in the terms of the wager. Laertes may score two points more than Hamlet and still lose the match. 275, 276. **let me see another:** Laertes picks out the unbated [sharp. EDS.] and poisoned foil.—**likes:** pleases, suits. 277. Osric may be unaware of the plot against Hamlet. 278–80. **stoups:** big goblets.—**quit...exchange:** repay Laertes (score a hit) in the third bout. 283. **an union:** a great and flawless pearl. 286. **kettle:** kettledrum.

Drum; trumpets sound; a piece goes off [within].
Give him the cup.

HAMLET	I'll play this bout first; set it by awhile.	295
	Come. (*They play.*) Another hit. What say you?	
LAERTES	A touch, a touch; I do confess't.	
KING	Our son shall win.	
QUEEN	He's fat, and scant of breath.	
	Here, Hamlet, take my napkin, rub thy brows.	
	The Queen carouses to thy fortune, Hamlet.†	300
HAMLET	Good madam.	
KING	Gertrude, do not drink. ·	
QUEEN	I will, my lord; I pray you pardon me. *Drinks.*	
KING	[*aside*] It is the poisoned cup; it is too late.	
HAMLET	I dare not drink yet, madam; by-and-by.	
QUEEN	Come, let me wipe thy face.	305
LAERTES	My lord, I'll hit him now.	
KING	I do not think't.	
LAERTES	[*aside*] And yet it is almost against my conscience.	
HAMLET	Come for the third, Laertes. You but dally.	
	I pray you pass with your best violence;	
	I am afeard you make a wanton of me.	310
LAERTES	Say you so? Come on. *Play.*	
OSRIC	Nothing neither way.	

---

298. **shall:** will surely. 298. **fat:** In modern times this adjective has given trouble. The Queen sees that Hamlet is panting and perspiring a little and remarks that he is fat. What she meant is not clear, but fat was not in fact denigrated as it is today. [There was a notion also that perspiration was melting body fat. EDS.] 299. **napkin:** handkerchief. 300. **carouses:** drinks a full draught. 301. **Good madam:** A polite acknowledgment of the Queen's toast. 304. **dare not:** Hamlet has no suspicion that the cup is poisoned. He merely does not think it wise to drink until the match is over. 307. **almost...conscience:** This aside makes the confession of Laertes in lines 324–31, 338–42, sound less like too sudden a conversion. 309. **pass:** thrust. 310. **make a wanton of me:** you are indulging me and not trying your best to win. A wanton is "a spoiled child." 312. **Nothing neither way:** Thus the third bout ends with a score of two hits for Hamlet (lines 292-7) and one draw.

---

†   Olivier's Gertrude suspects the King's plan to poison Hamlet, and drinks to save him. Scott's Gertrude seems reconciled to her husband and unsuspecting.

LAERTES	Have at you now.‡

[Laertes wounds Hamlet; then,] in scuffling,
they change rapiers, [and Hamlet wounds Laertes].

KING	Part them. They are incensed.	
HAMLET	Nay come. again.	*The Queen falls.*
OSRIC	Look to the Queen there, ho.	
HORATIO	They bleed on both sides. How is it, my lord?	315
OSRIC	How is't, Laertes?	
LAERTES	Why, as a woodcock to mine own springe, Osric.	
	I am justly killed with mine own treachery.	
HAMLET	How does the Queen?	
KING	She sounds to see them bleed,	
QUEEN	No, no. the drink, the drink. O my dear Hamlet.	320
	The drink, the drink. I am poisoned. [*Dies.*]	
HAMLET	O villany. Ho. let the door be locked.	
	Treachery. Seek it out.	

[Laertes falls.]

LAERTES	It is here, Hamlet. Hamlet, thou art slain;	
	No med'cine in the world can do thee good.	325
	In thee there is not half an hour of life.	
	The treacherous instrument is in thy hand,	
	Unbated and envenomed. The foul practice	
	Hath turned itself on me. Lo, here I lie,	
	Never to rise again. Thy mother's poisoned.	330
	I can no more. The King, the King's to blame.	
HAMLET	The point envenomed too?	
	Then, venom, to thy work.	*Hurts the King.*
ALL	Treason. treason.	

---

313. The First Quarto has the stage direction: *They catch one anothers Rapiers, and both are wounded, Laertes falles downe, the Queene falles downe and dies.* The Folios read *In scuffling they change Rapiers.* Just how this trick was managed is uncertain. In fencing with rapiers only (i.e., without daggers), there was a recognized series of plays in which each fencer seized the other's sword at the hilt and thereby exchanged weapons. 317. **as...springe:** like a fool, caught in my own snare. A woodcock, in its stupid curiosity, was supposed to fumble with the snare and thus achieve its own capture. 319. **She...bleed:** Claudius remains cool. See 4.5.120 ff.—**sounds:** swounds, swoons. 328. **practice:** plot. 332. **too:** i.e., not only "unbated" (as he now sees) but also "envenomed" [poisoned. EDS.]. 333. Thus Hamlet's vengeance is self-defense.

---

‡   Most actors who play Laertes announce here a foul blow.

KING	O, yet defend me, friends. I am but hurt.	335
HAMLET	Here, thou incestuous, murd'rous, damned Dane,	
	Drink off this potion. Is thy union here?	
	Follow my mother.	*King dies.*
LAERTES	He is justly served.	
	It is a poison tempered by himself.	
	Exchange forgiveness with me, noble Hamlet.	340
	Mine and my father's death come not upon thee,	
	Nor thine on me.	*Dies.*
HAMLET	Heaven make thee free of it. I follow thee.	
	I am dead, Horatio. Wretched queen, adieu.	
	You that look pale and tremble at this chance,	345
	That are but mutes or audience to this act,	
	Had I but time (as this fell sergeant, Death,	
	Is strict in his arrest) O, I could tell you —	
	But let it be. Horatio, I am dead;	
	Thou liv'st; report me and my cause aright	350
	To the unsatisfied.	
HORATIO	Never believe it.	
	I am more an antique Roman than a Dane.	
	Here's yet some liquor left.	
HAMLET	As th'art a man,	
	Give me the cup. Let go. By heaven, I'll ha't.	
	O good Horatio, what a wounded name	355
	(Things standing thus unknown) shall live behind me.	
	If thou didst ever hold me in thy heart,	
	Absent thee from felicity awhile,	
	And in this harsh world draw thy breath in pain,	
	To tell my story. *March ajar off, and shot within.*	
	What warlike noise is this?	360
OSRIC	Young Fortinbras, with conquest come from Poland,	
	To the ambassadors of England gives	
	This warlike volley.	
HAMLET	O, I die, Horatio.	
	The potent poison quite o'ercrows my spirit.	
	I cannot live to hear the news from England,	365

---

335. **hurt:** wounded. 339. **tempered:** compounded. 346. **mutes:** players without speaking parts. 348. **sergeant:** a sheriff's officer. [Death. EDS.] 351. **the unsatisfied:** those who are uninformed. 364. **o'ercrows:** overcomes. The figure is from cockfighting; the word was as common as the sport, in Elizabethan times.—**spirit:** vitality, life.

But I do prophesy th' election lights
On Fortinbras. He has my dying voice.
So tell him, with th' occurrents, more and less,
Which have solicited — the rest is silence.[†]

Dies.

HORATIO   Now cracks a noble heart. Good night, sweet prince,   370
And flights of angels sing thee to thy rest.

[*March within.*]

Why does the drum come hither?

Enter Fortinbras and English Ambassadors, with Drum, Colors, and Attendants.

FORTINBRAS   Where is this sight?

HORATIO   What is it you would see?
If aught of woe or wonder, cease your search.

FORTINBRAS   This quarry cries on havoc. O proud Death,   375
What feast is toward in thine eternal cell
That thou so many princes at a shot
So bloodily hast struck?

AMBASSADOR   The sight is dismal;
And our affairs from England come too late.
The ears are senseless that should give us hearing   380
To tell him his commandment is fulfilled,
That Rosencrantz and Guildenstern are dead.
Where should we have our thanks?

HORATIO   Not from his mouth,
Had it th' ability of life to thank you.
He never gave commandment for their death.   385
But since, so jump upon this bloody question,
You from the Polack wars, and you from England,
Are here arrived, give order that these bodies

---

366. **th' election:** The crown of Denmark was elective, but nomination by the reigning king had much influence in determining his successor, and Hamlet is now virtually King of Denmark. 367. **voice:** vote [support. [EDS.]. 368. **occurrents:** occurrences. 369. **solicited:** brought on (this tragedy). 375. **This... havoc:** These dead bodies proclaim that a massacre has taken place. *Quarry* is the regular word for the game killed in a hunt. *Havoc* was the old battle cry for "No quarter. " 270 ff. *Cries on:* "shouts." 376. **toward:** in preparation. Scandinavian warriors believed that, if slain in battle, they were translated to Valhalla (*Valhöll*), Odin's palace in the sky, where they were to spend their time in feasting and fighting. Shakespeare's knowledge of this myth is uncertain. [In any case, Fortinbras speaks metaphorically, not literally. EDS.] 386. **jump:** exactly.

[†]   Kozintsev suggests through music that the Ghost is satisfied. Scott's Hamlet, before he says this line, sees the Ghost standing enigmatically among the courtiers.

Zeffirelli's ending shows the ruling house destroyed. The high-angle shot distances the audience from the scene of death, and even the bystanders seem detached.

High on a stage be placed to the view;
And let me speak to th' yet unknowing world   390
How these things came about. So shall you hear
Of carnal, bloody, and unnatural acts;
Of accidental judgments, casual slaughters;
Of deaths put on by cunning and forced cause;
And, in this upshot, purposes mistook   395
Fall'n on th' inventors' heads. All this can I
Truly deliver.

FORTINBRAS   Let us haste to hear it,
And call the noblest to the audience.
For me, with sorrow I embrace my fortune.
I have some rights of memory in this kingdom,   400

---

393. **accidental judgments:** judgments of God brought about by means apparently accidental. This refers particularly to the death of the Queen and of Laertes. 394. **put on:** instigated. These deaths were those of Rosencrantz and Guildenstern. If so, *cunning* describes Hamlet's cleverness in changing the death mandate, and *forced cause* indicates the necessity of self-defense which prompted him. Possibly, however, Horatio alludes to Hamlet's death, craftily instigated by the King and by Laertes own "forced" (exaggerated) passion of revenge. 400. **rights of memory:** unforgotten rights, suggesting perhaps that Fortinbras is related to the Danish royal family. [He might also be referring to his father's losses of land that he had wanted to reclaim. EDS.]

	Which now to claim my vantage doth invite me.
HORATIO	Of that I shall have also cause to speak,
	And from his mouth whose voice will draw on more.
	But let this same be presently performed,
	Even while men's minds are wild, lest more mischance
	On plots and errors happen.

FORTINBRAS   Let four captains   406
              Bear Hamlet like a soldier to the stage;
              For he was likely, had he been put on,
              To have proved most royally; and for his passage
              The soldiers' music and the rites of war   410
              Speak loudly for him.
              Take up the bodies. Such a sight as this
              Becomes the field, but here shows much amiss.‡
              Go, bid the soldiers shoot.

Exeunt marching; after the which
a peal of ordinance are shot off.

---

401. **my vantage:** my presence (with troops) at this opportune moment. 403. **from his mouth:** See line 367. 404. **more:** more voices, more suffrages.—**presently:** at once. 405. **On:** on account of. 406–14. In Elizabethan tragedy, the person of highest rank among the survivors regularly makes the speech which brings the play to a formal close. 408. **put on:** advanced to the kingship, and so put to the test. 409. **To have proved most royally:** to have shown himself a true king—an important tribute from a warrior such as Fortinbras. [But of course he does not know Hamlet or his capabilities. EDS.] —**passage:** death. 413. **shows:** appears. 414. **ordinance:** ordnance.

---

‡   Zeffirelli's last take is a high angle long shot, the camera tracking back to display the bodies of Hamlet and his mother situated on either side of the frame, thereby emphasizing the personal rather than the political nature of Shakespeare's tragedy. On the other hand, Branagh's last take, also a long tracking shot, emphasizes the political theme by his camera's slow passage from Hamlet's soldier's bier to the methodical demolition of Old Hamlet's monolithic statue, which so dominates the film's opening scene.

HOW TO READ *HAMLET* AS PERFORMANCE

Since Shakespeare wrote his plays for the stage, the best way to enjoy *Hamlet* is to experience it as a performance. Fortunately, a performance in the mind, or a performance with classmates, of even small segments of the script can be an excellent way to develop a performance perspective. Once you by yourself have focused on performance choices or you and your friends or classmates have tried performing together and for each other, you will probably find it easier to understand and assess the performance decisions that directors and actors make in staged or filmed versions that you will see. Below we suggest some of the ways you can bring the *Hamlet* script to life as you are reading it by yourself (perhaps aloud) or with a group. It can be helpful to listen to an audio version of the play while you are reading it for the first time. There are audiotapes and CDs in which one actor reads the entire play; there are others that are performed by a full cast of actors. Either can work for you (see Bibliography).[1] Keep in mind that on an audio version, a director and actors have made decisions about how the words should be spoken depending on the effects they want to achieve: no one version can capture all the possibilities of the script.

It might be helpful to know that Shakespeare's stage was about as simple as it could be. Therefore, in imagining the play for performance, you don't have to worry about lighting, scenery or costumes. Shakespeare had to use language like "Where are you? I can't see you!" to inform the audience that the action was taking place in the dark, or props like torches to silently suggest darkness. Without scenery, which sometimes serves to indicate the setting of the action, Globe Theater productions depended on language to give a sense of place when necessary. Costumes, as far as we can tell from the few illustrations available from around 1600, were contemporary. That is, they didn't try to suggest a distant time or place, such as Denmark five hundred or so years before the play was being performed. So you are all set in any

---

1   A film on videotape or DVD with the picture left dark and sound alone can also work, but probably not as well as the audio versions because of the many cuts you'll find in films and the spaces sometimes left between words for action and scenic displays. Below, we suggest ways to read film performances.

sort of room using ordinary lighting and wearing your normal clothes. Props, on the other hand, could be important. For example, in the first scene of *Hamlet* most or all of the men entering might be holding some sort of weapon, because at least some of them are sentries, and perhaps one or more are holding torches, to indicate the night-time setting.

Your aim is to tease out what Shakespeare's purpose might have been in writing the particular segment you're considering: how does the scene advance the plot, illuminate the characters and explain their relationship to each other? Don't worry if your answers are different from anybody else's. There are hundreds of performances of *Hamlet* mounted world-wide each year because almost every director has his or her conception of how to answer these and other questions. The important idea to remember is that what you decide about any particular line should work with other lines. In any case, you will want to experiment with the action before you decide the answers to these questions. Your choices as you try out performance possibilities will uncover potential answers for you—and probably other questions as well. The play belongs to you, the reader.

Smaller issues also need attention. You must decide where characters will enter into and exit from the playing space, how close they will stand to each other, how their body language will indicate their feelings, how they will react to what others on stage are saying, how they are working to achieve whatever their goal is in the scene, how they would speak their lines and for what purpose. You'll notice in looking at the script that it overtly answers very few if any of these questions. Shakespeare, as one of the actors in his troupe, was probably around to guide the players, to say "I'd like you to do it this way." Not expecting his scripts to be printed for theater practitioners (or even most likely for readers),[2] he did not write extensive stage directions—all the better for us and for our imaginative engagement with the text. In the text of the play we use, you may notice that many stage directions are in brackets; these are the ones we and editors preceding us have added to the basic script we are using

Taking just the first 65 lines of the play, up to the first retreat of the Ghost, you can begin to see that the process can be very complex.[3] Fortunately, you are not mounting a whole production! You can learn a great deal about performance possibilities simply by focusing on one segment, one character or one motif (See Topics for Discussion and Further Study, p. 171). Our aim here is to provide a template that we hope will inspire you to select other segments and figure out their performance possibilities. It's best to do exercises like the one described below after reading the whole play, or at least reading an outline of the play (See "The Play's Timeline" (p. 167). The first segment is obviously extremely important to Shakespeare: he has to grab the audience

---

2   As near as scholars can tell about the printing history of Shakespeare's plays, it may have been in the players' best interest not to have the script printed and thus available to other companies, who might have performed it to the detriment of The Lord Chamberlain's Men. But this point is controversial.

3   The method described here can be used for any short segment of the play, such as the first 128 lines of act one, scene two; the dialogue between Polonius and Ophelia in 1.3.88-136, and so on.

and somehow, on a well-lit open-air summer stage, make them feel the dread and awe of the men on a cold night in Denmark.

The setting

Consider how the actors, in a well-lit space, can indicate to the audience that it is night and that it is cold? Try using body language.

The characters' goals

First, list the roles in the segment you choose; in 1.1 there are five: Francisco, Bernardo, Marcellus, Horatio, and the Ghost. Decide how many actors you will need. At least four are necessary in scene one, because four appear together; Francisco could double as the Ghost. What is Francisco's aim in 1.1? How do you know? What are the aims of all the others? Do the aims change during the course of the scene? You won't know the Ghost's aim until you know the whole play, and even then it can be rather iffy, but you probably can make guesses about the aims of all the characters in the segment you choose—and thus decide how you want the actors to express your suppositions. Are the character's aims successfully reached or are they frustrated in any way?

The variety of interactions

You might begin with the first two lines; the second, "Nay, answer me," said by Francisco, contradicts ("Nay" or "No") the first speaker, Bernardo. Most commentators think this shows that because Francisco is the sentinel on duty (as we discover from line 12) and because Bernardo is coming to relieve him, it is Francisco, not the new arrival, who should voice the challenge. Are there whispers in these lines or shouts or a mixture? To what effect? The fact that Bernardo doesn't speak according to military protocol could suggest that he is uneasy about something. You know from your further reading that he has encountered a ghost on two previous watches. When he enters he may fear that he is seeing a ghost—but it turns out to be only Francisco—or does he see something in the corner of the space that *is* the Ghost or that he might think is the Ghost? So how could you stage those two lines to convey the point of Bernardo's fear and Francisco's challenge? Line 13 suggests that Francisco is not in very good shape either. Why do you think Shakespeare gives this character a strange, unmilitary confession about his feelings when we are never going to see him again? How does Francisco's unease add to the emotional effect of the scene?

Voicing the choices

Try this circle exercise: a group stands in a circle. One person steps into the circle and acts out the first line, Bernardo's line. Another person steps into the circle to give Francisco's response. Bernardo starts each mini dialogue, and Francisco completes it and begins again as Bernardo, and is responded to by another Francisco. Each set of two should try to express the lines differently. Then the group might decide what seemed to work best. The original texts have a question mark at the end of the first line and a period at the end of each sentence (two commands) in the second line. Would it help to have an exclamation point at the end of one or both of the commands? Try expressing the second line with no exclamation point—neither one nor two. Try using the exclamation for the second half only. Editors often introduce punctuation not found in the original texts to convey to readers their ideas about how the line should be acted.

Even an armchair thinker about the play has to take into account the motives of the personages in the play, their tones of voice and demeanor, and the writer has to argue persuasively for his or her view of "how it would be" or "how we should understand what is happening."

Once you have worked on this first segment, even exaggerating to project your point—about how cold it is, perhaps, or how frightened Bernardo is, or how ill at ease Francisco is—consider this question: some productions omit this entire first scene because they need to shorten the performance and because Marcellus and Horatio tell Hamlet about the Ghost's visitation at the end of the next scene. Why do you think Shakespeare included this first scene in spite of the play's length and the repetition of some aspects later? The work you do on the first segment (or any short segment) can be a valuable introduction to reading any play in performance.

Films are an excellent medium to use to read the play in its many performance aspects. After deciding on the overall effect they want to achieve, filmmakers have to decide which Shakespeare text to use as a basis for their scripts: some combine features of all three original (First Quarto, Second Quarto, and First Folio). Many films change the order of scenes found in the printed texts and cut whole segments. Comparing such decisions helps to clarify the filmmakers' aims: why might a filmmaker have cut or transposed scenes in his version? Why might Shakespeare have wanted the order we see in the dominant text, the Second Quarto? Many other elements of a film performance bear noting. Consider background music and other sound effects, some meant only for the audience, some heard also by the characters; design of scenery and costumes, use of indoor and outdoor settings; manipulation of the camera and lighting, including close-ups, long shots, and more. By comparing a short segment of two films side-by-side, you will be able to notice many choices and speculate about their contribution to the whole experience of seeing the play. All these observations can make you more aware of possibilities—can make you, in short, a better reader of the play.

By reading the play as a performance you can begin to see the richness that delights audiences and that makes it possible to see multiple versions of the play over a period of years, and to learn something new about the play each time.

Historical Timeline

1509-1547   Reign of Henry VIII (b. 1491), first Protestant King of England.

1517   Martin Luther (1483-1546) posted 97 theses in Wittenberg, important to the Protestant Reformation.

1534   Under King Henry, Parliament established the "Act of Supremacy," disavowing the power of the Roman Catholic Pope and naming the English monarch as "supreme" head of the Church of England. Henry's breach with Rome enabled him to divorce Katherine of Aragon, Mary Tudor's mother, and marry Anne Boleyn (the mother of Queen Elizabeth).

1547-1553   Reign of Edward VI (b. 1537). An Edwardian Parliament established a strongly Protestant Prayer Book and enforced a new Act of Uniformity (1549). Many Catholics lost their power, possessions, and land.

1553-1558   Reign of Mary Tudor (b. 1516). Queen Mary restored Roman Catholicism to England. Many Protestants fled the country; those remaining in opposition were persecuted and many were burned at the stake.

1558-1603   Reign of Elizabeth I (b.1533). In 1559, an Elizabethan Parliament established, in two separate Acts of Supremacy, the Queen of England as supreme "governor in all spiritual things" and *The Book of Common Prayer* as the official national prayer book, which attempted to reconcile Protestant and Catholic liturgies.

1564   Birth of William Shakespeare in Stratford-upon-Avon.

1576   Francois de Belleforest rendered the Hamlet story into French, the version Shakespeare may have known, from the Danish history of Saxo Grammaticus, written c. 1200. An early dramatic version of *Hamlet*, possibly by Thomas Kyd (1558-1594), performed in 1594, could also have been a source.

1576   The Theatre, early public theater built by James Burbage and his sons Cuthbert and Richard, the much-praised actor who probably played Hamlet and other major roles.

1579   Katharine Hamlett, a young Stratford "spinster," drowned under circumstances similar to Ophelia's.

1582   William Shakespeare married Anne Hathaway.

1583   Birth of Shakespeare's daughter, Susanna.

1585   Birth of Shakespeare's twins: daughter Judith and son Hamnet, who died at age eleven, 1596. No direct descendents survive today.

1586   *The Spanish Tragedy* by Thomas Kyd set the pattern for a wave of revenge tragedies. In this play a father revenges the death of a son. Forerunners of revenge tragedy can be found in Greek tragedy and myth and in the plays of the Roman author Seneca, published in English in 1581.

1594   William Shakespeare and Richard Burbage became sharers (owners) in the Lord Chamberlain's Men (their title when they were sponsored by Queen Elizabeth).

1599   Opening of the Globe Theater. *Henry V* (1599), *Julius Caesar* (1599) and *Hamlet* (1601) were among the first plays staged there.

1601   Death of Shakespeare's father, John, around the time of the composition of *Hamlet*.

1603   Death of Queen Elizabeth. James VI of Scotland (b. 1566) succeeded her as King.

1603   The Lord Chamberlain's Men became the King's Men, sponsored by James.

1603   First Quarto of *Hamlet* published.

1604   Second Quarto of *Hamlet* published.

1616   Death of William Shakespeare (April 23); he had retired to Stratford c. 1611.

1623   Publication of the First Folio by Shakespeare's theater colleagues.

THE PLAY'S TIMELINE

Pre-play

Old King Hamlet has died and has been interred with due ceremony (reported 1.4.46-50). Historically, a royal funeral would take place some time after the monarch's death (time enough for luminaries to gather from far and wide), but Shakespeare's plays did not have to adhere to royal timing. The action of the play begins not quite two months after King Hamlet's death (mentioned 1.2.138). An indefinite time after the death, Claudius, King Hamlet's brother, was elected to the throne, and, according to Hamlet, somewhat less than a month after the death of his father Claudius began a relationship with his brother's widow, Hamlet's mother (1.2.145).

Day 1

1.1   The Ghost first appears at one o'clock in the morning (line 39), and Marcellus, Bernardo and Horatio break up their watch at dawn (line 166).

1.2   Since Marcellus says he knows where he can find Hamlet "this morning" (1.1.174), that is when he and Horatio meet Hamlet (1.2.160). The purpose of the court gathering seems to be to announce the marriage of the new king and his former sister-in-law, though some productions imply that it also marks the new king's coronation. Since Hamlet plans to join the men on the platform that night, we know that 1.4 will take place that evening.

1.3   Sometime during the interval between 1.2 and 1.4, the afternoon of the first day, we learn of a budding romance between Ophelia and Hamlet that both her brother and father want her to end. Since this relationship seems to have begun after Hamlet returned from Wittenberg, his father's death had not prevented him from wooing Ophelia—though the play does not invite logical inferences like this.

Day 2

1.4   After midnight that night, the second day (lines 3-4), Hamlet, Horatio and Marcellus wait for the Ghost's appearance; it motions Hamlet to go with it.

1.5   The Ghost reveals to Hamlet why it has returned from purgatory, and Hamlet responds. The scene ends after dawn (line 59) when Marcellus and Horatio rejoin Hamlet.

Interim

A viewing audience can be led to believe that the reported scene between Hamlet and Ophelia (act 2, scene 1) takes places during the morning after Hamlet has seen the Ghost, and directors can further that impression by having Hamlet wear the same clothes in both scenes. But the text later indicates that between Acts 1 and 2, Hamlet has acted upon his resolution to behave as if deranged —or he is actually teetering on madness—(2.2.4-7), and sufficient time has passed for the King to be worried about Hamlet and to have sent for Rosencrantz and Guildenstern. The exact time is vague in performance because it's not until Ophelia mentions the passage of time—and then so casually that many will miss it (3.2.136)—that we can begin to count the time. She says it has been four months since the death of King Hamlet. Her "four months" is a round figure but indicates that it's about two months since the end of act 1.

Day 1 of the second movement

2.1   Enough time has passed for Polonius to want to refresh Laertes's supply of money and for Ophelia to have avoided Hamlet. From here on to the exile of Hamlet (4.3), time proceeds smoothly.

2.2   Since Polonius is eager to tell the King about Hamlet's love for Ophelia, scene 2 takes place almost immediately. During the scene, the players arrive and determine the time of act 3, scene 2, because Hamlet says, "We'll hear a play tomorrow" (2.2.560).

Day 1 or 2 of the second movement

3.1   Polonius uses Ophelia as a decoy. This scene could take place early on the day that the play is to be performed or it could take place later in the same day as scene 2.2.

Day 2-3 of the second movement

3.2   The day after 2.2, the players perform and the King reacts. Hamlet's mother, through Rosencrantz and Guildenstern, asks Hamlet to come to her immediately.

3.3   The King determines to use Rosencrantz and Guildenstern to get rid of Hamlet, sees Polonius on his way to the Queen's closet to spy on Hamlet, and tries to pray. Hamlet has a chance to kill the King but rejects it and hurries on to his mother.

3.4   Minutes later, Polonius, in Gertrude's closet, hides as Hamlet enters; Hamlet kills him, possibly thinking he has killed the King. Hamlet then tries to accomplish one of the Ghost's behests: to urge his mother to avoid the King's bed and so keep the throne from being "A couch for luxury and damned incest" (1.5.83).

4.1   This scene seems to be a continuation of the previous scene and thus is in the same time frame. Q2 shows no exit for the Queen at the end of 3.4, but an entrance to her by the King (with Rosencrantz and Guildenstern in Q2, who enter later in F1). The King tells Rosencrantz and Guildenstern to find Hamlet.

4.2   A little later; Hamlet has hidden Polonius's body and is "captured" by Rosencrantz and Guildenstern.

4.3   Immediately after, the King tells Hamlet that he is to leave for England.

4.4   The same day or early the next day, on the way to the ship, Hamlet sees Fortinbras and speaks with a captain of Fortinbras's army.

Interim

Enough time passes for Polonius to be quickly buried without the usual formalities accorded to a high-ranking courtier, for Laertes to return to Denmark from France, for Ophelia's derangement to be noticeable, and for Hamlet to have aborted his voyage to England and returned to Denmark.

Day 1 of the third movement

4.5   Ophelia is mad and Laertes with a group of followers threatens the King's reign.

4.6   Horatio receives a letter from Hamlet, written while he was on his way back to Denmark.

4.7   In the meantime, the King and Laertes plot to kill Hamlet, and the Queen tells them of Ophelia's death by drowning.

Day 2 of the third movement

5.1   Hamlet and Horatio meet outside Elsinore, and see Ophelia being buried. The King speaks to Laertes of "our last night's speech," referring to the events of 4.7.

Day 2 or 3 of the third movement

5.2   Horatio listens to the story of Hamlet's escape from the death the King had intended for him. The fencing match that the King and Laertes planned in 4.7 brings the play to a conclusion.

Total elapsed time for the play: about two months and several days for the voyage towards England and back.

TOPICS FOR DISCUSSION AND FURTHER STUDY

A. Character study

Focusing on one character in *Hamlet* can yield important insights, as can be seen in many published studies of the play. Here we suggest a few ways to concentrate attention and to consider how each choice a director makes works for the play as a whole. Each of these suggestions could yield a paper, a class discussion, or a way into a classroom performance.

1. Where does the script imply that the Ghost is "good"? Where does it imply that the Ghost is "bad"? Does the script reconcile these opposite views? How are these questions addressed by film directors?

2. Some critics have asserted that though Claudius has committed regicide and fratricide, they consider him to be an excellent king. See, for example, Kittredge's view in his introduction (pp. x-xi). Can you find evidence in the text for other views? How do the films you have seen convey the King's nature? For extreme opposites, compare the BBC Claudius (Patrick Stewart) to the Richardson Claudius (Anthony Hopkins).

3. The name *Amleth* in the source story comes from an Icelandic word meaning "a simpleton" and in the early version of the story, the name fits well, for the hero gains protection from the murderous king by assuming the disguise of a fool. Shakespeare converts this device into Hamlet's pretended madness. What purposes does the madness serve in the play? Review the script where Hamlet indicates that he has been pretending madness or is mad (1.5.170-2, 2.2.396, 3.2.157, 3.4.141, 3.4.187-8; and 5.2.237-50). What effects does he achieve through his pretense? Note the reactions of the other characters. How do films treat Hamlet's madness? Consider Scott's film, in which Hamlet seems to be at least occasionally unhinged (but not after 5.1). What is the effect of overtly making Hamlet, intermittently, a madman? Other films show him playing the madman only with those he considers his enemies.

4. By mistakenly killing Polonius, Hamlet is indirectly guilty of the deaths of six others (seven including himself), at least some of whom are innocent. Does he retain your allegiance, and if so, how? Does your support for him vary from film to film? from time to time within films?

5. Several of the young people in *Hamlet* have remarkably similar problems and each responds to them differently. Consider the position of Ophelia, Laertes, and Fortinbras. How does the reaction of each to the death of a father illumine Hamlet's response?

6. How guilty is Gertrude? And of what? Hamlet seems to imply in the closet scene that her main fault was choosing as a new husband a man who is not as handsome and kingly as her former one. Did she commit murder? Adultery? How can we infer her innocence or guilt since either is to be found only between the lines? In the films that you have seen, does she change in her *feelings* for Claudius after the closet scene? Does her *behavior* toward him change? Compare two or three film depictions of her character in scenes 4.1, 4.5, 5.1 and 5.2 to note the development of her response.

7. At Ophelia's grave, Hamlet says that he loved her deeply. Is there any evidence to support this in the words and action of the play? Compare two or more films in this respect. See also the description of Caird's stage production in the introduction (p. xxv-xxvi). If Hamlet loved Ophelia as much as he says he did, does the play convey any reason why he treats her badly?

9. Polonius has sometimes been played as a foolish old man. Is there any evidence to support this interpretation? Can you find support for other interpretations of his character? For example, How do the other characters in the play regard him? How do films treat him? Scott's Polonius is dignified; Branagh's is corrupt; Kozintsev's is an honored statesman. How does a film's treatment of Polonius affect the characterization of Hamlet?

10. Consider the effect of each of the main characters on the interpretation of the play as a whole. Are there specific characterizations that will work only with other characterizations?

B. Language study

Next to the characters, probably the most important single aspect of Shakespeare's artistry is his language (some would place it first). Language is of course inextricably linked to characters because it's the characters who speak the language.

1. For those who hesitate to engage with Shakespeare because they fear his language, it is useful to notice how many of his words are common now. On one or two pages of your text, underline all the words that you know. There are probably more than you would have thought. See if a moment's reflection can reveal to you the meaning of other words that at first seem unknowns. Context can help. Take a leap. On the other hand, some words we think we

know have changed meaning rather drastically. That's where the notes below the text can be helpful.

2. Examine any short speech that seems especially significant. Listen to the speech in a film or on a recording. Provide a translation into everyday modern English using multiple synonyms to convey as much as possible about the speech.

3. Often Shakespeare will invert or twist normal word order to maintain rhythm, something popular music also does for the same reason. Find several instances of inversions and see if rearranging the words slightly will help to clarify the meaning of the sentences.

4. Hamlet's soliloquies are significant for their searching, thoughtful qualities, as he tries to decide what to do and who he is; they are among the most meaningful elements in the play. Examine one of Hamlet's soliloquies in detail, looking for shifts in his perspective. Compare the way two or more films treat the delivery of the soliloquy.

5. Claudius and Ophelia also have important soliloquies: Examine one for what it reveals about the character and how it contributes to the development of the plot. Compare the soliloquy you have chosen in two or three film versions and determine the actors' and directors' purposes (partly by noting the effect the speech has on you and others).

BIBLIOGRAPHY

Early texts

The Three-Text Hamlet: *Parallel Texts of the First and Second Quartos and First Folio.* Ed. Bernice W. Kliman and Paul Bertram. 2nd ed. revised and enlarged. Parallel columns of the three main *Hamlet* texts arranged for comparison. New York: AMS, 2003.

Texts based on screened productions

Ethan Hawke as Hamlet: *William Shakespeare's* Hamlet *Adapted by Michael Almereyda.* London: Faber and Faber, 2001. With director's notes.

Kenneth Branagh as Hamlet: *Hamlet* by William Shakespeare. Screenplay and Introduction by Kenneth Branagh. Film diary by Kenneth Jackson. Photographs by Rolf Konow and Peter Mountain. New York and Long: W. W. Norton, 1996.

Derek Jacobi as Hamlet: BBC TV and Time-Life Television Coproduction. William Shakespeare. *Hamlet.* Text ed. Peter Alexander (1951). New York: Mayflower Books, 1980. Originally published in England by BBC. Intro. by literary advisor John Wilders, with commentary and notes by the production team and a glossary by Graham May.

Criticism

Biggs, Murray. "'He's Going to his Mother's Closet': Hamlet and Gertrude on Screen." *Shakespeare Survey* 45 (1993): 53-62. Useful examination of 3.4 in the Olivier, Richardson, BBC, and Zeffirelli versions of *Hamlet.*

Bulman, J. C., and H. R. Coursen, eds. *Shakespeare on Television: An Anthology of Essays and Reviews.* Hanover, NH: UP of New England, 1988.

Cartmell, Deborah. *Interpreting Shakespeare on Screen.* New York: St. Martin's, 2000. Chapter 2 on *Hamlet* films.

—. "Reading and Screening Ophelia: 1948-1996." Klein and Daphinoff, 28-41.

Clayton, Thomas, ed. *The Hamlet First Published: Origins, Form, Intertextualities.* Newark: U of Delaware P, 1992. Discussion of the First Quarto.

Coursen, H. R. "Ophelia in Performance." 53-61."The Myth and Madness of Ophelia." A catalogue prepared for Mead Art Museum, Amherst College. Amherst, MA, 2001. Comprehensive critical survey of notable Ophelias.

Davies, Anthony. *Filming Shakespeare's Plays: The Adaptations of Laurence Olivier, Orson Welles, Peter Brook and Akira Kurosawa.* Cambridge: Cambridge UP, 1988. Has a chapter comparing theatrical and cinematic space, one on Olivier's *Hamlet,* and one on the film actor.

Dawson, Anthony B. *Hamlet: Shakespeare in Performance.* Manchester and New York: Manchester UP, 1995.

Donaldson, Peter S. "Olivier, Hamlet, and Freud." *Shakespearean Films' Shakespearean Directors.* Boston: Unwin Hyman, 1990. 31-68. Makes a compelling case for a Freudian reading of Olivier's film, illuminating the theory of Ernest Jones and Freud with biographical elements.

Empson, William. *Essays on Shakespeare,* Ed. David B. Pirie. Cambridge and New York: Cambridge UP, 1986. Includes an essay about Hamlet's delay.

Frye, Roland M. *The Renaissance Hamlet: Issues and Responses in 1600.* Princeton: Princeton UP, 1984. Situates the play in the socio-political context of the time, treating contemporary attitudes towards topics such as rebellion, regicide, revenge, incest, conscience, and mourning.

Goethe, Johann Wolfgang. *Wilhelm Meister's Apprenticeship* [1796] Ed. and trans. E. A. Blackall in cooperation with V. Lange. New York: Suhrkamp, 1989. The main character appears as Hamlet in a stage production.

Greenblatt, Stephen. *Hamlet in Purgatory.* Princeton: Princeton UP, 2001. Clear exposition of early modern beliefs about purgatory and ghosts.

Hale, David G. "'Did'st Perceive?': Five Versions of the Mousetrap in *Hamlet.*" See Klein and Daphinoff, 74-84.

Jones, Ernest. *Hamlet and Oedipus* [1923]. New York: Norton, 1949.

Jorgens, Jack J. *Shakespeare on Film.* Bloomington and London: Indiana UP, 1977. Reprinted: Lanham : UP of America, c1991. Illustrated. Credits and Outlines of the Major Films. Index. Olivier's *Hamlet* 207-17 (notes 327-8), Kozintsev's 218-34 (notes 328-30).

Klein, Holger, and Dimiter Daphinoff, eds. *Hamlet on Screen.* A Publication of the *Shakespeare Yearbook*, Vol. 8. Lewiston, NY: The Edward Mellen Press, 1997. 26 essays on screened *Hamlet* by an international gathering of scholars with end notes for each essay.

Kliman, Bernice W. HAMLET: *Film, Television and Audio Performance.* Rutherford, NJ: Fairleigh Dickinson UP, 1988. Available in full on www.hamletworks. org. Contains discussions of major and minor productions from the silent era through 1984 with comparisons to stage productions.

—. "The Unkindest Cuts: Flashcut Excess in Kenneth Branagh's *Hamlet.*" *Talking Shakespeare: Shakespeare into the Millennium.* Ed. Deborah Cartmell and Michael Scott. Houndmills: Palgrave, 2001. 151-67.

—. "*Hamlet* Productions Starring Beale, Hawke, and Darling From the Perspective of Performance History." In *A Companion to Shakespeare's Works*. Vol. 1. *The Tragedies*. Ed. Richard Dutton and Jean E. Howard, Malden, MA and Oxford: Blackwell Publishing, 2003. 136-57. The comments on Almereyda and Beale within derive from this essay.

Lake, James H. "The Effects of Primacy and Recency upon Audience Response to Five Film Versions of *Hamlet*." *Literature/Film Quarterly*. 28. 2 (2000): 112-17.

Maher, Mary Z. *Modern Hamlets and Their Soliloquies*. 2nd ed. Iowa City: U of Iowa P, 2003. Interviews actors who played Hamlet and discusses their approaches to the soliloquies.

Manvell, Roger. *Shakespeare and the Film*. South Brunswick and New York: A. S. Barnes and Co., 1979. A slightly updated version of the 1971 hardcover first ed. Discusses Shakespeare films knowledgeably.

Newell, Alex. *The Soliloquies in* Hamlet: *The Structural Design*. Rutherford, NJ: Fairleigh Dickinson UP, 1991. Provides a handy collection of soliloquies, 165-72, omitting only the Queen's aside in 4.5.17-20.

Nettles, John. "Customary Suits of Solemn Black Rubber: Hamlet as Contemporary Action Hero." *Shakespeare and the Classroom* 7, no. 2 (1999): 44-47. Compares Hamlet to postmodern action heroes, from *Batman* to *The Mask of Zorro,* and suggests using such heroes to introduce students to *Hamlet*.

Ottenhoff, John. "Hamlet and the Kiss," See Klein and Daphinoff, 98-109. An example of how a critic can observe variations among films by focusing on one element.

Prosser, Eleanor. *Hamlet and Revenge*. 2nd ed. Stanford: Stanford UP, 1971. Author does not think that Hamlet is morally obligated to kill the King.

Tarkovsky, Andrei. "On *Hamlet*." *Time within Time: The Diaries* 1970-1986. London: Verso, 1993. 378-84. Influenced the Almereyda film.

Tibbets, John. "Breaking the Classical Barrier: Franco Zeffirelli Interviewed by John Tibbets." *Literature/Film Quarterly*. 22.2 (1994): 136-140.

Trewin, J. C. *Five and Eighty Hamlets*. New York: New Amsterdam, 1989. Orig. ed. 1987. A chronological review of stage productions from 1908 to 1987.

Other References Consulted

Bullough, Geoffrey, ed. *Narrative and Dramatic Sources of Shakespeare*. Vol. 7. *Major Tragedies*. London and Henley: Routledge and Kegan Paul; New York: Columbia UP, 1973.

Rothwell, Kenneth S. *A History of Shakespeare on Screen: A Century of Film and Television* Second Edition. Cambridge: Cambridge UP, 2005. Descriptive analyses of many productions.

Shakespeare, William. *The Tragedy of Macbeth*. Ed. Annalisa Castaldo. The New Kittredge Shakespeare. Newburyport: Focus Publishing, 2008.

—. *The Tragedy of Romeo and Juliet*. Ed. Bernice W. Kliman and Laury Magnus. The New Kittredge Shakespeare. Newburyport: Focus Publishing, 2008.

Websites

Hamletworks.org: http://www.hamletworks.org. Contains *Hamlet* texts from 1603 to the nineteenth century (including complete works), essays, books, illustrations, notes on individual words of the play, and more.

The International Movie Database: http://imdb.com/ a rich source of information about film and TV productions.

The Internet Shakespeare Project: <http://internetshakespeare.uvic.ca/ At the University of Victoria, Canada, with many valuable resources

Massachusetts Institute of Technology sites, entry from: http://shea.mit.edu/ ramparts/ A thorough approach to *Hamlet* act 1, scenes 4 and 5 and much more.

Rothwell, Kenneth S., and Annabelle Henkin-Melzer. *Shakespeare on Screen: An International Filmography and Videography*. New York: Neal-Schuman, 1990. A revised and updated Internet edition by Kenneth S. Rothwell, José Ramón Díaz Fernández and Tanya Gough is available at <http://internetshakespeare.uvic.ca/Theater/sip/spotlights.html>http://internetshakespeare.uvic.ca/Theater/sip/spotlights.html.>

The World Shakespeare Bibliography Online, ed. James L. Harner. This searchable electronic database consists of the most comprehensive record of Shakespeare-related scholarship and theatrical productions published or produced worldwide between 1962 and 2008. Containing over 115,260 annotated entries, this collected information is an essential tool for anyone engaged in research on Shakespeare or early modern English literature.

Audiobooks

Beale. *Hamlet* by William Shakespeare. Simon Russell Beale as Hamlet, Imogen Stubbs as Ophelia, Jane Lapotaire as Gertrude, Bob Peck as Claudius, Norman Rodway as Polonius. Distributed by the Penguin Group from the Pelican Shakespeare series. 2 cassettes. 3 hrs., 25 mins.

Branagh. *Hamlet* by William Shakespeare. The Renaissance Theatre Company, in association with BBC Radio Drama. Audio production on tape and CD. 1st broadcast 26 April 1992. Kenneth Branagh as Hamlet, Judi Dench as Gertrude, Richard Briers as Polonius, John Gielgud as the ghost, Derek Jacobi as Claudius, Sophie Thompson as Ophelia. Worth comparing with the 1996 Branagh film. 3 CDs, with booklet. 3 hrs., 30 mins.

Muller. *Hamlet* by William Shakespeare. Unabridged narration by Frank Muller, who takes on all roles. Prince Frederick, MD: Recorded Books, n.d. 3 cassettes. 4 hrs.

FILMOGRAPHY

1948   Lawrence Olivier as Hamlet. Directed by Lawrence Olivier. With Eileen Herlie as Gertrude, Basil Sydney as Claudius, Jean Simmons as Ophelia, Felix Aymer as Polonius. B&W. 2 hrs., 35 mins.

1960   *The Bad Sleep Well.* Directed by Akira Kurosawa. With Toshirô Mifune as Koichi Nishi, the Hamlet figure. Original Music by Masaru Satô; Cinematography by Yuzuru Aizawa Contemporary Japanese business world. B&W. 2 hrs., 15 min.

1960   *Hamlet.* Directed by Peter Wirth with Maximilian Schell as Hamlet, Wanda Rotha as Gertrude, Dunja Movar as Ophelia. 2 hrs., 7 min.

1964   Richard Burton as Hamlet. Directed by John Gielgud with Hume Cronyn as Polonius, Eileen Herlie as Gertrude, Alfred Drake as Claudius, and Linda Marsh as Ophelia. B&W. 3 hrs., 19 mins.

1964   Directed by Grigori Kozintsev. Screenplay by Grigori Kozintsev. From the translation into Russian by Boris Pasternak (subtitled in English). Music by Dmitri Shostakovich. With Innokenti Smokhtunovski as Hamlet, Mikhail Nazvanov as Claudius, Elza Raszin-Szolkonis as Gertrude, Yuri Tolubeev as Polonius, Anastasia Vertinskaya as Ophelia. B&W. 2 hrs., 28 mins.

1969   Directed by Tony Richardson by special arrangement with Woodfall Ltd. Produced at the Roundhouse Theatre. With Nicol Williamson as Hamlet, Judy Parfitt as Gertrude, Mark Dignam as Polonius, Gordon Jackson as Horatio, Anthony Hopkins as Claudius, Marianne Faithfull as Ophelia. 1 hr., 57 mins.

1980   BBC-TV-Time-Life Production for television, produced by Cedric Messina. Directed by Rodney Bennett with Derek Jacobi as Hamlet, Claire Bloom as Gertrude, Eric Porter as Polonius, Patrick Stewart as Claudius, Lalla Ward as Ophelia. Color. 2 hrs., 30 mins.

1984   Directed by Ragnar Lyth for Swedish Television. *Den tragiska historien om Hamlet, prinz av Denmark.* With Stellan Skarsgaard as Hamlet. 2 hrs., 40 min. Not presently available.

1990   Mel Gibson as Hamlet. Directed by Franco Zeffirelli. Screenplay by Christopher DeVore and Franco Zeffirelli. With Alan Bates as Claudius, Paul Scofield as the ghost, Ian Holm as Polonius, Helena Bonham-Carter as Ophelia. Color. 2 hrs., 15 mins.

1990   Kevin Kline as Hamlet. Film version for TV directed by Kevin Kline and Kirk Browning, based on the stage production directed by Kevin Kline at the Public Theater, New York. With Kevin Kline as Hamlet, Dana Ivey as Gertrude, Brian Murray as Claudius, Diane Venora as Ophelia, Michael Cumpsty as Laertes. 2 hrs., 47 min.

1995   *In the Bleak Midwinter* (in the U.S. *A Midwinter's Tale*), a theatrical production of *Hamlet* within the movie. Directed and written by Kenneth Branagh. Michael Maloney as Hamlet; Richard Briers as Claudius, Ghost, Player King; Nicholas Farrell as Laertes, Fortinbras, and Messengers; Mark Hadfield as Polonius, Marcellus and First Gravedigger; Julia Sawalha as Ophelia. B&W. 1 hr., 38 min.

1996   Directed by Kenneth Branagh. Kenneth Branagh as Hamlet. With Derek Jacobi as Claudius, Julie Christie as Gertrude, Kate Winslet as Ophelia, Richard Briers as Polonius, Judi Dench as Hecuba, John Gielgud as Priam. Color. 4 hrs.

2000   Directed by Michael Almereyda. With Ethan Hawke as Hamlet, Julia Stiles as Ophelia, Diane Venora as Gertrude, Bill Murray as Polonius, Sam Shepard as the ghost, Kyle MacLachlin as Claudius, Liev Schreiber as Laertes. Color. 1 hr., 52 min.

2000   Directed by Campbell Scott and Eric Simonson. With Campbell Scott as Hamlet, Blair Brown as Gertrude, Roscoe Lee Brown as Polonius, Lisa Gay Hamilton as Ophelia, and Jamey Sheridan as Claudius. A Hallmark Production, with original music by Gary De Michele and cinematography by Dan Gillham. Color. 3 hrs., 10 min.